A PLUME BOOK

LOVE & WAR

JAMES CARVILLE is an American political consultant, commentator, educator, actor, attorney, media personality, and prominent liberal pundit. He gained national attention for his work as the lead strategist of the successful 1992 presidential campaign of Bill Clinton. Carville was a co-host of CNN's *Crossfire* until its final broadcast in June 2005, and is currently a Fox News contributor. Carville is the author of several books, most recently *It's the Middle Class, Stupid!* (coauthored with Stan Greenberg). He teaches political science at Tulane University.

MARY MATALIN served in the Reagan, George H. W. Bush, and George W. Bush administrations and as counselor to vice president Dick Cheney. She is a bestselling author, television and radio host, and currently the cohost of the national radio show *Both Sides Now* with Arianna Huffington. Mary and husband, James Carville, were 2013 NFL Super Bowl Host Committee co-chairmen and Loyola University of New Orleans Centennial co-chairmen, where Matalin was recently appointed Visiting Distinguished Lecturer.

Praise for *Love & War*

"A solid memoir of political lives from both sides of the spectrum."
—*Kirkus Reviews*

"Compelling . . . The voices are the glue for and the animating features of an ultimately tender book that shines a light on their successful union, not to mention the Crescent City, and shows how big and small a role politics plays in our lives."
—*USA Today*

JAMES CARVILLE & MARY MATALIN

LOVE & WAR

Twenty Years, Three Presidents,
Two Daughters & One Louisiana Home

A PLUME BOOK

PLUME
Published by the Penguin Group
Penguin Group (USA) LLC
375 Hudson Street
New York, New York 10014

USA | Canada | UK | Ireland | Australia | New Zealand | India | South Africa | China
penguin.com
A Penguin Random House Company

First published in the United States of America by Blue Rider Press, a member of Penguin Group (USA)
LLC, 2013
First Plume Printing 2014

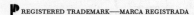
THE LIBRARY OF CONGRESS HAS CATALOGED THE BLUE RIDER PRESS EDITION AS FOLLOWS:
Carville, James.
Love & war : twenty years, three presidents, two daughters and one Louisiana home /
James Carville and Mary Matalin.
p.   cm.
ISBN 978-0-399-16724-9 (hc.)
ISBN 978-0-14-218125-6 (pbk.)
1. Carville, James.   2. Matalin, Mary.   3. Carville, James—Marriage.   4. Matalin, Mary—Marriage.
5. Political consultants—United States—Biography.   6. Married people—United States—Biography.
7. New Orleans (La.)—Biography.   8. United States—Politics and government—1993–2001.
9. United States—Politics and government—2001–2009.   10. United States—Politics and
government—2009–   I. Matalin, Mary.   II. Matalin, Mary. All's fair.   III. Title.
IV. Title: Love and war.
E840.6.C37   2014   2013042532
324.092'2—dc23
[B]

Printed in the United States of America
10   9   8   7   6   5   4   3   2

Original hardcover design by Stephanie Huntwork

JAMES

For Tim Russert

MARY

*To Gabriel and Michael,
angels always*

JAMES

There are a lot of places I like, but I like New Orleans better.
  —*Bob Dylan*

MARY

I am the wisest man alive, for I know one thing, and that is that I know
nothing.   —*Socrates*

What has been will be again,
what has been done will be done again;
there is nothing new under the sun.   —*Ecclesiastes*

LOVE & WAR

FAQ

SOME PEOPLE IN POLITICS INSPIRE CONFIDENCE. We seem to inspire curiosity. And not too much concerning the field we are known for: politics.

Being asked strange and highly personal questions is normal life for us. We promise you that every single answer to the questions below can be found in vivid and occasionally lurid detail in the pages to follow. Think of this book as *James and Mary for Dummies*. Or, better yet, think of this book as a scavenger hunt. The only question not answered is whether James has any hobbies apart from sex.

Not that we think you are dummies, by the way—unless you don't believe in honest politics and true love.

- Is your marriage a sham?
- Is your marriage a political stunt?

- Are your politics a sham/stunt?

- Do you have offspring, and if so, Republicans or Democrats?

- What could you possibly see in each other?

- Is your wife as big a bitch as she seems to be on TV?

- What is Dick Cheney really like?

- Is your husband weird like that at home?

- He must be good in bed, otherwise why would you be with him?

- Is this all about good make-up sex?

- What is sex with a Republican like?

- Do you have any friends in common?

- What do you fight about the most?

- How close to divorce have you gotten?

- Do you have hobbies?

- If you had hobbies, what would they be?

- Why did you move to New Orleans?

1.

You Can Always Go
Home Again

MARY

IT WAS A NEW ORLEANS SUMMER NIGHT IN 2007. Dusk was just ending and the air was thick, like a cocktail of air and water. I ventured outside to walk the dogs. The street was dark, weirdly quiet. I looked back at the empty house we'd just moved into, a rambling mansion by my standards, but certainly not by the standards of New Orleans, a world unto itself, a distinctly American city with a romantic European grandeur.

I wondered what the new house, and a new city, would bring us. After twenty years of holy and unholy matrimony—including storms, hurricanes, wars, disruptive house moves that James always hated, raising two daughters into teenagehood, and our own separate moments on the frontlines of political battles, presidential elections, punditry pontification and, yes, if I can go braggadocio on you, even history—we had worked out a way of living together, staying together and being happier.

There had been too many trials. Even more errors. One thing we learned: if peace could visit us, even illusively, it required well-thought-out living arrangements.

James and I needed space. Mostly from each other.

To be happy under the same roof, we required our own offices, our own bathrooms and our own closets. We needed a well-functioning kitchen with a double sink, a big icebox and enough room so our family, all of us—true foodies and amateur cooks—could concoct our meals. We needed a dining room for big gatherings, a lair for mass viewings of TV football games, and a hangout place where our daughters, Matty and Emerson, could be with their friends, inclusive of but not restricted to pajama parties.

I had my own personal requirements: windows that open for fresh air, a garden where all my animals could run. I needed bookshelves, lots and lots of shelves for my old books, loved and cared for and purchased over a lifetime, way before I had girls who grew up to be book junkies and collectors themselves. Once it had seemed like a huge luxury, but I was now dependent on a soaking tub for temporary escapes from reality. A fireplace wasn't mandatory but greatly appreciated.

James had his own list of must-haves. He gave me explicit instructions: if we were going to move to New Orleans, we couldn't live in the French Quarter (tough for kids), we could not be on St. Charles (too much traffic), and we had to be near his work (he was going to try teaching at Tulane) and a place for his daily jog.

But there was more: the house had to have super air-conditioning (Southerners are psycho about their fake chilled air), a killer shower with strong water pressure (no longer available in the era of environmental wackos and efficient toilet flushing). And most of all, he needed a private space where he could close the doors and never have to interact with any of my animals. And a special "steam" component in the shower was not mandatory but greatly appreciated.

Nobody got 100 percent of the must-haves on their list. These were the grounds for opening negotiations.

On a family visit to New Orleans, I had gone house hunting alone. This gave me a distinct advantage. But there was no other way. James hates shopping for real estate almost as much as he hates snow. He opted instead for daytime drinking and lamenting with his sisters over his wife's out-of-control materialism. I didn't expect to find the right house immediately—who ever does? But after viewing five or six houses that were in the realm of possibility, and thanks to the astoundingly astute Realtor queen, Carmen Duncan, I discovered the grand vintage New Orleans home of my dreams.

I was sure.

I was in love.

My father had just died and I had a feeling that the house was his parting supernatural gift to me. It happened so suddenly, so easily: it was meant to be. I'll admit, it was a tad pricey given James's parameters, but the house called to me. And the neighborhood called to me, and all around it, the shattered city, a place I loved.

I telephoned James, breathless with excitement and flushed with victory. "You have to come immediately and see this house!" He complied, and soon afterward he pulled up with his sisters in tow—so many Carvilles squeezed together in one vehicle that they could barely exit in a civilized manner.

JAMES

AFTER HURRICANE KATRINA, I couldn't stop thinking about the fragility of New Orleans. What really sets it apart from almost anywhere else in America is this: its survival isn't guaranteed. Washington is going to be there fifty years from now. Dallas is going to be there. Nashville might get a flood or a tornado, but it'll be there. Atlanta, Houston, Chicago, they're not going anywhere.

In New Orleans, that's never a given. The city's permanent existence is never assured. It's environmentally fragile, it's economically fragile and it's politically fragile. After Katrina, it really could have gone either way.

I couldn't believe the stories I was hearing back in D.C. I understood what it meant that the levees had broken and that the water was going to go to the level of the lake. But it wasn't only that two-thirds of the city had flooded. It was that the whole culture could go under. So many musical instruments had washed away, and the musicians who owned them were scattered all across the country. Hundreds of doctors left. Schools closed.

I started having visions that New Orleans would wind up as a little spit of land on the Mississippi, the size of Key West. I could imagine us sitting around a piano thirty years from now, playing a couple of old songs and telling the kids how it used to be.

I'd been raised sixty miles up the river in Carville, a little town named after my grandfather, who was the postmaster. I'd already witnessed pieces of old Louisiana disappear. My mother was Cajun, descended from the Acadians who settled in Louisiana, and she and my grandmother would talk to each other in French. I remember being kind of embarrassed by that as a kid. I wasn't the only one. After World War II, everybody just wanted to be an American.

These days, there are relatively few French speakers in Louisiana, but that wasn't the case when I was growing up. I worked offshore on a dredge boat, and I'd hear people say, "You know what, I just can't explain it to you in English." There were some French-language radio stations, but they've largely gone off the air. As I got older, I couldn't believe that we were so stupid, as a people, to lose that part of our culture.

Culture is everything in New Orleans. If you live in Washington, you have three airports nearby. You've got stunning parks, breathtaking public spaces. The museums are world-class, not to mention free. You've got a world-class subway system. There's a real quality of life.

But nobody does culture like New Orleans. Most people know exactly what a Mardi Gras carnival krewe looks like. You've probably got a pretty good idea what a New Orleans funeral looks like. Our food, our music, our architecture, our second-line parades—it's all very distinctive. Think about it. Who ever went to an Ohio restaurant and listened to Oregon music?

After the storm, the thought kept gnawing at me: what if that culture doesn't last? I had come to New Orleans and used it and abused it as a young man. I'd go down to the French Quarter to get drunk and stupid. Years later, Mary and I got married there. I always had a deep affection for the place. But

I'd never done that much to really support it. For so long, I had taken for granted that it would always be here, all of that emotion and passion and creativity.

When it dawned on me that it might not, I went from simply missing New Orleans to feeling this gripping fear that it might fade away before I could get down there for good. As much as anything, I wanted to get back home before home disappeared.

MARY

JAMES TOOK ONE LOOK at the grand old vintage mansion that I'd found and loved, and he started laughing. Then he started crying. He refused to even come up the stairs. I should have known. When I gave him the address on the phone, he had gasped.

I had to drag him inside. He stood in the center hall and looked up the grand staircase and started crying anew. He looked to the left and right, to rooms adorned with their original Italian frieze borders, to the majestic fireplaces in every room—mantels of sculpted marble, mantels of intricately carved old wood. More tears. Almost wailing. No laughing now.

What were his first words?

"Oh, Mary, love of my life, bride of my dreams, mother of the century to my beloved children, wizard of home and hearth. Angel. Your wonders never cease to amaze and delight me!"

Guess again.

What he actually said was: "Way too expensive. *Not gonna happen.*"

Did I mention that it was one block from his favorite cousin, Anne Milling, and her wonderful husband, King?

Did I mention his sisters were racing around the house in all directions like screaming banshees—emitting oohs and aahs and moans of approval?

Did I mention it was twice the size and half the price of the house we would be selling?

Three months and multiple miraculous machinations and manipulations later, interspersed with several bouts of manly-man haggling over the price—three months of haggling was a blink of an eye in our household—Chester James Carville was heading *home again*. And loving every square inch of his house and his wife.

Did I mention his bathroom had a steam shower?

But we did find ourselves saying to each other, "Are we being stupid? Will this really work? Can we really move away from Washington like that, so easily?"

Right decision?

Wrong decision?

Only time would tell.

JAMES

I NEVER WAS *NOT* FROM LOUISIANA. Whenever I said "home," everyone knew exactly what I meant. When people see George Stephanopoulos on television, they don't think of Cleveland. When they see Wolf Blitzer, they don't think of Buffalo. On the other hand, I reek of Louisiana. You can smell it all over me.

Truth is, I always feel slightly off anywhere other than down South. Even after two decades in Washington, I never quite felt like a citizen. I lived there, and I did the normal things people do when they live in a place. But that doesn't make it home.

MARY

A CHURCH BELL TOLLED, and the faint sounds of other church bells farther away could be heard, tolling all across New Orleans, as they did every hour on the hour. Noise cops be damned. It was nine o'clock when I started my walk into the nighttime neighborhood.

Gorgeous and Cherrie, my two long-haired dachshunds, ambled down the sidewalk, unaccustomed to the moist heat and fat misty air that sparkled with a weird ambient light. The dogs were doing that romping, excited, doggy-smiling thing that always attends an off-leash adventure in new terrain with fresh smells. We were sharing a moment, my precious pets and I. While they were sniffing and investigating, I took a deep breath and—for the very first time— smelled night-blooming jasmine. My senses were waking up for the first time in years, decades. A few steps down our block and suddenly I had the super-heightened sensory perception animals enjoy as a birthright.

Like so many wives and moms, I deal with the logistics of family life—getting the practical things done. I came down to New Orleans ahead of James to get things ready in the house. I was buying pots and pans and gadgets for the kitchen (not that we needed any more, but it was a mandatory part of my moving ritual). I was finding schools for Matty and Emerson, who were going into the fifth and eighth grades. I was getting the gas piped in, the electricity turned on, ordering cable and the James-mandated Direct TV (so he could have 1,001 sports channels), all the things you have to do when you move to a new place. (Did I mention that James thinks people just walk into any new home and ESPN appears by magic?)

I was still waiting for our furniture and clothes. It's easy to forget what that's like—to live in an empty house before your stuff comes. It's awful but wonderful. The girls and I love camping out on the floor, but James is a good mattress and crisp, fresh bedding snob.

Thinking about all this now, I feel like launching some fireworks, a tribute to mother–movers across the land.

Behind me in the dark grass and bushes, I heard new sounds. The many cats of the neighborhood, left homeless by Hurricane Katrina, but fed and protected by everyone, were trailing the dogs and me. I could hear them skulking in the shrubs and see their moving shadows as we walked ahead.

I didn't go far. In the daylight hours, sunny Uptown seemed safe, but at night, it became a mysterious place that I didn't know at all. Katrina had devastated the Crescent City and many blocks were still in ruins, where the inhabitants couldn't or wouldn't come home.

Unlike so many neighborhoods, where ruined and uninhabited houses were spray-painted with various warnings, our neighborhood was mostly intact. The worst of the physical devastation had been removed but the psychic toll was still palpable. Nobody whined, but there was a silent residual feeling of fear. In the post-Katrina chaos, homes on our block had been looted and most of our neighbors had guns and ammo. The block had even pooled money to hire a neighborhood security patrol. As for me, I had a baseball bat and a couple of vintage army knives and bayonets that brought me little comfort. They were still in transit.

On a more primal level than personal safety, though, I really fear getting lost. My sense of direction is notoriously bad. And James, the human GPS, had been telling me for years that I couldn't follow the normal compass directions—north, south, east, west—to find my way around New Orleans. Even street maps confused me.

The city works off the mother ship: the Mississippi River, which gives it its distinctive crescent shape and the neighborhoods and districts that flow into each other. New Orleans is ordered not so much by numbers and letters—there's nothing like a grid system—but more by human metrics: original ethnic settlements, wards, parishes, neighborhoods and districts of certain activities, each encompassing multiple intricacies and idiosyncratic names or known by events that just stuck. Major streets and avenues are reference points rather than landmarks.

Each street name tells a story. In the French Quarter, for instance, all the streets named for royals, particularly illegitimate sons of the kings of France, are flanked and separated by streets named for saints.

And just when you think you know where you're going, a street will arbitrarily change names when it crosses into a new 'hood. Because, well . . . just because.

For example, we live in Uptown—upriver from the French Quarter—referred to by some as the University District because it houses Tulane and Loyola universities. Our house is on Palmer Avenue, which is the "lake" side of St. Charles Avenue (named for Carlos III of Spain) and the "river" side of Freret Street, where Katrina's floodwaters stopped. Palmer Avenue becomes Webster Street on the river side of St. Charles because Reverend Webster was run over by a streetcar there and it seemed fitting to name a street after him. And St. Charles turns into Royal Street downriver when you cross into the French Quarter, and it becomes River Road upriver above Uptown/University. The name of our church is St. Stephen, which is in the Good Shepherd parish because the Katrina devastation resulted in the conflation of three churches into one new parish. And where we live is considered "organized."

Confused?

In our first weeks in New Orleans, it was too overwhelming to think about all this. Instead, I determined my safe zone—where I could walk safely and how far I could go without getting accosted or lost. The safe zone was to the end of our block, where I could actually see our house. I walked only that far, and then I walked back.

And I always locked our doors.

But, just a few steps away from the house, even in that short distance, not even one-eighth of a mile, I was overcome by the beauty and breadth of the junglelike foliage. I stared in wonder at the gigantic live oaks with their long arms sweeping high above the house and down to the street. I inhaled the new fragrances, so many all at once. I watched the lush fronds move in the breeze. All I could think was: Jurassic Park.

At the end of our block, I was struck by a feeling that I hadn't had since my childhood. When I was a girl, well before I hit puberty, I had the decorating bug already and had papered the wall above my top bunk with dozens of color photographs from *National Geographic*. I liked to pretend I was an adventurer, and at night and in the early morning, when I awoke, my eyes traveled to exotic places I doubted that I would ever see.

And now, here I was: the adult me, on a most unexpected exploration with my menagerie of domesticated dogs and semiferal cats. I had always dreamed life would be one seamless adventure, destination un-known. And now, the journey was just beginning.

Naturally, there will always be forces that make you want to stop in your tracks. They're not necessarily evil; they're just obstacles. For in-stance, my kids weren't sure about moving. Washington was the only home they'd known. And all their friends were there. My husband—even though James was born and raised and loved Louisiana with every cell of his being, and we'd been married in New Orleans—wasn't totally sure it was the right thing either.

After twenty-eight years for me in Washington, and twenty years for him, it was unthinkable that we'd leave the place where we'd made our careers, had our babies, had so many friends and experiences. Who *leaves* Washington?

All of my friends were unified in their response.

"What? You're doing *what*? You'll be back. You'll be back in six months."

Right decision? Wrong decision?

How would everything turn out?

My previous operating principle in life was to figure things out as quickly as I could—check that task off my list. Make the unknown known. Get the lay of the land. I am a quick study. New Orleans taught me—demanded of me— a different way of living, the way I had always hoped to live. I learned to stop trying to have all the answers, and delight at new discoveries every day instead.

Let mysteries unravel at their own speed.

JAMES

I NEVER HATED WASHINGTON. And I didn't move away because I wanted to run away from something. I just discovered that I didn't want to live there any-more. People in D.C. tend to care very much about the latest political fight or the next campaign, but nobody gives a crap whether LSU wins or loses. Most people didn't even know the line on the game. That alone was enough to make me feel like an outsider at times.

That's not to say I didn't enjoy Washington. I loved being in the center of the storm all those years. I was very close to a president and the people who worked for him. A lot of good things happened during Bill Clinton's tenure in the 1990s, things I'm very proud of. I wouldn't trade those experiences, even the dark days, for anything.

But I never was going to be that guy in his seventies, living out his last days in some apartment building on Connecticut Avenue. I was coming home. I didn't know when, and I didn't know under what circumstances. I just knew it would happen at some point. It always lingered in the back of my mind.

Who am I to say whether Washington has gotten better or worse over the years? That depends on your perspective. All I knew was that it had begun to change in very tangible ways. The whole media landscape had grown so fractured; the news cycles had become constant and too often devoid of any real substance. So many people we'd known and grown to trust—in the media, in politics, in local business—began to die off or move on.

That's not necessarily a bad thing. It's just change, and it's inevitable. But it also forced us to think about whether we'd been there long enough.

By late 2006, I think Mary and I both were growing a little weary of D.C. Twenty years in the pressure cooker will do that to you. I'd fought and clawed to get there. I'd had a good run. I wasn't mad at anybody. But I was kind of losing interest in the conversation.

MARY

JAMES FLEW INTO LOUIS ARMSTRONG AIRPORT the next morning and I drove to pick him up—quite proud of myself for getting there on time in spite of being directionally challenged. James got behind the wheel and I felt instantly safe again. *Daddy's home.*

We were yammering away, catching up, holding hands, scared and excited to be starting yet another unexpected adventure. Of course, food being central to James, he made an immediate beeline to our neighborhood grocery store to get his favorite homegrown Louisiana specialties.

His cell phone started buzzing, a sound that usually sets my molars to grinding since it is the ceaseless sound that accompanies James everywhere, anytime—he jawbones on the phone way more than any girl I've ever known—but I was so happy to be with him and be home, I let it go.

He was all smiles. "Hey, man! Just pulled into town!"

Then silence.

"Tim Russert is dead?"

My instant and only thought: they must mean Big Russ, Tim's daddy in Buffalo—not Tim himself. It was too much to take in. We couldn't believe it. *We didn't believe it.*

His phone buzzed again. It was Tim's MSNBC producer, and she was weeping and weeping, barely able to get out the words. James and I couldn't speak either. That day we fell into pieces that couldn't be picked up.

JAMES

I REMEMBER IT LIKE IT WAS YESTERDAY. June 13, 2008. Friday the thirteenth. Day one in our new home in New Orleans. I'd just gotten to town that morning. Mary had come the night before. The boxes were unpacked. The refrigerator was empty.

We had hopped in the car to pick up a few groceries at Langenstein's, a little family store that's been there forever down on Arabella Street. Bread, milk, eggs, coffee. The basic stuff you need just to get a house started.

That's when my cell phone rang. It was Al Hunt, a longtime Washington reporter and an old friend.

"I've got the most awful news you can imagine," he said. "I think Tim just died."

"That can't be true," I said.

Another call was already coming in. I recognized the number. It was

Barbara Fant, Tim's executive producer at MSNBC. She was weeping. That's when I knew.

Here's the thing. I talked to Tim Russert every day, including most weekends. For years, we hardly ever missed a day. Sometimes it was about politics. But most times it was about sports, about our families, about all kinds of other stuff. He'd call me sometimes when LSU scored a touchdown, just to say congratulations.

I can't tell you the number of conversations I'd had with him about moving back to New Orleans and what it would mean. He was a Buffalo boy at heart. He knew all about having deep roots. He understood the pull of home.

I'd been connected to Tim and *Meet the Press* for decades. That was one of the strongest ties I had to Washington.

And then, boom. Out of nowhere, he was gone.

It was almost like somebody slapped me and said, "All right. You want to move? You want to leave Washington after all these years? Fine, I'll sever one of your biggest connections to it."

In life, you sort of get over everything. My father and my mother died. I lost a brother. It's certainly never the same after that, but you move on.

Still, Tim's death hit me hard. Not only because he was such a dear friend, but also because in some strange and visceral way it marked an end and a beginning. The before and the after. Washington and New Orleans. We were leaving behind a world we had known for a new one filled with uncertainty.

I'll never forget that day. Even now, I take a different route when I go to Langenstein's. I still won't go down Arabella Street.

MARY

I DON'T REMEMBER WHO SAID, "You have to come do the show on Sunday. Brokaw's hosting it." All I remember, besides an all-encompassing pain, was my aching heart for Maureen Orth and Luke Russert, Tim's wife and son. Of course we had to do it. How could we not?

Maureen and Luke are like family to us. Maureen had long been an incredible gal pal and Luke was forever the son we didn't have. There wasn't any other thought but *We gotta go.* There isn't anything you can really do for a grieving family. But, still, you have to try. Unfortunately, from personal experience, I knew Maureen and Luke would be deprived of the normal quiet grieving process, of somberly being surrounded by family and close friends.

Washington, D.C., culture dictated that the Russerts put on a lavish, multitiered televised event where all the D.C. Doyennes and Masters of the Universe could make an appearance and put on a good show of personal grief. I don't mean to suggest that Tim's passing didn't strike deep pain and shock into the hearts of his legions of friends and colleagues. But I was also certain his funeral would be attended by far fewer who *knew* Timothy John Russert of Buffalo, New York, than those who simply knew of the famous man and his coveted Sunday show. And, as if they weren't in enough pain already, dealing with the clamoring "This Town" crowd would be tough for his family.

So we got on a plane and went back to Washington—the city we'd literally just left behind. My heart was sinking. And just because God likes to rub it in sometimes, almost all my wardrobe was in transit, so I was forced to go power shopping for a suitable made-for-TV funeral outfit. Even in my pit of despair, I realized the standard moving garb of shorts and flip-flops wasn't gonna cut it.

Appearing on *Meet the Press* was the last thing I wanted to do, but I consoled myself with the thought that our love for Tim would make the whole ordeal a cakewalk. I was wrong about that.

The Sunday show was horrible. James could not stop crying, so I had to keep it together and be coherent. (Please don't remind me that I wasn't.) The set felt foreign and soulless without Tim. For me, the whole thing was the worst kind of good-bye ever created. And I hate good-byes. I have avoided them all my life. My mom must have been the same way. She had cancer when I was young and she never told any of us, my dad or my brother or my sister or me. She just got thinner and thinner, more and more exhausted, until she left us for good.

All the new losses in our lives trigger painful memories of the old ones.

Misery upon misery, I had just been reunited with Tim—another of God's gut shots, I guess. He and James spoke every day on the phone, usually more than once. But during the long and tortured Scooter Libby investigation and trial, a display of prosecutorial excess the likes of which I hope to never see again, but know I will—Tim and I weren't allowed to speak because Scooter and I had worked together in the Bush/Cheney White House. Scooter had been falsely accused of leaking the identity of CIA operative Valerie Plame, and the case more or less turned on a long forgotten and irrelevant conversation he'd had with Tim, who had been called to testify against Scooter, and I got grilled by the FBI and called before a grand jury.

I am not going to rehash this travesty of justice here, otherwise I will get riled up again over the utter havoc wreaked upon innocent lives in a political parlor game. But the point is, while the ugly circus was going on, nobody in a massive radius of the White House was permitted to talk to most anybody in the D.C. metro area, including Tim and me.

When the trial was finally over, and we could talk again, I called Tim and we both cried and cried into the phone, because we were family, a family ripped apart through no fault of their own. Because I loved him like that.

And then he dies on our first day in New Orleans. To me, leaving God out of it, this was definitely not a good sign. This wasn't a good omen of any kind. And it made me ask myself again: Right decision? Wrong decision? I really wanted an answer.

The funeral was at Tim's Georgetown church, Holy Trinity. He was super Catholic. As expected, everybody who was anybody in the political and power world—and plenty of straphangers—showed up. We were aching to say good-bye to our dear friend, but it wasn't so much Tim's funeral as a generic Important Washington Person funeral. Non-Catholics and known atheists stood in line for Communion and somberly walked out, square in the line of the camera.

I guess if you are seen at an important Washington funeral it means you are worth something, that you matter and count. It might even determine your per-hour billing charge at a law, lobbying or PR firm. I don't know why I was so upset by it; I had already endured the funereal extravaganza of my late boss and mentor, Lee Atwater, as well as one of my very best friends, Ann Devroy. Atwater was the RNC chairman and Ann was a White House reporter for the *Washington Post*, but they were first and foremost a father, a mother, a son, a daughter, a husband, a wife, a beloved friend. And I hated those send-offs.

But there we were.

The church service was followed by a big to-do at the Kennedy Center, and I said, "I cannot go to that." We had front-row seats, we were told. I said, "I'm not going." And James was of the same sorrowful sentiment. But, of course, we did go. We sat in the back in undesignated seats and cut out early before the "after-party." We went to the Palm and got drunk and even then we still couldn't talk about it, but we sure could cry.

JAMES

THEY HAD CALLED AND ASKED if Mary and I would come on a special edition of *Meet the Press* honoring Tim that Sunday, two days after he died, so we turned around and flew back to Washington. Tom Brokaw was going to host the show. Doris Kearns Goodwin was coming, along with Mike Barnicle and a few others.

Neither of us felt much like going on national television at that moment. We both were a mess. But how could you say no? I don't really remember what I said that day, other than talking about how Tim genuinely loved politics and how he was actually even a better guy than people imagined him to be. Mostly, I just remember trying not to cry on air.

There's a word that's used in Washington in a way that is seldom used in other places. And the word is *relationship*. The relationship-to-friendship ratio in Washington is really skewed. It would sound odd in most places if you said, "You know, I have a relationship with that guy." People don't blink at a sentence like that in Washington. I had a relationship with people in the press. I had a relationship with political people in Washington. I had a *friendship* with Tim Russert. We talked probably a dozen times a week. We had basketball tickets together, baseball tickets together. I did a radio show with his son. I did his show God-knows-how-many Sundays. Our families spent holidays together.

So when he died, different people had different reactions. Some people lost a colleague. Some people lost a TV personality they watched every Sunday morning. Some people lost a guy they had a relationship with. I lost a damn good friend. I was grieving profoundly. By Monday afternoon, we'd done *Meet the Press*. I'd done some other interviews about his death. We'd been to the funeral at Tim's church in Georgetown. And afterward came this big see-and-be-seen event at the Kennedy Center, which I think would have amused Tim, the spectacle of it all.

Mary and I left early. We'd just had enough. We didn't feel like seeing or being seen that day. What we really felt like was getting the hell away from everybody else and wallowing in our misery for a while. So we left. I honestly don't even remember where we went. Even now, it's all kind of a blur.

MARY

THE REST OF THAT SUMMER was a blur too—an inferno blur of heat and humidity while we were settling in. Our dogs were very happy to have us home. And my safe zone expanded. Each week, we walked farther into our neighborhood, exploring more. Everywhere I looked, there was something mind-blowing to study. My senses were still in heightened doggie mode. My sound library was building up. In addition to the mellifluous around-the-clock tolling church bells, there were jungle insect sounds—buzzing, crackling, chirping—and the low *clackity-clack* of the streetcars on St. Charles Avenue at the end of our block, plus the random but frequent outbreaks of indigenous local music.

People drove down the street in broad daylight with an entire musical ensemble playing away, right in the back of their pickups. In the middle of Audubon Park, a few blocks from us, there was an old guy on oxygen, a senior citizen attached to some kind of portable breathing device, playing the violin every afternoon.

Like in all of New Orleans, there are countless places of worship in our neighborhood. We have a synagogue on one corner, a Catholic church next door to that, Presbyterian or Episcopalian churches across the street. Along with the inescapable bells, you can't fail to feel a sense of the sacred and other invisible realms around you. Even before I was officially religious, before I had a concrete framework or an easier way to discuss it, living in New Orleans made me acutely aware of our connectivity to something beyond the limiting boundaries of the material world. Of stuff. Of self. I could feel a natural, timeless order to the world, even if it was unrevealed.

James started running in Audubon Park every afternoon. It was just down the street, really, across from Loyola and Tulane. By midsummer I had started walking there, usually alone with the dogs. The land was purchased for a city park in 1871, became a site for the World's Fair in 1884, and was blasted to the ground by the hurricane of 1915. It was rebuilt following a design drafted by John Charles Olmsted, one of the brothers in the revered family firm that created Central Park in Manhattan. It was laid to waste yet again by Katrina, but it is quickly regaining its timeless glory. So it's gorgeous, a bit mysterious—the way all great parks are. It isn't like D.C. and Alexandria's Old Town were without amazing natural beauty of their own, but I rarely had time to slow down, let alone just stop and be absorbed in it.

Many of the giant live oaks there didn't survive Katrina, but the new plantings were taking off like Jack's beanstalk. New Orleans is a paradise for vegetation. After a rain, everything explodes. You can almost hear it, the sound of growth; a day or two later the trees are another foot taller.

The first time I went to the park alone, I noticed the nesting trees near the alligator pond. Egrets would swoop in at dusk, when you could see the diffused light of the setting sun through the Spanish moss. I made a nightly vigil to watch them—hundreds of these magical primordial birds—and studied their varying plumage and tried to discern their pecking order. Their cackling was loud, deafening. And then, suddenly, they'd all grow quiet at the same time.

Very few of the other park walkers and runners paid much attention to this airborne circus. The nesting trees were no big deal to them—just another everyday New Orleans occurrence. But the dogs and I would stand and stare, watching the egrets swoop in with their long legs hanging behind them as they immediately went to their predestined hierarchical positions.

Later on, I realized that the ones on the top of the tree had the greatest plumage, and the little birds with less plumage were on the bottom. Here, I thought, was one piece of the natural, timeless order revealed. What would come next?

JAMES

MY WIFE WAS HAPPY IN NEW ORLEANS. I mean, truly, deeply, instantly happy. More than I could have imagined when we first cooked up the idea of moving back to Louisiana.

Although she's from Chicago and spent nearly three decades in Washington, almost everything about New Orleans fits her personality, from the food to the religion. After all, she insisted on getting married here in 1993. This was always one of her favorite places even before we met.

In part, I think she's drawn toward tradition. She likes subtle noises and the smell of magnolias and jasmine. She likes the tolling of old church bells, the rumbling of the streetcar clapping its way along St. Charles Ave, the sound of a distant gospel choir. She loves spiritual, mystical, ancient things, and New Orleans is all of the above. If you're that kind of person, you're really going to like it down here.

If you're the kind of person who's into modern things, and you don't like bugs and you prefer low humidity, this ain't the place for you. It's not Phoenix. It's not Denver. There's weird stuff that goes on here. There's voodoo and screwed-up streets and rickety old houses and second-line jazz funerals and the eternal threat of hurricanes and floods.

New Orleans definitely isn't for everyone; I'd be the first to admit that. But if it's for you, it's *really* for you.

For our girls, those first days and weeks were daunting; it must have seemed like a different country to them altogether. To them, it must have seemed like an utterly strange land, like when Dorothy arrives in Oz and everything about it seems foreign and foreboding.

They were so young. Washington was the only life they'd really ever known. They were the new kids in school, and everything about the move was a huge adjustment.

I've always been a creature of Louisiana. I'm a brown-blooded American—cut into me, and my blood comes out the color of the river. When we got down here, Mary and the girls were still red-blooded creatures of Washington. But I hoped it would only be a matter of time before their veins started to turn brown too.

MARY

ONE DAY THAT FIRST SUMMER, I took the girls outside and I said, "Come explore the neighborhood with me." So we walked down the block to Audubon Park, which was becoming central to their father's physical and their mother's spiritual daily life in our new home. As soon as we got to the first grove of live oaks, it started to rain.

Except it didn't just rain—it was a full-fledged, hurricane–velocity, gusting storm replete with nonstop lightning and thunder. *Ba-boom! Ba-boom!* The dogs were freaking out and pretty soon the girls and I were freaking out. You really don't want to be in Audubon Park when a summer storm hits. The lightning began striking closer and closer;

the thunder was deafening. There were sheets and sheets of sideways-blasting rain, a real tsunami deluge. Even if we could have seen more than a foot in front of ourselves, we didn't know where to go or what to do. We were stranded in the park, drenched, freezing, huddling together. We didn't have a phone. And nobody knew where we were.

But I had faith. Not the God kind. The Carville kind . . . not that I am making any comparisons whatsoever. I just instinctively knew James would find us. I didn't know where he was . . . heck, I didn't know where we were by then. But when he got back from wherever he was, even though he had no idea where we could be, I knew he would figure out precisely where we were, realize it was a dangerous storm, and he would find us.

James is like a homing pigeon for his family, especially in danger. It's a good thing too, because somebody did get hit by lightning that day.

I said to the girls, "Let's just stay right here and Daddy will come find us."

And he did.

JAMES

AFTER WE MOVED HERE, my children said to me one day, "Dad, would you give us a ride to Pinkberry?"

I said, "Pinkberry, what the hell is that?"

They said, "It's a yogurt place."

So I told them, "We do not eat frozen yogurt in this family. We have snow-balls, goddamn it. I don't want any yogurt in my house."

They were like: "Geez, we just asked the man for some yogurt." They didn't realize it was blasphemy. So I took them down to Hansen's Sno-Bliz to help them understand the majesty of a good snowball.

Hansen's doesn't look like much. It operates out of a little old shack off Tchoupitoulas Street, where it's been for seventy years. But it is an institution. The high cathedral of snowballs in New Orleans. The Taj Mahal. The duomo.

You can get damn near any flavor, from coconut to cream of peach. I usually go with satsuma, which is a little citrus fruit similar to a mandarin.

A few years back, there were like three places in the country with a 29 rating in Zagat. One of them was a restaurant in suburban Chicago. I think another was the French Laundry out in California. The third was Hansen's.

Now my kids know. They don't ask for rides to Pinkberry anymore.

MARY

OF THE MANY WACKY things about James that the girls and I love—or are at least amused by—is his fanaticism over his many rigid epicurean dictates. Like Hansen's snowballs or Domilise's poor boys or Leidenheimer's bread or roadside creole tomatoes or Antoine's oysters or Manale's shrimp, to name just a few. God forbid you get caught sneaking a frozen yogurt or fast-food sandwich. And, truly, anyone who eats a store-ripened tomato is damned to eternity.

JAMES

FOR ME, moving back to New Orleans was like taking an old bike out of the garage after twenty-five years. You haven't been on it in a while, but you never forget how to ride it, so you just hop on and go. I knew the culture. I knew the streets. I knew a lot of people, and most of my family lived right up the road. The heat didn't bother me. I loved the sports teams and the food. I slipped right back into Louisiana life.

In Louisiana, I know everybody and everybody knows me. One of my favorite stories—and this shows you the difference between Washington and New Orleans—is about going to get my driver's license after we moved.

In Washington, if you're a public figure, you have to be awfully careful about throwing your weight around. I've always been cautious about relying on fame or celebrity for any kind of special treatment.

So, right after we moved down, I went to the DMV to get a new license. I take a number and sit down with a stack of newspapers, prepared for a long wait. All of a sudden, the lady working the counter says, "Mr. Carville, come on up."

And I'm like: "Oh, no, no, I'm sitting here with everybody."

And the people in line start saying, "Man, go on up there. This man ain't got time to fool around. Go on up!" The crowd was almost shoving me toward the front of the line.

In Washington, you have to say no to something like that. Somebody will snap a picture and post it on a blog. It will end up in Reliable Sources in the *Washington Post*.

It's a different world. Part of that is that they simply revere older people in this culture. If you get old and retire in Washington, they'll just run you over at the DMV or anywhere else. It's just the way it is. If you think that people will say, "Oh, that guy was Bill Clinton's campaign manager," and then open a door for you, no way. That's relevant for some time, but it has a shelf life.

Obviously the transition wasn't quite so smooth for everyone else that first year, especially the girls. I knew Matty and Emma felt apprehensive about settling into a new school in a new city. Who wouldn't be at their age? Matty was going into eighth grade, and Emerson was starting fifth grade. But they were wrestling with more than just the usual challenges and anxieties of being the new kid in class. There was a real tightness among the kids who had lived there during Katrina and endured the storm. They had been through the fire together; they had a bond. It was hard at times to break through and make friends if you didn't have that shared experience.

On top of all that, New Orleans is a hard city to explain to someone who's never lived there. Socially, ethnically, racially—it's a very complicated place that's not given to simple explanations. So we spent a lot of time talking with them about why things were the way they were.

It definitely could have been tougher. If your daddy is a gunnery sergeant in the Marine Corps, he might be shipped off to Afghanistan for a year, and then you might get stationed in North Carolina or Okinawa or any number of places. You're *always* the new kid on the block. The girls weren't totally surrounded by strangers. They had their aunts and uncles and cousins all around. We had a nice house in a nice neighborhood, and people threw parties welcoming us to the city.

Still, I know it wasn't easy. I suspect they shared more about their struggles with their mother than with me. But as a father, you just know. You notice every detail—how many friends they have over or don't have over, their daily demeanor, everything. It's not like they were out-and-out miserable. But I could tell it took a while to find their footing. At the same time, I think on some level they understood it was important that we were there, that part of the reason for coming back was to help rebuild the city. I think they also recognized that they were in a unique place.

But me? It was just a matter of dusting off the bike and going for a ride.

MARY

I AM FORBIDDEN TO SPEAK, write, discuss or even *think* about the girls with anyone without their prior approval, which is harder to obtain than the top security clearance I used to have at the White House. So when I write about our family's transition to New Orleans and what those first days and weeks and months were like, I am writing entirely about me.

For my sake—and possibly your own—assume we are talking about an entirely *hypothetical* and *fictional* universe, one in which two middle school girls are ripped from the only home they have ever known and flung blindly into another middle school in a distant galaxy by already certifiably crazy parents.

And imagine this hypothetical middle school girl having no lifeline or anything like a real or imaginary friend, except her sister—with whom she may or may not be speaking at any given time. And without the comfort of her posse of friends back in Old Town Alexandria who'd been with her since preschool, and without the reliable protection of an Iron Man suit of armor—or even Harry Potter's cloak of invisibility—I guess we can all agree that this would be a daunting experience.

And it was.

But not for any of the reasons I'd anticipated.

My first mistake was presuming these two girls, who have wildly divergent personalities and worldviews, would react in lockstep to their new universe.

Emerson—if I may call the youngest daughter that, although it bears no resemblance to her real name—had a super-close, high-octane, barrel-of-monkeys cast of characters back in Virginia. Now deprived of them, she tried valiantly not to complain about having moved to a place where everybody in town knew everybody else, and each other's cousins and ancient ancestors to boot. Compounding her discomfort, she was at the stage of hyper self-consciousness, which you wouldn't think would be so tortuous, as she had a closet right out of *The Devil Wears Prada* and is blessed with a long sumptuous mane of straight, silky, shiny, dark auburn hair and a flawless face. But apparently none of those, or her many other blessings, counted. Still, she did not complain. Nor did she complain about being three feet taller than the other students in her class, except she did confess to me—under duress—that she was singled out at her new school as "freakishly tall." And I will say, in the defense of the mean-spirited child who described the beautiful Emerson this way, that she did stand literally head and shoulders above her classmates.

"Embrace your height, honey!" It sounded like a mother's cheerleading, but I meant it. "Everyone would kill for legs to the ceiling—and glossy auburn hair to the waist. You are beyond beautiful!"

But the mother's and the daughter's perceptions don't always line up, particularly when one of them is in fifth grade. Still, not once did Emerson complain. But mothers don't listen so much to what their kids say as watch what they do, and I was tracking her like a Reagan National air traffic controller at rush hour.

Emerson was tough and poised to the casual witness, but to her mother it was heartbreakingly clear this previously gregarious, fun-loving, witty girl was withdrawing due to her removal from her "true place."

Being a mother is often similar to being a manager (or a wife, I guess): to get your people to do their best, you have to know how they process information and tackle problems. The trick in being effective at this, according to the great and wise Carville, is to "think like they think."

But I have never been great at thinking like anyone other than myself. And my process does not work for everyone. (Behind my back, on campaigns, I was often referred to as a "ballbuster," which I am not sure was meant as a compliment. My foxhole buddy on the campaign cycle, Bill Canary, once presented me with a little trophy of a winged angel on a marble pedestal that was inscribed, SHREW BITCH FROM HELL.)

But Emerson is no shrew bitch. She is thoughtful, contemplative and resists confrontation, preferring instead to consider carefully thought-out corrective options.

One night, while I was tucking her in, rather than say what I was thinking—*How in the name of everything that is holy could anyone not love this magical place?*—I carefully said, "Honey, this isn't prison; we can go back if you want. I will split time between here and Virginia." (Where we still had a home we couldn't sell, thanks to the Obama economy.)

"But you love it here, Mom," she replied, with true thoughtfulness. "Going back would make you so unhappy."

This stopped me in my tracks. My sweet, young daughter had put my happiness above her own and suffered rather than cause her selfish old mother discomfort. I tried to make her understand nothing could make a mother more miserable than having an unhappy child—especially such a thoughtful and caring one. What had I done to my precious baby girl? I really was a shrew bitch from hell and not in a good way.

For Matty, or the girl whom we shall refer to as Matty—even though she has beautiful alabaster skin, naturally curly and naturally blond locks, not to mention a wit and spark that could light up any room—the transition adjustment process was completely different.

The hardest part of her arrival at the prestigious Academy of the Sacred Heart on St. Charles Avenue—grandmothers "penciled in" their unborn grandchildren when their daughters married and alumni families traced their connection to the institution to the Dark Ages—wasn't just being an unknown nonlegacy, it was being an overly known nonlegacy legend, *the daughter of James Carville*.

It had always been confusing to both our girls—and uncomfortably so—that James evokes strong emotions in people; they *really* love him or they *totally* despise him. And nobody seems capable of refraining from sharing their excessive opinions about him with his daughters. He is what they call in our home state, *a Louisiana legend*. And the point is, while I could pretty much predict what kind of reception the mention of him would elicit, depending on where we were, the girls were always walking on eggshells.

Matty's love and devotion to her father is deep and serious (for the most part), but she got plenty sick of hearing ad nauseam about how great he was. (And who wouldn't?) The two of them can fight like cats and dogs (or worse, since we have regular canine-feline contretemps in our home and they are never as bad as Matty and James going at it), but when exposed to the slightest lamentations of outsiders, she defends him with fierceness and passion. Worse than either situation, though, is being prejudged as a "daughter of" rather than as her own unique person.

To make matters worse, in those early days of our new life, James was in the local newspaper almost every day, a daily paper with 68 percent readership penetration. He was on a warpath to save New Orleans, fix New Orleans, heal New Orleans and be there for New Orleans. The man loves this city; every person here loves this special place. But barely a day passed without everyone reading about Citizen James Carville in the *Times Pic* before they brushed their teeth in the morning, which made every day another fresh new hell for Matty.

Which she kept to herself, of course, to avoid hurting our feelings. But no one had to tell her mother. Matty's heart beat in mine. Both Matty's and Emerson's did. And, by my reckoning, the pain and suffering of the opening days of their new life were frying their tender hearts to a crisp. What kind of selfish, heinous parents would drag their happy young girls from their own paradise to one that was ours? Confronting this question provoked the most heart-searing and painful mother moments I've experienced.

Some of the pain was made worse by the uniform.

The Catholic girls' school uniform.

This part is not fiction: Catholic girls' school uniforms are itchy, sweaty, ugly, stiff and too long—oppressive Christian-style burkas that require so little care or cleaning that they can be slept in and worn the next day, looking spotless and smooth. All you have to do is get out of bed and scrunch your unbrushed, dreadlockian hair into one of two ubiquitous styles: the high bun or the low bun. That completed "the look."

At first, when the girls complained about *the uniform*, I defended it. It seemed like a high-performance protective shield along the lines of Harry's cloak of invisibility.

My argument was that if every girl looks exactly the same, from all threads down to the shoelaces, then wouldn't all girls effectively disappear? (And what about the furniture people in Sherlock Holmes? If the uniform didn't render complete invisibility, wasn't it good enough to just blend in? Heck, even Dr. Watson didn't recognize his famous detective partner.)

The girls were fans of Harry and Holmes but, like teenage girls from any planet, did not see the particular relevance of them to their own sartorial existence.

Matty, always favoring efficiency over fussiness in her wardrobe, quickly came to worship her uniform—customizing it with handsome ink drawings, strategic rips, a triple-wrapped waistband. But Emerson, a fashionista from birth, never stopped loathing such undistinguished garb. Her painstaking attention to dressing always rivaled that of Renaissance master painters.

And there was no comfort in being reminded that, in Emerson's previous existence back in Virginia, there were years and years of mornings where she said, "I don't have anything to wear, Mom," while peering into a closet as big and messy as Filene's Basement, and years of coming downstairs to model completely different, fully accessorized outfits with the "how does this look" look on her face. To which I always replied, "Just darling, darling," which turns out to be the *totally not right* thing to say.

Each morning of our old life culminated in the old mother nag having to shout, "Girl, you are *not* going out of the house in that!" while I was slaving over a hot breakfast. (The girls may tell you this entire chapter is complete fiction, but they can't deny under oath that they were often served my famous breakfast of champions—Kraft mac and cheese and canned pork and beans—even if it wasn't always piping hot.)

Time heals all. If only I had listened to my own internal maternal voice telling me that in those early days in New Orleans. Instead, I got caught up in bribery, in taking the girls on multiple shopping extravaganzas (did I mention Catholic girls need a lot of clothes?), spa days, getaways, return trips to Virginia, as well as helping to plan massive sleepovers in hopes of helping them settle in—none of which Matty remotely wanted or Emerson needed. So as the new gravitational force set in, peace did not reign in the land of our fictional solar system.

In a classic bit of overreaction, with only a few strands of hair left unpulled from her already dwindling, graying mane, our fictional mother resorted to the nuclear option: transition counseling. I sought out, found and put us in the hands of a real professional.

The opening chapter of our little fictional tale concludes: After one session, the professional transition counselor calls in the overwrought mother and says, "Mrs. Carville"—even though her real last name is Matalin—"your daughters are fine; you are nuts."

Okay then.

JAMES

I KNEW MARY WAS NUTS A LONG TIME AGO, but I loved her in spite of it—and probably because of it.

When we tied the knot back in 1993, a lot of people thought it was some kind of stunt marriage. They wouldn't exactly come up and tell you that to your face. But we knew. We heard the whispers.

Mary and I had a big raucous wedding on Thanksgiving Day in New Orleans. We led a dancing, swinging jazz parade through the French Quarter. Bystanders threw Mardi Gras beads down from the balconies. Imagine Rush Limbaugh and Paul Begala waltzing down Bourbon Street at the same time. It was a hell of a lot of fun.

But I think the general feeling among some people was that this was a great party, a nice wedding, but also kind of a big joke. We'll all have a good time, have a good laugh, and then move on to the next thing. It never would last.

It wasn't like that at all, not for me.

One of my most satisfying moments came the next year when the book Mary and I had written about the 1992 campaign came out. We'd called it *All's Fair: Love, War, and Running for President*.

Jonathan Yardley, the influential critic at the *Washington Post*, had gone on a rant when Random House and Simon & Schuster had announced they would jointly publish the book as a political and romantic memoir. He'd called it "a nonevent staged in order to announce the impending arrival of a nonbook." He said it was "virtually certain" that the book would be a dud and that "hype is really the only thing that matters in an enterprise such as this one."

When the book finally came out and we saw that he'd reviewed it, we expected to just get slaughtered. But here's what he wrote: "Fry it or bake it, broil it or barbecue it: No matter how you cook your crow, it's still an indigestible meal. But when it's the only dish on the table, there's no choice except to suck it up and chow down." He called the book "entertaining, engaging and—here comes the fattest piece of crow—interesting."

I sent Yardley a bottle of Old Crow whiskey with a note that said, "Better to drink crow than eat crow."

What he didn't understand—what a lot of people haven't understood over the years—is that our marriage never was a stunt. Sure, we have the Republican-versus-Democrat dynamic, sleeping with the enemy, however you want to describe it. It's true that I don't agree with her politics, but we agree on plenty of other things. And what two married people have ever been exactly alike? How boring.

I got married when I was forty-nine years old. It's the first and only time I've ever been married. I didn't enter into that lightly. This never was a lark for us. We knew what we were getting into, and we stuck with it.

A lot of people have eaten a lot of crow about that over the years.

MARY

I CONFESS THAT I AM NOT completely unsympathetic to the cognoscenti who were skeptical about our blessed union—even the ones who had never met us but confidently accused us of pulling off what they were certain was nothing more than a sideshow gimmick. To them, ours was a tawdry low-life romance and "stunt marriage" designed to get positive press attention. As one critic wrote in a book review in the *Washington Post* in 1996:

> Political consultants have long cultivated the press through leaking and quippery; in 1992 Carville went them one better by flaunting his own eccentricity and pouring out lyrical streams of expletives. His stunt marriage to Republican operative Mary Matalin, and his stunt book about his stunt marriage, only underscored the point. If Carville outshone others in his field, it was a through his genius for self-promotion.

It's not as though contemporary culture doesn't produce a steady parade of look-at-me marriages—or prop children—at least the "culture" heralded by the East Coast elite and the West Coast arbiters of fine Hollywood taste does. In turn, this cockeyed value system is pumped into the American cultural bloodstream around the clock. And considering what most of America has no choice but to consume in mass-media

products—thanks to the Barnum and Bailey world of "infotainment"—
why would anybody think we were real people with real convictions
and a real marriage, or even real children? So "stunt life" became our
"narrative."

Our romance didn't become public by some master Machiavellian
plan, or even with our consent, originally. We were just two longtime
trench-warfare politicos whose paths crossed by chance, two people who
had more in common due to the nature of their work and passion than
most normal people, even though we happened to be true believers in
diametrically opposing political philosophies, which, by the way, is way
less unique in the real world than is commonly claimed.

And then, like a bad random traffic accident, we found ourselves in
love and together at the same time that we were both lucky enough, and
hardworking enough, to be chosen as campaign pooh-bahs in opposite
camps in an epic battle for the presidency in 1992.

James led the charge for the wayward, I-never-inhaled, Southern-
fried-but-elite-educated, liberal-in-centrist's-sheepskin candidate, Bill
Clinton. I was the one who stood by the ultimate statesman, an honest
man and lifelong public servant, George H. W. Bush—aka "Poppy" to
me—the fantastic, accomplished incumbent who deserved victory but
had it snatched away by a perfect storm generated by a next-gen Southern stud and an old-gen crackpot, Ross Perot.

Due to the length of presidential campaigns, the media found it had
to fill an inordinate amount of airtime and column inches. There are
only so many scintillating diversions to cover in the daily grind of an
endless campaign with its nauseatingly repetitive stump speeches and
canned talking points, even though no one could deny what, between
Clinton and Perot, 1992 was stacking up to be not your predictable
garden–variety presidential contest.

I guess in that context a seemingly impossible romance between two
oddballs was a juicy press tidbit, gussied up to be the story of a
modern-day Romeo and Juliet on the road to the White House.

I would not deny we were, and remain, offbeat creatures. I would also not deny we are unlikely celebrities. But we didn't plan it, nor did we encourage or discourage it; we just went with it. From our perspective, coverage was coverage and we were always trying to disseminate the messages of our respective sides as far and wide as possible, by whatever vehicle available. There didn't seem to be much wrong in that. Any sane pol could (and should) take easy access to media for their candidate. But in the end, becoming famous or, in our case, mostly *in*famous—even mildly so—is a life-changing thing and can feel like you've both won and lost the lottery at the same time.

2.

Fame,
Failure and TV

JAMES

I DON'T THINK THAT I had any idea the day before Bill Clinton was elected what life would be like the day after. It wasn't like anybody sat me down and said, "Starting tomorrow, you're going to be famous." Nobody prepares you for that transition.

Right after Clinton won, I came back to Washington and picked up Mary, and we went to Venice. We both needed a vacation after such a long, grueling campaign, and we'd planned to take that trip no matter who won. But when we got to Italy, there were paparazzi camped out there waiting for me. It was insane.

When I got back to Washington, everybody was calling me for interviews. Or inviting me to dinner parties. That sort of thing. Katie Couric had my mother on the *Today* show, which was an awfully big deal back home. Then there was the inauguration itself. It was all very heady stuff.

I'd spent the better part of fifty years being anonymous, like anyone else walking down the street. I was thirty-three years old before I ever went to Washington, D.C., or New York. I was forty-two before I won my first political campaign. All of a sudden, that anonymity had vanished, and I was being hailed around town as the guy who engineered Bill Clinton's improbable run for president.

The first real celebrity political consultant was probably Lee Atwater back during the 1980s, who was a mentor and dear friend to Mary. Michael Deaver was pretty well-known back during the Reagan days. Both of them had become famous in political circles, but they never really became famous in the larger world.

Things had changed by the time I arrived in Washington. Clinton's election coincided with the rise of cable television and nonstop, around-the-clock news. He was the first baby boomer president, which brought with it another layer of hype. In many ways, my own fame arose out of that new media environment and all the attention being showered on a new, young president.

The only kind of fame I'd ever sought was to be respected in my own little world of political consultants. Even before 1992, I'd won a bunch of races—Bob Casey in Pennsylvania, Frank Lautenberg in New Jersey, Wallace Wilkinson in Kentucky, Zell Miller in Georgia, Harris Wofford in Pennsylvania—and I'd built a solid name for myself in the business. I always dreamed about making a name for myself professionally. But this was something else entirely.

MARY

I'VE WORKED ROUTINELY at home from the time I could walk and outside the home since I was eleven. Working is what our family did. Our credo was everybody had to pitch in and nobody got anything for nothing. And by the time I was an adult, work was the only thing I was reasonably good at.

Not just any kind of working, but a very specific narrow kind of working: I kept getting drawn to intense, driven, seven-days-a-week, warp-speed, hyperconnected work situations, getting lost completely in nonstop pressure and being on call every second of the day.

My whole life had been structured—my whole adult life, even before graduating from college—around high-pressure situations. That was what I loved and knew. When I was working on a campaign, every day had purpose and meaning and a quantifiable objective, namely, to fight with every fiber in every cell to elect good solid conservatives. Sometimes you lose and it's devastating. But the fight goes on. I never planned for the next job. Another campaign would always materialize.

That's one of the beautifully reliable things about politics. A campaign ends, you take a breath, maybe you get a vacation. You pay all the credit card bills and mortgage payments that you missed while you were in the trenches, and you call your friends who have almost forgotten you exist. But before you have time to call all of them or get your big backside reverse engineered into shape—or even before you join a gym—there's another campaign. And you jump on it like a moving train. In no time at all you are miles away from your home and life and mortgage payments. Maybe it doesn't sound like it, but it's a beautiful thing.

Except in 1993. There was no beauty. There was no moving train to jump onto. For the deputy campaign director for Bush 41, losing the presidential election was the kind of loss that people don't recover from quickly in Washington, D.C., or least they didn't then.

That particular loss made me the poster child for failure and disgrace.

A year before, Poppy Bush had been a beloved president. Everybody enjoyed his amusing antics and thought he was a charming, stately, earnest, honest, accomplished shoo-in for reelection, a reelect campaign we kicked off with a 91 percent approval rating.

He had managed the messy collapse of the Communist bloc with prudence and strategic foresight. He'd led us stoutly through the first Gulf War with seamless leadership. There were pockets of localized recessionary problems, but the overall 1992 economy grew at 5.7 percent (after a half decade of Obamanomics, you probably don't recognize that number). He launched A Thousand Points of Light, leveraging the American spirit of compassion and service to others.

Further, he had unprecedented experience in more fields than any three normal people could accomplish in three lifetimes, including successes in business, intelligence operations, and diplomacy as well as local, state and national politics. And most impressive of all, he excelled professionally while maintaining a first-rate marriage to a firecracker and universally beloved wife and raising five exceptional kids. Oh yeah, he was also a super athlete and a refined man.

Whenever I see the man—then or now—these words spring to mind.

Duty
Honor
Country

Besides all those things, I loved Poppy for personal reasons too. As I said in *All's Fair*, he took me under his wing in my worst days, right after my mother died, and, secondly, he was unfailingly loyal to his people and a genuinely good guy.

When our campaign death-spiraled, this historic president and stand-up statesman was caricatured as a one-term loser, and everybody associated with him—or at least those who didn't jump on the trash-Bush bandwagon—degenerated into radioactive toxic material. And politics being politics, when the chips were down and Poppy started sinking in the polls, very few people—his family and oldest friends aside—seemed eager to go out and publicly defend him.

So it became my job to go out—on TV, radio, in print and even on target-state street corners—and defend, defend, defend, along with making plenty of take-no-prisoners attacks on his opponents, which came pretty naturally to me. My ubiquitous and annoying presence, combined with the persistent focus on the whole Romeo-Juliet parody with James (even though the star-crossed lovers hadn't been in the same city or state for months) raised my profile while tripping up my life.

We lost and I dive-bombed overnight, splatting on the public pavement like an overripe rotten tomato. After twelve years of steady ascent in national Republican politics, I naively hoped everything I had built in my professional life—all the political miles and commitment and eons of invested time and decades of hard-earned relationships—would add up to *something* (in a just and merciful world).

But that's not the way it works in politics. And I can't honestly say that I didn't know this or expect this—or even not deserve it. But still, the lightning speed of my professional disintegration left me unmoored and lost. Especially painful were the fair-weather foxhole buddies who dumped me as if I were yesterday's smelly garbage. Overnight, it seemed, my whole world imploded. Washington is brutal that way. And to my credit, I guess, I didn't whine about it. No one would have listened anyway.

Besides, I couldn't wallow around in a one-man pity party, since credit card companies and mortgage holders are notoriously not into excuses for nonpayment.

So I was a loser girl without cash reserves, rich relatives or employment prospects. And I was deluged by payment-due notices. For the first time in my life, I was truly unemployable, at least as far as jobs I wanted, political jobs. I suppose I could have beaten the bushes for a corporate job or lobbying contract or knocked on Capitol Hill doors. But all I really wanted was to do what I always did: go back to the Republican National Committee and work toward the midterm and next presidential elections. But due to my radioactive status, that was no longer an option.

So I sat around my apartment reading cookbooks until I could come up with a better idea. Preferably something that paid.

And while I was adjusting to life without a job and days without purpose, James was beating off endless opportunities and accolades with a baseball bat. And getting every freaking award known to mankind just for being him.

JAMES

SOME OF IT WAS FUN. Some of it wasn't. But I'd never experienced anything quite like it. You walk into a restaurant, and people want to stop by and talk with you or take a picture together. Not that I didn't enjoy the attention. I've never been one to shy away from the spotlight. But you can begin to feel a little bit like an animal at the zoo, always being gawked at by passersby. I can see how some famous people become reclusive.

I figured out pretty quickly that if you didn't want to be nice to people don't go out. But once you went out, you'd better be a gentleman. If people see you being rude to someone, those kinds of stories travel a hell of a lot faster than any story of kindness. You could end up looking like a real asshole. I was pretty determined not to do that.

One thing that helped keep my head out of the clouds was seeing how raw Mary still was from the election. It had taken a lot out of both of us, of course. But to go through all that and lose made it even tougher for her. As thrilled as I was about the results, as much as I was enjoying my newfound celebrity, seeing her struggle with it sort of tempered my excitement.

Plus, it didn't take long for reality to set in. Clinton had a stimulus package that failed a few months after he took office. There was an uproar over the "don't ask, don't tell" policy on gays in the military. Then there was the midterm election disaster in 1994, when Republicans took back control of Congress.

That's how it went during the Clinton years. You were constantly up and then down. Something good would happen; something awful would happen. The reelection in 1996 was joyous. Whitewater and the Monica Lewinsky episode were abysmal. Along the way, Mary and I got hitched in late 1993. Matty was born in 1995. Emerson came along in 1998.

It was all a blur. Most days, I was just trying to keep my head above water.

MARY

NOT WORKING TOOK A TOLL ON ME, not just financially. It also took a toll on my spirit. Even in college, I had a job in a bread factory, worked in my mom's beauty shop and had a dog-breeding business on the side. *I need to work.* It would be a disservice to the truly clinically depressed to compare my abject misery and hyperpurposelessness to how they suffer. But I was suffering. I was lost. I was totally out of sorts. I had never ever not worked.

If I did get a chance to go out, it was to one of the two thousand James-victory-lap events, where he'd be getting another golden award or speaking to an audience of movie stars. His mother, Miss Nippy, would be always there, treating him like he was the Christ child and being an example of the sort of unconditionally loving presence that I never could be. (I just wasn't that kind of girlfriend—never mind wife.) Every single event I went to, trying to be supportive of James, was a miserable, painful experience. It wasn't just like ripping a scab from a healing wound. It was like sticking hot spikes into a wound and twisting the skin and pouring vinegar on it.

I can't begin to describe the painful confusion—because it was concomitant with my love for him. I wanted to be proud of him and applaud for him without all this ambivalence, but every award he received involved an incredible description of the brilliant campaign he ran against *us* and, more specifically, against me, which . . . come on . . . wouldn't you agree that it's just bad form for the James groupies to relish rubbing it right in my face?

That became the narrative. He was brilliant. I was inept. He was cool. I was a steaming pile of doggie doo. This undisputed narrative, which went on interminably, resulted in a schizophrenic world in which I was madly in love with him but simultaneously hated every inch of his skinny Cajun being.

Week after week passed with the glitterati swirling around him; Hollywood stars swooned over him, like the actress Kim Basinger—who is so beautiful even I had trouble keeping my eyes off her. The whole interplanetary system waited in line to tell him how incredible he was. And here I am: no job, no prospect of a job, no money, mounting debt and a relationship that was so absurdly confusing I couldn't even think about it . . . not that I wanted to.

Then one day I'm sitting alone in my apartment—again—and a woman named Ann Klenk calls and says, "Would you like to do a TV show?"

"I hate doing TV," I say.

"Come on," says Ann Klenk, "it's not that bad."

JAMES

I THINK I MADE A series of pretty smart decisions that kept my head on straight even after the initial burst of fame and that set me on a good path. Some were more serendipitous than anything deliberate on my part. There's that old expression that God protects drunks and fools. I guess, because I was both, I had a lot of protection.

First off, I didn't take up with a whole new crowd in Washington. I went to a few parties, of course, but I wasn't overly social. I didn't settle into the Georgetown dinner scene. I didn't buddy up to many movers and shakers on Capitol Hill. Most of my friends in town were people from the campaign, only they were in the White House now instead of Little Rock. I'd go over and hang out with them.

Mary and I got engaged that spring of 1993 after Clinton's inauguration. That was a blessing in more ways than I can count. It settled me and kept me out of trouble. I was a pretty active guy during my single days. The last thing I needed now that I had a much higher public profile was to be out chasing women all over Washington.

The book that Mary and I wrote together after the 1992 campaign turned out to be another good decision. She started on her own television show with Jane Wallace, on CNBC, and was becoming well-known in her own right.

Though I stuck around as an adviser to the president, I chose not to go into the White House full-time or become a lobbyist. That surprised some people, but it felt right. I was almost fifty years old by the time Clinton got to the White House. I didn't have a hell of a lot of money in the bank. Neither did Mary. I figured I had to go out and make some money while I could. So working in the government didn't seem like a wise choice, and the lobbying world just didn't appeal to me.

Bob Barnett, one of the best lawyers and deal makers in D.C., told me I should go talk with Harry Rhoads, who had cofounded the Washington Speakers Bureau back in the late 1970s. I began traveling all over the country giving speeches, and I've never really stopped. I've probably given 1,500 speeches over the years. It became a big part of my income and something I really enjoy, certainly more than I'd have enjoyed endless meetings at the White House or lobbying on Capitol Hill.

Finally, I was determined not to do any more domestic political consulting. I decided I would only work on foreign campaigns, and that's a decision that I've always been thankful I made at the time.

I just trusted my gut, and I'm glad I did. It kept me out of a lot of stuff I could have gotten into that would have been unpleasant. For instance, I'd encounter people who were hoping to take advantage of my ties to Clinton to win influence in some way. But I could always say truthfully that I didn't work for the White House, and that I had no real decision-making power there. Likewise, when candidates would approach me about other U.S. campaigns, I didn't have to make up excuses for somebody I didn't necessarily want to work for. I'd just say I didn't do domestic campaigns anymore, period.

I can't tell you that I sat up one night and planned the whole thing. But I do give myself credit for making some wise choices during those days when I could have gone a lot of different directions. In a town like Washington, not all of them would have turned out well.

MARY

I DIDN'T WANT TO do a TV show. I *never* wanted to do a TV show. But in 1992 and early 1993, before James and I were married, or had a book contract, I was broke. Stone-cold out of cash, out of work and out of favor. If necessity is the mother of invention, then for me, desperation and starvation were the accidental parents of wacky TV shows.

And so, quite randomly, the spawn of my epic political failure was a groundbreaking, cult-producing, girl-gab show, something called *Equal Time*, on CNBC. It was ostensibly political. And it was ostensibly an actual "show." And it starred me, as the humiliated, disgraced and not particularly photogenic politico, and Jane Wallace, as the awesomely beautiful superstar and Emmy Award–winning television journalist who knew what she was doing in front of a camera.

Many have claimed that Jane and I paved the way for *The View*, and all the subsequent chick-fight shows, which were suspiciously copycat. Okay, I'm bragging, but I'm not exaggerating. Before one reviewer described our show as "*Wayne's World* on estrogen," there were few if any women on TV giving it to you straight up, or at least on the rocks.

And that was the concept: a loose and relaxed show with two smart women being honest, being comfortable in their own skin, and having deep and honest unrushed conversations with people on all sides of the issues. It was five nights a week. Prime time. That sounds a little more glamorous than it actually was, though. CNBC was still a fledgling operation and I was being paid just enough to cover the mortgage. It was about one-third of my campaign salary, which, in those days, was already nothing to write home about.

The "show" was equally low budget, a bargain-basement production literally—it was shot in a D.C. basement—and it looked it. Jane and I did our own hair and wore whatever we wanted, which was frequently and arbitrarily just pulled from a dryer. We didn't have decent furniture, or even much of a set. Every night before the cameras were turned on, we had to drag in chairs and a rickety dime-store table from the nearby waiting room.

CNBC was still figuring out what it was—and who its audience was. It was the anything-goes era of cable, like the Wild West, way before the whole political-junkie-around-the-clock universe had been created, and before the true TV god, Roger Ailes, took over and gave CNBC a soul and purpose. At the time, the random suits in charge tried experimenting with every sort of show. They wanted to see what worked and they tried having a "this" show and a "that" show, and we were the *girl* show.

They gave us no guidance, other than the original girl-show concept, and left us alone. We became a neglected orphan show, which must be how hits are made, stars are born and cults created. (So to those of you who dream of launching your own hit TV show, there is your answer. Except I wouldn't try it in your own basement.)

The dynamic between Jane and me had nothing to do with political tension, left versus right. It was more about attitude. I was intense. She was carefree. We came from different professional worlds and had no respect for each other's careers. I couldn't imagine anybody wanting to be a TV reporter; it seemed like the most unserious, *insipid* and vain thing to do. Jane was even more hateful of politics and politicians, and considered my work pointless, uninspiring and silly. The whole Washington scene was beyond ridiculous to her. It was unserious to her and deadly serious to me. I mean, I'd devoted my entire adult life to it and was still trying to heal an open, oozy wound from losing a presidential election.

Not surprisingly, Jane and I got into nightly on-air fights. It made me nuts when she'd make fun of Dan Quayle or do what journalists do in their sleep—make sweeping assumptions and global statements patched together from scraps of misinformation. I'd call her out on stuff, to her great delight. The girl could really take it. And the girl could really make me laugh. That's how we complemented each other. Every night was a genuine love-hate bitch-fest bonfire, which all you women out there know is the foundation of a deep and profound friendship.

We were both pigheaded, forceful, and had a beast-of-burden work ethic. I was used to campaign life, had worked alongside legends such as Lee Atwater and Rich Bond. If I hadn't actually "seen it all," then I had seen a pretty expansive swath of it all. Jane was a chain-smoker with a truck driver's mouth, a single mother of what seemed like a passel of urchins to me (being the single, childless know-nothing that I was at the time). Jane's kids were adorable, actually, and she was a crackerjack mom, always worried about their runny noses and all that mom stuff that gave me a headache.

We'd all pile into Jane's car, with the kids sniffling in the backseat, and she'd light up. And as if I was some kind of Mother of the Year, I'd admonish her, "What? You're smoking? Are you sure that is approved-for-urchin behavior? Open the window at least, *beeatch*. And give me a butt, babe."

We drank on the set every night. We put wine in our coffee cups and eventually we joked about it openly on air. What the heck, nobody was watching anyway. At least we didn't think they were. We were just doing the chick chat-rap that CNBC said it wanted. And somehow we got really good guests. *Really good*. Even if the politicians were oblivious to cultural happenings, their staffs were onto us like a rat on a Cheeto.

Once *Equal Time* got a buzz going, we were able to bring on anybody we liked. All-night cable shows didn't exist in those days, so we had our pick of politicos—the same people who wouldn't give me the time of day, let alone a job, just months before. People who had lied to me. One should never let a crisis go to waste, as they say, and now they came in droves to try to tap into our politically active and astute cult audience. We called our fans "Loopsters" because they were following such a loopy TV show.

Jane and I were not trying to do good TV. We *were* trying to do real thinking—mimicking the kind of thought process and conversation that goes on every day inside a campaign, though surely that would have royally pissed off Jane if I had pointed it out to her. It was purposeful gabbing to get somewhere, a destination unknown as far we knew. It was a sincere and intense conversation, and politicians loved it. How often are they asked to do that?

I was on a mission—a deep-dive journey into understanding policy—and I felt a fervent obligation to convey it in an understandable, accessible way to our audience. But I am pretty sure it would have been a yawner if not for Jane's professional and skeptical but bemused probing. While we talked, the cameras seemed to disappear, as though the cameramen were truly enchanted.

In the campaign world in those days, politics and policy were kept separate, parallel universes with very little interaction. I had always been an operations person and, by tradition and necessity, had zero time or desire to delve into policy much. But preparing for *Equal Time*, I did hours and hours of research, called up friends and various "smart" people, and asked them to come on the show and 'splain things for us Lucy types. Soon enough I was sucked into a centrifugal force of policy. I fell fast for it, and fell hard. I started loving policy like I'd never loved anything before.

It wasn't long before our fans began sending us stuff, which was how we discovered we had fans at all. They sent us furniture. They sent us tchotchkes. They sent us artwork. They sent us two life-size papier-mâché models of Jane and me, a coffee table in the shape of a reclining nude holding a timepiece. (Get it, equal *time?*) Those nutty Loopsters were over-the-top decorators, which is also how we figured out that we had a massive gay male following.

I did not—and do not—like to insult the glory of individuals by lumping them together and assigning them a group identity, but by my empirical reckoning, gay men, by and large, do seem to possess superior taste and are, more often than not, the ultimate arbiters of fine taste, fabulous fabrics and smart decor. And terrific gardeners too. When they turned out in droves for *Equal Time*, I discovered true loves, soul mates and fantastic creative mentors.

Who doesn't want to be loved by men who otherwise have no use for you? It's a purer love, because it's not filtered through the endless guy-mind loop, "I wonder what she's like in bed."

And when we complained that CNBC wouldn't cover the costs of subscribing to *The Hotline*, the Washington political bible at the time, decades before *Politico*, I asked the Loopsters to send in a penny each so we could buy a year's subscription. We got hundreds of thousands of pennies! We loaded up a wheelbarrow with them, on camera, and pushed it down to *Hotline* to buy a year's subscription. I know this is vaguely Norma Desmond–esque, but thank you, beloved Loopsters, for all eternity. You made me so happy.

We bonded, the Loopsters and I, and it felt like we were on a journey together, much of which turned out to be my real life. I got married on the show. I got pregnant on the show. I lactated on the show. (I asked the producer once, "Why are you only doing a head shot?" Her response was to cast her eyes downward. When I followed her gaze, there were two giant round wet spots displayed on my made-for-TV jacket. The sound of hearing Matty offstage had produced an involuntary on-air mammary response.) There was also a deep and super-loyal following of "women of a certain-age" who came along for the ride. We exchanged letters, recipes, and photos of our kids, grandkids, and tales of odd husband behaviors.

The show was less a planned television production than a carpe diem thing along the lines of *Dead Poets Society*. Then suddenly—very strangely and unexpectedly (and nobody was more aghast than Jane and I)—we had a cable hit.

JAMES

WHEN MARY STARTED ON the CNBC show with Jane Wallace—which was a really good show, by the way—it became the first all-chick cable talk show. It had a cult following, and it really paved the way for a lot of shows that came after it.

While she was off spending her days in front of a television camera, I was spending more and more of my time 30,000 feet in the air. I was still an unpaid adviser to President Clinton and one of his fiercest defenders. But the paying jobs I had—writing books, giving speeches and advising foreign political campaigns—increasingly kept me away from Washington.

That last gig was undoubtedly the most interesting and exciting. Before 1993, I'd never thought much about doing foreign campaigns or aspired to work for politicians overseas. My specialty was domestic politics. That's the world I knew. That's the world I liked.

But after Clinton won in 1992, it started to look like an attractive and appealing opportunity. As bizarre, unfamiliar, annoying and enjoyable as my newfound fame was, it didn't take me long to realize that I had a real problem on my hands: if I kept working on domestic campaigns the way I'd always done, I would become part of the story. I'd draw attention just by joining a campaign. That's never what you want as a political consultant. The candidate should be the focus; the candidate should get the spotlight. I felt if I kept running campaigns in America, I risked becoming a distraction.

That said, I didn't want to give up campaigns altogether. I love working on campaigns. It's what drew me to politics. It's what had defined my career. Besides, I've never been one to sell a product—a poll or direct-mail advertising or a television spot or some sort of software to target the right voters. That is the difference between me and a lot of other consultants in the political world. I'm not selling anything but my own bullshit. There's nothing tangible that comes with it. No staff, no infrastructure, nothing. Just a guy with a mouth and, I hope, some smart ideas and sound counsel.

I decided to take that same approach to working overseas. I'd been asked about working on foreign campaigns a few times before. It seemed like a way to see cool places and an interesting challenge to try to figure out new, unfamiliar political systems. Early on, because I was so closely associated with the Clinton White House, I exercised a lot of caution. I didn't want my foreign work to cause any trouble back home. Most of the people I worked for were pretty moderate candidates. Some were more liberal, some more conservative. You have to understand that a conservative somewhere else in the world might be more liberal than a Democrat in the United States, so our descriptions don't always translate elsewhere.

I certainly wasn't about to work for someone who was on the fringes or somehow anti-American. But in those pre-Internet days, you didn't always know a lot about the people seeking out your counsel. You had to be careful. Shady people sometimes wanted to hire you because they believed your presence would confer legitimacy on them. I remember being approached about consulting for General Sani Abacha in Nigeria not long after Clinton got into office. They were offering me a ton of money. It didn't take a lot of digging to figure out that this guy was an authoritarian dictator suspected of all sorts of corruption and human rights abuses. Thanks but no thanks.

When you work in different countries, you come to realize fairly quickly that established democracy is the exception, not the norm. And even where you have a democracy, that's a relatively new development in many places. Take Indonesia, where I've worked in the past. They never had a political convention before. They had to start from scratch. You ask people, "Well, how are you going to choose delegates? How are you going to select a nominee?" The basic answer is "We don't know." It's a totally new experiment for them.

Wherever you are, you can count on the fact that a lot of voting behavior is tribal. In the United States, for example, a general rule of thumb is that 45 percent of the people are going to vote Democratic and 45 percent are going to vote Republican no matter what. You're always trying to win as much of a sliver of the remaining 10 percent as possible. These days, people are so polarized that the sliver is more like 5 percent, but the same principle applies. However, in a different country there might be eight viable parties, with the vote divided between them in any number of ways. That presents all sorts of complications. You have to figure out who's likely to vote for which parties, how you can build coalitions and get enough support to win a majority. It's a totally different equation than in the United States.

Another lesson you learn is that you can give great advice, but if it can't be executed, it's no good. You have to work within reality. Campaigns in other countries, for example, often don't have advance teams like we do here to help get people out to events and to measure how many people and what type of people show up. So if you have a strategy to barnstorm the countryside to get your message out but nobody's showing up at any given stop, then that's a stupid strategy.

On the other hand, some countries naturally draw large crowds at political rallies. When I was working for the New Democracy Party in Greece in 1993, somebody from the campaign called into headquarters and said, "We had 300,000 people turn out for the event in Salonika yesterday." And I said, "Holy shit! That's unbelievable, man. We got some momentum!" And the guy said, "No, no, New Democracy always gets 300,000 in Salonika. It doesn't mean anything." If you're in the United States and you have 300,000 people show up at an event, you're shitting yourself because you're so happy. In Greece, people just go to political rallies. It's like a social gathering. It doesn't mean they're going to vote for you.

Cultural differences like that take time and patience to understand. You learn to look at countries you thought you knew in entirely new ways, and you begin to understand more about the ones you never knew. The Greeks, they like to meet all day and drink coffee and smoke cigarettes forever. Israel is a much cooler, thriving, modern place than people imagine, especially Tel Aviv. In Afghanistan, you feel the absence of order. There's no real emergency phone line, like 911, to call, no stoplights, no normal cops. When I was there, you had to have a tail car when you were driving because if you broke down or got in a wreck, you were entirely on your own.

Starting out, I knew there would be wins and losses, just like back home. The worst loss I ever had was down in Mexico in 2000. The Institutional Revolutionary Party, or PRI, had won every presidential election for the past seventy years. They hired me to work on Francisco Labastida's campaign, and he promptly lost to Vicente Fox, who was a compelling guy in his own right. There were a lot of factors at play, but a loss is a loss, and that one stung.

Being a foreign campaign consultant also exposes you to some disturbing realities about how the world works. I did some work for James Michel, the president of the Republic of Seychelles, which is basically this string of little islands way out in the Indian Ocean east of mainland Africa. They're actually not that far from the coast of Somalia, so they've had problems with pirates at certain times of the year.

In any case, I'm there on a visit helping him prepare for their version of the State of the Union Address, and I ask some of his people, "Would you give me a ride around? I just want to see what the parliament looks like." So I hop in a car with this guy, and suddenly we're rolling down this grand boulevard, and I see this brand-new ornate building up ahead. And I'm thinking, *What in the world is this?*

It was the parliament building. And I said something to him like "Man, are you guys crazy?" The International Monetary Fund was there helping out, and the government was raising taxes and cutting social welfare to get its fiscal situation in order, and they went and built this Taj Mahal of a parliament? I couldn't believe it.

"It didn't cost us anything," he said. "The Chinese paid for it. They do that everywhere."

It was my first real encounter with the fact that the Chinese actually go all over the world paying for stuff left and right to get in the good graces of political leaders. You need a new building for your government? You need a luxurious place for your politicians to park themselves? Boom. In many places, the Chinese will write that check.

It wasn't the only time I've seen that phenomenon up close. In Afghanistan, where so many of our young people are getting banged up fighting the Taliban, and where we're spending all this money on training police and building infrastructure, the Chinese have put their energy and money into building a railroad into eastern Afghanistan, where there's like a trillion dollars' worth of minerals just waiting to be taken out of the country. They are spending money hand over fist around the world to further their interests. I saw it in Seychelles; I saw it in Afghanistan.

At the end of the day, I learned pretty quickly that being successful at foreign campaign consulting boils down to sound judgment. You pick the candidates you believe in. You pick the candidates you think you can help. You steer clear of the ones who make you a little uneasy. You go in knowing that you're going to win some and lose some. Ultimately, it's not so different from working on domestic campaigns.

Have I made the right choice in every instance? No, but I didn't make any horrifically bad choices, either, and that's every bit as important. You can make some bad freaking choices, representing dictators or authoritarian regimes or bumbling idiots who generally just shouldn't be in power. I've avoided all that.

I would say that along with good judgment, I've had good luck. You need both to be successful, whether in work or in marriage.

MARY

IT TURNS OUT, when your ratings are lousy and nobody's watching, you are left alone to die a quiet TV death. It's when you have a hit that the problems start. Once we were "discovered" by the TV critics, the CNBC suits appeared like Death Eaters and tried to suck the blood and soul from *Equal Time*, hoping to renovate us into a bad version of *Crossfire*. What they wanted was everything that doesn't work on TV. And it was the antithesis of what we had been doing.

We did get a better set. And it was decided that we needed to be given a wardrobe budget, which led to free designer clothes—okay, that rocked—until it became obvious that the guys in charge didn't want my own personal taste displayed. They wanted me to be "dressed," kinda clone gal, TV monochromatic. I was supposed to look the same every night, same hair, same lipstick—*bleh, bleh*, you know the rest. I get it. This is how on-air people are successfully "branded" on TV. But in the end, free cool duds or not, I couldn't do the whole processed cheese thing.

For one thing, it was suddenly not okay for me to be constantly changing my hairstyle. What? I'm the daughter of a beauty salon owner, I grew up in a beauty school and am a trained cosmetologist who's been doing my own as well as all my friends' hair for twenty years. Out of boredom and curiosity, I consider my own hair as ever evolving. And it became a recurring joke on the show. Hillary of the 1990s had nothing on me. My nonstop hair transitions were the star of many a spoof. The suits at CNBC were horrified.

The last straw was O. J. I didn't want to do shows about that moronic murder trial, let alone night after night after night. The rest of television was doing the O. J. trial *nonstop*. What intelligent or edifying thing could

I possibly add to that? What intelligent or edifying thing could *anyone* say about that? The O. J. trial clearly marked the early stages of cable crapdom: the dumber the story, the greater the coverage.

So I announced to Loopsterville: "If you're tuning in to talk about that moronic event, change the channel or turn off the TV, because this is an O. J.–free talk-show zone."

That really enraged the cable gods. They felt we were tampering with the vital life source of their cable kingdom: ratings. I held my ground. "I'm not going to do this night after night. Actually, I am not going to do this one single frickin' night. Period." Their response was to tell our producer, Ann Klenk, that her job was on the line if we didn't get with the O. J. program.

I was like: "Hell, well, that's fine! Let 'em fire you." The problem was they did. So that wasn't good. I mean, Ann was like a sister to me by that point. She had looked after me through a marriage and a zillion melt-downs. After my first miscarriage, she really took care of me, sent me home, found substitute hosts for me. We were very, very close. And she was the sole breadwinner at home, the single mother of a sweet baby girl.

So when the suits fired *her* and not *me* because I refused to verbally mud wrestle in the O. J. pit, it was a soul-sucking gut punch. And as hard as I tried, I couldn't get Ann rehired. It was such a blatant injustice, so wrong, that I never had the same energy or commitment to the show again. Is there anything worse than when somebody else gets punished for your misdeed? Answer: big fat no. It's beyond horrible. And it wasn't even a misdeed. By then, you could get your O. J. fix all day, all night, and this was before blanket cable.

By then I also had a three-hour radio show during the day, a far more gratifying way to spend my time. Five nights a week I was dragging Matty and the dogs to the TV set, and then we were eating dinner at the Palm with James when the show was over at nine-thirty. By the time we got home, and I'd watched the rebroadcast of *Equal Time* at eleven, it was well past midnight. It wasn't a normal babyhood. I wasn't a normal baby mama either. I was an exhausted forty-four-year-old postpartum and perimenopausal sixteen-car-pileup of a wreck. And guess what? Baby number two was on her way. When it was time to renew my contract, I didn't.

Not long afterward, Jennifer Block called from *Crossfire*. She asked if I'd like to do the show as a regular.

"No," I said. "I don't want to do TV. I hate TV."

But, of course, I did it. At CNN, I had tons of support, great money, great research and a decent schedule that worked with my kids and their lives. And I stayed there until 2000 when I got another kind of call.

JAMES

WHATEVER YOU THOUGHT OF *Crossfire*—plenty of people loved it and plenty of people hated it—I never did agree with the assessment that it was some sort of evil show.

I would concede that it probably wasn't a very good television show in its last year. CNN pulled back on the resources, and it showed. We probably got a hundred little things wrong. But in the end, we got one really huge thing right: the Iraq War. I'll always be proud of that. I would argue that *Crossfire* was probably the most consistently anti–Iraq War talk show on cable TV. Paul Begala and I, obviously, were never for the Iraq War, and neither was Robert Novak. Tucker Carlson was for it for maybe a couple of months at most, until he realized the Republican hawks who were trying to convince him it was a good idea were just dead wrong.

I never did feel that *Crossfire* was somehow "hurting America," as Jon Stewart famously said when he came on the show with Carlson and Begala one night in 2004. Even CNN's president, Jonathan Klein, told the *New York Times* in 2005 that he wanted to move the network away from "head-butting debate shows."

That's perfectly fine. CNN can do whatever it wants with its programs. But I didn't see any truth to the notion that what's wrong with Washington are the cable news shows where partisan pundits go back and forth at each other about politics. No, what's wrong with Washington is all the money and all the power that the interest groups have. What's wrong is the mindless gridlock on Capitol Hill and a general lack of leadership. It's not some TV show that airs in the late afternoon and is eventually going to get canceled. That's an asinine conversation, and it misses the bigger picture.

It also misses a much more significant and disturbing shift: the fragmentation of the media. Today, conservatives can get all their information from conservative outlets, and liberals can get all their information from liberal outfits. And you can spend your whole life never being challenged, never having to hear or think about or confront viewpoints that are different from your own.

Back when I went to LSU a million years ago, we got the Baton Rouge paper. But if you wanted to read the *New York Times* or the *Wall Street Journal*, you had to go to the reading room of the student union, and you got the edition several days after it had been published, and you had to read it on a wooden stick. *Meet the Press* was already on television. You had the nightly news on the networks. That was about it for news sources.

I tell my students today, look around you at Tulane. They give away copies or online access to the *Times* or the *Journal* or the *Washington Post*, not to mention all the local papers. No more wooden sticks. These kids have access to hundreds of TV channels and an infinite number of websites without ever leaving their dorm rooms. They have Twitter feeds and news apps on their smartphones. They're never more than a finger swipe away from answering almost any question they might have about the world.

Compared to the information available to me in 1962, kids today have way more information at their fingertips. Endless amounts of information. But do they have more knowledge? Not really. They aren't any more informed than I was then. I wasn't even that good a student, but I knew what was happening in the state and in the country. I knew the names of every senator. I could talk halfway intelligently about most any current event. A lot of kids today don't have that capacity or don't have a deep interest in understanding the world around them.

Seeing that makes me believe the proliferation of information has actually been a bad thing because people don't use it properly. They use it to become more insular instead of more engaged in the world. So if you are a liberal, you never have to look at, read or consider a conservative thing for the rest of your life. You can visit *Daily Kos* or go to *Talking Points Memo*. You can watch Rachel Maddow. And if you're a conservative, you have all kinds of liberal-free media to choose from. You can listen to Rush Limbaugh. You can surf Townhall.com or RedState.com. You can watch Fox News to your heart's content.

Instead of taking all this information and using it as a window on the entire world, a big part of the media industry now exists in large part to confirm your beliefs. People have figured out that there's a lot of money to be made telling you that you were right in the first place. It makes both sides more dug in.

On *Crossfire*, at least you had to face the other guy. My job was to defend or articulate a position. Not just preach to the choir.

MARY

JAMES HAS BEEN OFFERED all kinds of television shows over the years, but he has always said he couldn't do it every night—or every week—that he has no attention span for that. It would be too hard. But he makes it look easy to me.

Over the years, before going on Russert's show, I had to know six weeks out so I would have time to prepare. I'd be tormented and stressed the whole time and studying like crazy. I'd wake up every morning with an anxiety headache from just anticipating going on Russert's show in the distant future, and it would continue all day, thump-thump-thumping at my temples like a drumbeat. *Russert, Russert, Russert.* I'd read newspapers, magazines, briefs, anything I could get my hands on, and start scouring the Internet. Then I'd call friends for inside stuff, things that hadn't gone public yet. It was a total grind.

After every show, I'd feel like I'd been hit by a car. Since I was actually hit by a car when I was thirteen, I know what I'm talking about. (This reminds me of one of Tim's favorite jokes—he had a vast repertoire of them, repeated regularly, a personal iPod shuffle inside his head—"If Mary Matalin ran over James Carville in their driveway, in full view of their entire neighborhood, then backed up and ran over him three more times, a jury of her peers would acquit her.")

Tim liked to laugh. I like to laugh. James is a laugh (in a good way). This might not always have made the most sophisticated Sunday morning television, like the time Tim and I convulsed in a laughing fit while discussing the sexual orientation of various Teletubbies, which, believe it or not, was once a serious D.C. political topic.

When he first started booking us, Tim got a lot of grief from members of the chattering class who ascribed to the narrative that ours was a stunt marriage. It tickled him and reinforced his affection for the audience he loved best, normal people outside the Beltway. He also knew how to get the best out of his guests. He delighted us and everyone who came on (except BS'ing pols).

Though a source of high-pitched horror for TV reviewers, Tim loved booking our whole family at the holidays. We had standing Thanksgiving, Christmas and Mother's Day appearances. Tim always had an anniversary cake for us at Thanksgiving, Santa gifts for the girls on Christmas and roses for me on Mother's Day. Tim was a real family guy; the girls came to all the shows—they adored him. That part of those Sunday mornings was always joyful, except for the Mother's Day that fell three weeks after Emerson was born. In the customary postshow photo, I tried to hide my exhausted, blubbery mug behind the roses.

So we had plenty of laughs and lovefests on *Meet the Press*, which did mitigate the angst of those shows, but afterward, no matter what, I was always wiped out on a cellular level—and, believe me, I have never been able to watch a recording of any of our appearances later. It is like reliving a near-death experience.

James is another story. He has the confidence and coolness of a natural raconteur. Before he goes on Russert, or any show, people send him briefs, which he *might* (at most) give a cursory glance. He doesn't do briefs, doesn't need to. For one thing, James is never *not* gathering intel;

from dawn till dusk, if he is breathing, he is on the phone. On top of that, TV leverages his ADHD, I think—because it offers the kind of intense stimulation that he needs to focus really well. The whole experience is just a walk in the park for him. He loves it, feels good doing it. It's his sweet spot.

On the mornings of *Meet the Press*, after a night that I hadn't slept a wink, James would pop out of bed, take a run, skim the *New York Times* and the *Washington Post*, ignore the briefs, and then plop down in front of the camera and deliver one amazing line after another.

He's the Zen master of sound bites. He can say the most pointed things in the least number of words of anybody you've ever known. He has coined more expressions that are in ubiquitous daily use than you can count. Take "It's the economy, stupid." If we had a nickel for every time that appeared, we wouldn't have to work anymore.

TV is a *cool* medium and James is as hot as a jalapeño. He thrives in overheated conditions, like an exotic hothouse orchid. TV is a *visual* medium populated by stud muffins and cleavage, and James has been likened to everything from ET to Skeletor. He always tells me how good I am at TV, but we both know I'll never be in his league.

But I do have better hair.

JAMES

YOU NEVER KNOW WHAT will bring you lasting fame. I played a big role in getting a U.S. president elected. I've won Senate campaigns and gubernatorial campaigns. I've consulted to candidates from Israel to Ecuador. I've been on every political talk show more times than I can count.

People know me for more than just politics. They know I'm a rabid LSU fan, that I chaired the Super Bowl committee when it came to New Orleans. I had a sports talk show on XM Satellite Radio. I've been parodied on *Saturday Night Live*.

But of anything I've ever done, the one thing that got the most reaction—the one thing people still ask about more than almost anything else—is my cameo in the comedy *Old School*. Its staying power is remarkable.

Todd Phillips, the director, had called me and asked if I wanted to do it. It sounded fun. I had made an appearance in *The People vs. Larry Flynt* several years earlier and enjoyed that. So why not do it again? What the hell.

I flew out to Southern California, and we filmed it at a studio there. The scene involves a debating competition, in which I get brought in by this ass of a dean (played by Jeremy Piven) to make sure these frat boys lose a debate. I'm supposed to be the ringer. As I'm about to answer the first question, something about America's investment in biotechnology, Will Ferrell's bumbling idiot of a character interrupts and says he'd like to give it a shot.

"Have at it, hoss," I say.

To everyone's amazement, he comes up with this incredibly articulate answer to a question about America's investment in biotechnology. Our side is speechless.

"We have no response," I say. "That was perfect."

The audience goes wild. The frat boys win the debate. That was it. Those were the lines. It took half an hour to film, if that, and I was on my way.

That was a decade ago, and I've never stopped hearing about *Old School*. I got invited to give the graduation speech at Cornell University. "Everybody wants you to come because of *Old School*," one of the organizers told me.

It's a lesson in fame. Just when you think you're hot shit in your chosen field, something comes along to remind you that whether you like it or not people might remember you for something else entirely.

3.

Mysteries of Marriage

MARY

THE TOP TEN THINGS WE FIGHT ABOUT:

10. THE GIRLS. And the twenty-first-century teenage wasteland. How to raise our kids is more of an obsessional conversation rather than full-blown argument at this point.

9. AIR-CONDITIONING

8. THE BATHROOM. Just because you remembered to put the seat down does not absolve you from other potty etiquette, like flushing.

7. HIS NEED FOR TEDIOUS ROUTINE VS. MY NEED FOR NEWNESS (see ADHD section)

6. THE IRAQ WAR. For a long time, it was number one or number two, but then it became a case of either shut up or move out.

5. RELIGION. James delights in playing devil's advocate on all subjects, but he thinks because he's a cradle Catholic, he's entitled to some special indulgence permitting him to subject me to endless soliloquies about every doubting Thomas in history, the creation of the universe, the existence of evil, guitar Masses, women priests (or the lack thereof), contraception, thirteenth-century popes, Church collusion with the Nazis, the right way to do an examination of conscience, whether or not Mary and Joseph had sex, why Jesus was a liberal, etc. And just because he can recite the entire Mass in Latin—frontward and backward—does not give him the authority to deny that my guardian angel's name is Alphonso. This subject hasn't been relegated to the never-bring-it-up-again pile, which I wish included the ones you will be reading about soon.

4. ANIMALS (see below, this chapter)

3. REAL ESTATE. Every roof we've put over our heads—every apartment, condo, house, garden, barn, dog house and shed, including every renovation project and *inch of sod*—that we have jointly purchased has been precipitated by massive meltdowns over money. This happens in penniless and flush days, no difference.

2. FURNITURE and DECOR. Every stick we have put under our roof—or in proximity to it—every rug, lamp, table, shred of fabulous fabric, houseplant, dish, appliance, garden hose, piece of patio furniture, pool cleaner and every spectacular one-of-a-kind antique I've painstakingly researched, fully considered and judiciously purchased has been debated like the Florida recount. Not to mention every painting, piece of sculpture, any and all vintage silver or crystal from highball glasses to chandeliers. No matter what *it* is, from the attic to the basement, no matter how life-enhancing, how beautiful, how hard to get— even if he loves *it*—does James ever think we *need* it?

1. MONEY. James sometimes talks to me, and about me, as though he were living with Marie Antoinette or Catherine the Great. Do I wear a different gown every night of the week? Do I have any rooms covered in giant ancient amber? Not that I wouldn't love to live like a queen for a day, but I am a working-class girl from South Chicago. Despite our similar shoot-the-moon, go-big-or-go-home tendencies on everything else, when it comes to money, James doesn't practice healthy, oxygenated, vital behavior. With money, he doesn't believe in energetic movement; he likes stagnancy. Once it comes in, he never wants it to go out. Unless it's your tax money.

So now you know why our move to New Orleans was a perfect storm. Money, real estate, furniture, fabrics, religion, teenagers, air-conditioning and animals . . . all in a new time zone.

Some years later, when every corner of the house was done (or almost done, since you never say never when it comes to decor), I would frequently find James standing in the central hall, looking around with a smile on his face, talking to himself, his chest all puffed up. He couldn't believe how beautifully it all turned out.

When people visit, he tours them around, so proudly, admiring every single thing as if for the first time. The details, the colors, the dining room mural, the antique silver tea service, and vintage creamy white Oushak rug, every source of his former torment and tumult. Now he's gloating and giddy with his own good fortune.

The coup de grâce was last spring when President Clinton was visiting for a fund-raiser. I left after exchanging pleasantries, but before I did, Bill Clinton grilled me in his customary way about an antique Italian corona, which James never understood. As it turns out, the former president has a vast knowledge of obscure furniture and fabulous taste to boot. Not that I would ever vote for him, but I will be eternally delighted with the quote from the fund-raiser that made the *Times Pic* the next day.

"Carville," the former president told the newspaper, "has obviously done well since I let him escape government service. There were parts of his home here in New Orleans that made the White House look like public housing . . . His wife could at least take comfort from the fact that he is now living like a Republican."

JAMES

THE ANIMALS. God help me, I will never understand Mary's obsession with animals. We had one dog that I really liked, a King Charles spaniel named Reyes. But the rest of the dogs and cats, I tolerate them out of necessity.

We're up to four dogs and who knows how many cats—too many to count. There's also a bird or two. I don't even know all their names, nor do I care to. It's not that I hate them. It's just that I don't really care for them. They're in my house, always barking and pissing and smelling up the place. They add absolutely nothing to my life. I wouldn't lose a moment's sleep if they all vanished into the ether tomorrow.

But somewhere along the way, I decided that Mary loves the animals more than I hate them. That's not the hill I wanted to die on. For anybody who's married, that's always a good question to ask yourself before you pick a fight: are you sure that's a hill you want to die on? Because I'm pretty confident I could get the dogs and cats out of the house if I really, truly wanted that. But the price I'd pay—the immediate anger on top of long-term resentment—isn't even close to being worth it. So, the dogs and cats remain. I tolerate them and they tolerate me; and Mary and I stay happily married.

The need to be surrounded by a small army of animals is just one of so many things I still don't get about Mary, even after two decades together. For instance, why do we have to turn on every light in the house? I grew up Catholic, and they taught us a Latin phrase, *tantum quantum*. It means "so far as." Basically, "as needed." That's how I feel about lighting. If you need a light, turn it on. If you don't, turn it off. Not Mary. She has to have lights all over the house blazing for no apparent reason. Also, no overhead lighting. It's all lamps and diffused lighting. Every room has to have at least four lights, and every single one is turned on. It's hardly anything to get a divorce over, but that kind of thing drives me nuts.

Another thing: she used to open the doors and windows, and put the air conditioner on wide open. I'd say, "Look, you can't do that. You've got to go one way or the other. Because the air conditioner will pull the hot air in and over-work itself." Mechanically, morally, financially—however you looked at it, it didn't make any sense.

True story: I have seen her with a fire in the fireplace, the doors open and the air conditioner on full blast.

I don't know how many air conditioners we had to bust before she finally figured out you can't do stuff like that. We even did a series of commercials for Mitsubishi air conditioners. The premise was that I was always trying to sneak around and turn the air lower, and she was the one trying to save power. Art does not always imitate life.

I can count quite a few little battles like those that we have fought for years. But what's more important are the battles we haven't fought.

MARY

I DO NOT BELIEVE IN RELATIVITY; there is real truth and real beauty, and they are not altered by the whim of time or trends.

What has always been true and beautiful to me from my very first childhood memories is a love for animals. All animals. I remember being pained as a little girl when I watched the brightly lit tails of lightning bugs being pulled off by the all-male preschool gang in my neighbor-hood. Not that insect mutilation is a gender-exclusive activity, but the boys did seem to relish squishing every winged, crawling, hopping or buzzing thing they could get their sweaty hands on.

Because my father was allergic to cats, we always had dogs when I was little. So naturally I presumed that I was a dog person until my best college friend, Katie O'Hara, introduced me to the wonders of the feline world. Katie and I also shared a passion for reading and gardening and cooking. We had multiple dogs, cats and quite a few other creatures that regularly procreated under our watchful care to our utter delight. It's a wonder we graduated.

You can never have just one cat. And it isn't true that the presence of multiple cats is proof of crazy cat lady syndrome, an affliction my entire family accuses me of having. But there are dog people and cat people. You all know who you are.

I can accept that, but I never, ever expected there were no-animal-no-way (NANW) beings walking the Earth.

Until I met James Carville. In south Louisiana, there is a certainty that God created all creatures great and small but that none of them were meant to live indoors. This went beyond the beasts of burden, which the Carvilles grew up with. James never had a bicycle, but he always had a horse as a kid. To this day, he can ride like the wind and talks about horses like he's the son of the Horse Whisperer. So imagine my surprise to learn he was a fervent NANW acolyte.

There have been only three events in our twenty-two years together that have threatened permanent separation, and about which no reconciliation was possible: (1) my going back into the White House in 2000; (2) the Iraq War; and, honestly, the most troublesome one, (3) our disparate views of the animal kingdom.

James could put up with a hound or two, and he did develop, to his own surprise, a sincere affection for our first Blenheim King Charles spaniel that he named Reyes after his then-favorite red wine. And he even tolerated the second spaniel, a tricolor that he named Buckminster and called Buck-Buck, which remains his password for many apps despite Buck-Buck's passing long ago.

But our long-haired miniature dachshunds, the completely irresistible Gorgeous and Cherrie; our chocolate Lab, Paws; the corgies, Jack and Lilly; the Yorkiepoo, Bieber (yes, named after Justin during that phase of Emerson's tween life); and especially the amazing Skeeter, the rescue poodle-mutt, give him fits. Those fits, which manifested themselves in hollering, shouting, prolonged pouts and moans of misery, finally gave way to glaring hatred. This evolved, due to James's strong survival instinct, into begrudging tolerance.

"Come on," I'd coo. "How cute is Skeeter!?"

James would snarl back, "Get them out of my room."

After he falls asleep (usually four or five hours before me), my whole animal kingdom tiptoes into the bedroom with me and slithers under the blanket on my side of the bed. But as quiet and cuddly as we are, his NANW alarm goes off—and the menagerie is banished. If he somehow sleeps through our nocturnal raids until his customary 5:00 in the morning (which is often about an hour after I've finally gotten to sleep), he makes a big show of his doggie-disgust.

But the Carville NANW gene is too dominant to consider the possibility of house cats, although we have many. And, as is the wont of cats, who are the most ironic of creatures, they gravitate to those who detest them most—or whose allergies produce swollen eyes and closed throats (like my BFF, Maria Cino, whose allergies to all animals are so severe that her very presence in my home always produces an instant veritable Noah's ark, as all of the Matalin creatures race to cling to, hang off of or sit on her, even as she begins wheezing and her eyes swell up like Rocky after a bad fight).

Once, accidentally, during one of Maria's attacks, I sprayed what I thought was liquid antihistamine up her nose only to discover—after her eyes rolled back in her head and she fell to her knees—that it was *topical* Benadryl, with these words prominently printed across the bottle: UNDER NO CIRCUMSTANCES TO BE INGESTED OR INSERTED IN NASAL CAVITIES.

There is no one more beloved in our family than Maria, the devoted godmother to both the girls, so the girls and I aren't proud of the fact that we were laughing so hard at Maria's wheezing and eye rolling after the Benadryl mishap—and her crawling around on the kitchen floor—that we weren't able to breathe either. The fallout: Maria never leaves home without her own Benadryl tablets now.

James has zero allergies. Cats are simply Satan incarnate to him. This is partly because he is Mr. Fastidious—compulsively washing his hands with Purell—and becomes really, really upset when he finds cat hair on the butter (which he bitches about anyway because he likes his butter always in the icebox, while I must have access to soft butter at all times in case I have an urgent need to make Marcella Hazan's pesto pasta, which calls for six softened sticks of it).

James can't comprehend why cats should have the run of the kitchen countertops to begin with. But our cats' habit of licking butter—which makes complete sense to me, since it is the best part of cream, or life, for that matter—reduces him to tears. Or worse.

One morning, I came downstairs and discovered the whiskers of one of my favorite kitties, Black Cat (it's hard to creatively name dozens of kitties), were singed and mangled. James was unable to deny that he had turned on the burner while Black Cat was standing on the stove. Initially, he claimed this had been an accident but later fessed up. He wasn't even appropriately remorseful or defensive about this act of feline pyromania, even after I dug into him and pointed out that Black Cat had long hair and could have spontaneously combusted. This possibility—he claimed—hadn't occurred to him at the time. Although James did seem to experience a visible shudder of pleasure as he thought about it.

If it weren't the butter licking, something else would set him off on random antikitty tirades. James hates that Bagpipes, our other aptly named cat, screeches every time she wants attention, which is always. Even the melodic purring of our Siamese, aptly named Simon, makes him leave the room.

But his greatest antipathy is reserved for the forty-pound black-and-white tabby, whom we call Fat Cat or sometimes Killer Cat, depending on his mood. (He was originally named Robbie, but he never lived up to that.)

In James's defense, nobody really enjoys the company of Fat/Killer Cat. Our beloved friend and priest, Monsignor Christopher Nalty, tolerates Fat/Killer Cat because (I suspect) his profession actually obliges him to love all God's creatures.

Of course, Fat/Killer—being a member in good standing of the ironic feline species—adores the good monsignor. Fat/Killer could be MIA for days, but the minute Monsignor Nalty takes a seat to relax after a long week of marrying, burying, baptizing, forgiving and inspiring, Fat/Killer magically appears and with the accuracy and destructive capacity of a heat-seeking missile, he dive-bombs Monsignor. Fat/Killer leaves fuzzy swatches of white fur up and down the monsignor's black clerical garb (not to mention the hair sticking to whatever appetizer or beverage he may have in his hand). I always offer to dry-clean his clothes, but he maintains his own regular dry-cleaner schedule, which takes into account that dinner at our home means he will return to the rectory "Rogained," as he puts it.

The monsignor is a brilliant theologian, civil and canon lawyer, and a 100-percent believer, not just in the obvious things, but in all of the Roman Catholic Church's teachings. James is more of a cafeteria Catholic, picking and choosing what he'll go along with. The two of them can really go at it, which was fun the first one hundred or so dinners. Neither of them seems to care if their fellow diners get up and leave while they keep dancing on the heads of boxfuls of theological pins. But they are in lockstep agreement when it comes to their lack of fondness—okay, *disgust and horror* would be a more accurate description of their feelings—for another two of God's creatures that inhabit our home: Matty's pet rats, Hattie and Stella (named after classic characters from New Orleans literature).

As I said, "lack of fondness" doesn't adequately capture James's and the monsignor's full-on revulsion to Hattie and Stella, who like to sit on my shoulders while I'm mixing up another batch of yummy pesto pasta with my always available soft butter minus cat hairs.

Despite his polite but consistent and well-articulated revulsion to the rats, the tremendously loving and faithful monsignor didn't hesitate for a nanosecond when I called, weeping, to tell him the terrible news that Hattie had not survived her mammary gland surgery (rats bleed out easily in major surgeries because, well, they don't have much blood) and beseeched him to perform a funeral for her.

I prepared a Mass card of sorts for Hattie, and while Matty and I stood holding hands and praying in our backyard animal cemetery, the monsignor delivered one of the most heartfelt and appropriate eulogies of all time. We should all be sent off so well.

It was a memorable evening, even though the rodent-intolerant James missed it. (He claimed he was otherwise indisposed on a Saturday night at a "business commitment.")

There are many more tales of the beloved creatures under our roof—we have swimming ones, feathered ones, not just furry and scaly-tailed ones—and while none have enjoyed James's affection since Reyes and Buck-Buck, more than a few have been favored by his heroism. I have lost count of the times he has raced me to the emergency vet after one roadside calamity or another. As I wept, holding the body of a furry victim, only once did I hear him say to the vet under his breath, "You think these dumb bastards would learn how to cross the street."

It doesn't surprise me one bit and it is just oh-so-typical that a liberal could dispense with his bleeding heart the second it doesn't serve his purposes.

JAMES

I DEAL WITH MARY'S animals like I deal with her politics: I generally dislike them, so I tend to ignore them.

I understand why people are curious how our polar-opposite politics affect life at home. It's what we still get asked about most after all these years. But the answer has seldom changed: it really doesn't matter. As with any marriage, part of the trick is realizing you can't change your spouse even if you wanted to, and it's better simply to let her be who she is.

I learned a long time ago to stay away from politics at home. She'll watch Fox News or listen to Rush Limbaugh. I'll head to another room and flip on *SportsCenter*. I don't pay much attention to it. I rarely watch her when she's on television, and I'm pretty certain she rarely wastes a minute watching me.

That doesn't mean I'll ever quite understand Republicans. Conservatives— and I know this because I live with one—literally view it as a kind of weakness to talk to people other than themselves. Nothing would bore me more than to sit around talking and listening to a bunch of liberals all day. Just shoot me. But conservatives never seem to tire of one another. The conservative media landscape is the biggest echo chamber going. They love to reinforce their beliefs, day after day.

I just don't get it. Then again, I don't really care. Honestly, I don't. Mary can listen to what she wants. She can watch what she wants. She can talk with whomever she likes. If you want to believe that the government's coming for our guns or that Obamacare signals the end of civilization or that cutting taxes for rich people is the path to a better America, that's your choice. It doesn't affect me. I'm never going to believe in any of that shit. But I also know I'm not going to change it. So if it pleases her, then fine. I'd rather stay happily married than pick a fight with my wife over politics.

4.

How Do We Raise the Kids?

MARY

THE COMMON ASSUMPTION IS that two people with wildly divergent views on politics would have wildly divergent views on parenting. But James and I have always had the same approach to child rearing, even though we had different reactions to their arrival.

My anxieties and concerns about childbirth were trifling compared with James's off-the-charts anticipation. For one thing—and it was a major one—he is of the generation when fathers waited for the arrival of their new miracle with a box of cigars in the hospital hallway; they were not partners in the birthing room, let alone anywhere near the "action end" of the bed, as James kept calling it. When someone asked him if he wanted to videotape the crowning, all color drained from his face. When he realized it wasn't a joke question, his knees started buckling. (He is an aficionado of the "Louisiana Buckle," which is brought on by boozing, not birthing.)

When Matty was born, he began screaming—"It's a baby! It's a baby! It's a baby!"—more loudly and insanely with each repetition. Even in my daze, I could hear nurses all down the hall laughing. "As opposed to what? A puppy?"

I considered keeping him out of the "action" for Emerson, but he appeared to be manning up for the event. Emerson was a one push, easy-peasy birth, but James's previous experience didn't seem to have much assuaging effect. When he started buckling, I stopped pushing and ordered him an epidural.

JAMES

GETTING MARRIED IS NO BIG DEAL, at least for a guy. The day before you get married ain't a whole lot different than the day after. Maybe you're that rare bird who has waited until you get married to have sex. Maybe you're one of the few people who hasn't already lived with your soon-to-be spouse. Fine. But for most guys, it's not a sea change. It's nice to be married. It's comfortable. Life proceeds largely as it did before.

Fatherhood alters that balance entirely and permanently. When Mary got pregnant, I didn't fret much about having a child. What's the big deal? Well, the day after the baby arrives, you realize right away: it's an entirely different deal. The relationship with your wife, the power in the relationship, everything changes. The woman has been through the turmoil of childbirth. Everyone is tired and irritable. It is a transformational experience.

MARY

OUR DIFFERENCES CONTINUED. When Matty was born, I was constantly overcome by emotion, holding her twenty-four hours a day, singing *You Are My Sunshine* to her, and crying. I couldn't do a thing except that because I was a big fat lumbering blob and, for the most part, my brain had switched off. I was lost. I was weird. I couldn't even take a shower. In my entire life in politics, I had only cried twice: when Poppy

Bush lost and much later, in 2001, when I was so disappointed by how Cheney's brilliant, seriously comprehensive energy policy was received by hydrocarbon-hating tree huggers, including some in our own camp. But now I was sobbing for no reason and I couldn't stop, which was double crazy because I knew for a fact I'd never been happier. I had never loved anything more in all my long life the way I loved that baby. I couldn't put her down.

Meanwhile, James was back to normal, zipping around, off on his regular life, but even more so. He was fueled by a manly need to provide. And I didn't want to go anywhere—partly because I didn't want to hand Matty over to anybody else, particularly James. I know this was selfish of me, and I'm sure I robbed him of one of the great joys in life, but he was just hopeless at baby stuff. Like diapering—even creatures without opposable thumbs could whip on today's disposal diapers. As far as James was concerned, these modern wonders might well have been nuclear centrifuges. He was clueless. He put them on Matty upside down, backward, inside out, every which way but right side up. He couldn't mess with powder or ointment. He said that he was afraid he had germs on his hands or something. In short order, my mother calculator registered James + diaper = diaper rash. And since I was nursing, he couldn't do the feeding either. So I was tethered and he was not. He resumed his happy-go-lucky globe-trotting as if the screaming baby and crazy woman in his bed were just another day at the office.

This might sound angry, but I wasn't. Not one bit. I was ecstatic. Even if he'd *begged* to hold, feed or diaper Matty—which he didn't, he was totally happy just to marvel at her—he never had a chance. And I am not ashamed to admit it: I was one completely neurotic mother (and may still be).

I did read the parenting and baby books, because my tendency is to overprepare, while James is totally instinctual. And it quickly became obvious the books were like looking at a Google map of where you want to go, but at 50,000 feet. The best source of information was other mothers. Only other mothers could really tell me something smart and wise and helpful without making me feel like a crackpot, and assure me I wasn't doing anything that would scar my angel for life.

Soon, I was a total font of information and mother wisdom myself. And James had total and complete trust in me. He has the highest regard for maternal wisdom. He never questioned a thing I did. He was, and is, a crazy mother's blessing, which in no way should be construed as a commentary on his own mother.

JAMES

DON'T GET ME WRONG. You love your baby. You don't mind changing the diaper. But it's just a different existence. If your wife's been at home with the baby all day and she's tired and it's a Saturday night—it doesn't matter what plans you might have had, you stay your ass home. Or some nights the baby is up crying and she turns to you and says, "I can't deal with it. I had to deal with it all last night. You deal with this." And maybe you have a busy day ahead or really need the sleep. Doesn't matter.

I don't know of anybody who's had children who wishes they hadn't done it. I'm certainly grateful for our girls. It's just that before they arrived I could not fathom the deep and fundamental changes that were coming to our house. Changes that make life better, but not necessarily easier.

Then again, my first child was born when I was fifty. I had half a century to do basically whatever I wanted. Most people don't get anywhere near that amount of freedom. So a little deep and fundamental change wasn't necessarily a bad thing at all.

MARY

I KNEW WHAT A terrible mother I'd be to somebody like me. And if you put my eggs and James's sperm together, what else would that produce but another crazy person?

That's what I thought, what we both thought, actually. Not that we thought much about it at all when we got married at ages forty and forty-nine. We assumed we were beyond the point of having babies and didn't even try to have kids at first. Then one day, I felt like I was getting the flu and discovered I was pregnant. Who gets *accidentally* pregnant at forty? See, I told you. Crazy people.

Children weren't even part of our mutual attraction or any life plan— not that we had any identifiable plans. And waiting until forty to have babies wasn't part of a career strategy either. It was just how my life naturally went. In my office at the RNC, I had a poster on my wall: OOPS, I FORGOT TO HAVE A BABY.

In reality, if you really want something, you arrange your life to make it happen—whether or not you're doing it consciously, subconsciously or unconsciously. I didn't feel a void in my life. Nor did I never give it a thought. Of course, as we were racing through our childbearing years, the topic would occasionally come up in girl chats. But having a baby was like: *Yeah, sure, I'd like to fly to the moon someday too.* To me, mothering was a *big* deal, the highest calling. It's like a religious conversion. You don't enter into that lightly. It's a lifetime commitment. And I had doubts I could do it—physically or emotionally.

You can turn off your job. You can turn off your siblings, your neighbors, your friends—and put them out of your head. But you can't stop being a mom. You are always thinking of your children, always loving them, always caught up in their emerging lives and concerns and discoveries. When that much of your brain and heart is involved in anything— although it's hard to imagine what else would be so captivating—it is hard to shift gears and go whole hog for something else.

I guess many aspects of creating life are mind-blowing for everyone, but I was completely out of my element. *Everything* about it blew me away. I couldn't adjust to the fact that a subject to which I'd barely given a thought was suddenly the obsession of my every waking moment and all my sleeping ones too. *Nothing else* mattered. *Nothing else* was worthy of serious consideration. I never got over the wonder of pregnancy, but it barely registered on the emotional Richter scale compared to actually *having* a baby. It was an all-engrossing, completely fulfilling, never-ending miracle.

Though everything else in my life had been incomparable to having kids, I can now see parallels to receiving the gift of faith—how indescribable joy and peace sprang from a place in your heart you didn't know existed. In both cases, it never ceases to astound me. It is always totally unexpected. I never take it for granted. It is inexpressibly humbling and exhilarating at the same time.

The first time I looked at Matty's tiny little face, her perfect miniature fingers, heard those small soft noises she made, inhaled her whole intoxicating baby being, I was teleported to another dimension from which I hope never to return. It's a place of joy that makes me laugh and cry and swoon.

And it's a good thing, because without the joyous counterbalance, no one could withstand the sheer terror of being 100 percent responsible for the very existence of another living being.

Getting into the car for the first time after Matty was born, I couldn't even release her to the newborn-baby car seat, which would have actually protected her from injury or death far better than my arms. And when we got home, the grip continued.

This child never left my arms. We took her everywhere with us—to congressional parties, Sam Donaldson's birthday party, Tim Russert's Christmas party, anybody and everybody's dinner parties. When I went back to work, the poor baby came with me to TV sets and radio studios. After work, we brought her to the Palm Restaurant and plopped her car seat on our regular table under the political caricatures papering the walls while we had dinner. When I went around the country to speak, I carried her along. That infant had 31,000 air miles before she was three months old.

This isn't exactly normal behavior, but my friends were so cool that no one told me I was a tad over the top. Or maybe they just expected it of me. Whatever, all my girlfriends were enchanted with "our" baby. I'd like to think this was because Matty was so extraordinary, but it probably had something to do with her being the *only* baby we all had.

You think I am exaggerating? Because I never put that baby down, she never learned to crawl. She went from my arms to walking. And did you know that if you don't crawl you don't develop some of the processing tools you need to write and perform other small motor-coordination tasks? Me either. Well, now you do. Take it from another mother.

So one day she just pushes out of my arms and starts walking and talking and singing. It was like she had aged two years in a blink. She began talking nonstop at an unusually young age, maybe because she was constantly around adults who never shut up.

There wasn't one second of baby mothering that I didn't adore, or one baby task I wasn't over the moon about. I loved changing diapers, loved breast-feeding, loved singing to her, loved reading to her, loved rubbing her impossibly soft belly, which always made her emit the baby version of purring. I was never bored. She was my constant companion, the light of my life, song of my soul. She was a bliss I never even dreamed of. And you know what? I felt exactly the same way about her sister when she was born two years and nine months later, though I like to think I was less neurotic, despite both girls' insistence to the contrary.

From their first breath to this very afternoon, and every day in between, I look at the faces of my girls and think to myself, *This is the face of God.*

JAMES

PEOPLE OFTEN ASK ME: did having kids make you more conservative? The truth is, I just don't know. There's no way I can know how I would have evolved without them. I think there's a certain way to raise children right, and it really doesn't have much to do with your politics.

Mary and I have faced the fundamental question that every parent faces:

Do you allow your children to engage in the world—and by the world I mean movies and TV shows and the Internet and all the good and bad of our culture? Do you expose them to this secular, sinful, selfish world? Or do you try to protect your kids from the larger world? Do you try to shield them from the worst of it?

There are plenty of people who opt for the latter. It's perfectly understandable. But our approach has always been to expose them to the world rather than hide it from them. I think we both feel like our culture is what it is, for better or worse. And so if they ask about something we do our best to answer.

If a couple doesn't agree on that basic question, it can cause real problems in a marriage. But Mary and I always have been on the same page as far as that goes. We took the girls walking down Bourbon Street with us when they were only toddlers, and they saw every stripe of humanity there. We took them to Amsterdam, where they saw prostitutes in the windows and marijuana bars and such. When they asked, we explained. There are very few enclaves where everybody is in some idealistic nuclear family, where the world is ideal and perfect. I don't see the sense in pretending otherwise.

MARY

JAMES AND I WERE IN TOTAL AGREEMENT: the girls were to get a better education than we had. We wanted them surrounded by beautiful things, by flowers and art and culture. At the same time, we didn't want them to be sheltered the way James and I had been as kids. We wanted them to see the world, even difficult things. And we wanted them to have street smarts, often more critical to a happy life than all of the above. We agreed that they should make as many decisions for themselves as possible, and we would trust them as much as we could until their judgment proved otherwise.

JAMES

AND YOU KNOW, for all they might have learned from us, they've taught us plenty in return. One of my great satisfactions is that our generation has not been able to infect my daughters and their peers with our prejudices. If you bring up somebody's race or sexual orientation, they don't even know why you're talking about it or why it matters.

That's one reason I believe that very few young people identify with the hard-core social conservatives in this country. Young people think the conversation is totally irrelevant when conservatives rail on about gay marriage or whatever. It would be like somebody coming up to them and saying, "Hey, you better watch out for those sneaky Japs."

Those are prejudices from another time and place. And my children, thankfully, are part of a generation that has left them behind and moved on to better things.

MARY

RAISING A CHILD IN D.C.? Well, since I'd given no thought to even having a kid in D.C. or anywhere else, I was slow on the uptake to figure out that Washington, D.C., was not Andy Griffith's Mayberry in terms of child rearing.

I had no mother, no mother skills, no mother friends and even fewer maternal instincts, but I did have the requisite village it takes to raise a child in the form of great girlfriends, including Maria and my own sainted sister, Renie, not to mention a plethora of awesome avuncular types such as Tim Russert. And when my daughters were little, there was a pretty cool day-care center inside my office, the Old Executive Office Building (OEOB) next to the White House.

But once they hit the age of exposure to politics D.C. style, I confess the village started falling apart. There was no way to shield them from the worst of the place. And the best of the place was a constant distraction.

Despite the traumas of their uprooting from D.C., the girls were the compelling reason to leave.

The best part of a D.C. upbringing—with weird, plugged-in parents like us—was their hands-on experience with politicians as real people. The girls learned early that the famous and powerful are human beings just like anybody else. They saw Dick Cheney as the grandpa who had lots of dogs that he loved more than anything. The girls didn't see Poppy Bush that often, but they thought of him as a faraway grandfather and heard lots of funny stories about him from me. Bill Clinton was a hoarse-voiced uncle who could talk to them about anything, and even better, about things they wanted to talk about.

After a marathon conversation with Matty about all things Beatles related (she had inherited the *all or nothing* gene and possessed every known factoid about every Beatle, their time and place and girlfriends and influences and mother issues, every lyric to every song, including obscure bootlegs . . . well, you get the drift), Clinton gave her his entire Beatles vinyl collection. I have to admit even I coveted it.

And because James is James, there was a regular stream of other famous friends in our house—from Barney to Popeye the Sailor Man, and anybody else his Hollywood pals could send. It wasn't normal, but to start with, when you have a dad like Carville, I think your gauge of that becomes a little skewed. To this day, hanging with the Muppets is just another Take Our Daughters to Work Day in James's world.

My own Take Our Daughters to Work Day happened a lot more often, and was slightly more grounded in real life. After we had an unfortunate caregiver issue, I brought Matty and Emerson to day care at the OEOB all the time. Once in the West Wing, when she was still a toddler, Emerson ran into the president and in her normal fashion offered her gross, slobbery bottle of God-knows-what to him. Without missing a beat, President George W. Bush said, "Thanks, but I'm off that stuff now." She tried to follow him into the Oval Office before tod-dling back to my office.

Another good thing about their one-dimensional D.C. world was their inescapable exposure to current events, although some of it was more like a bleak Grimms' fairy tale than a Cinderella story. One of our rare family "vacations" occurred when the first Intifada erupted and I spent the entire holiday in front of the tube as the horror unfolded live. After a couple of days of bomb lobbing and surreal analysis, Emerson took out her *ʐoo-ʐoo* (our term for her pacifier) and offered the best advice I had heard, "That guy Arafat needs a time-out!" Another time, after overhearing way too many Mommy-and-Daddy "discussions" about Iraq, she asked me with the wisdom of the ages: "How can they say we lost the Iraq War before it's over?"

My reply: "That's right, kid!"

On the downside, D.C. is a highly competitive place. Competition is healthy and learning to deal with it is necessary. I have a real problem with fraudulent self-esteem schemes devised by liberal child "experts." But that doesn't mean kids need to face every day as if they were Fortune 100 CEOs.

James and I have never been pushy parents. We set standards, we know what our kids are capable of—and they have to answer to us if their efforts fail to match our expectations. We provide lots of opportu-nities for exposure to the big wide world and we're both good listeners and good at being guiding hands. But we don't push our preferences on them and we discourage them from self-judgment based on the stan-dards and whims of their peers or pop culture. Find your own place and space. Explore your options. These are different and unique for each individual.

D.C. childhood reflects D.C. adulthood. Infused with adult compet-itiveness and ambition and aggressive type A personalities, it's a hard place to find yourself as a young person.

But so many of the D.C. kids were on a boot camp schedule—

enrolled in all manner of activities and sports. They took music, language, dancing and social etiquette classes as well as being provided with the coolest playgroups, the best concerts, designer clothes and fine dining. I wondered if they'd be burned out before their time—overwrought, overworked and played out.

They didn't have time for the moments in life we like best—baking a German chocolate cake, concocting a new pasta sauce, watching *Doctor Who* or just hanging out.

Another inevitable and unavoidable characteristic of D.C., for good or ill—for kids as well as adults—is the omnipresence of politics. This is terrific if you are a political junkie with few other interests, but Matty and Emerson were not political junkies—in fact, they were fastidious avoiders of politics—and had multiple other interests. It was bad enough they had a mommy and daddy who could lock horns on topics completely irrelevant to them, but it became too common for schoolmates and neighborhood kids to goad the girls about politics. Fortunately, the girls had learned by osmosis how to dispatch a weenie kid on any given current events topic without breaking a sweat. But when adults jump in—and get hostile—that's another thing.

Here's a real-life story:

On Emerson's first day of first grade, we were holding hands and standing in line at the bookstore with our arms full of gym shorts, notebooks, first readers, colored pencils with pink feathers where erasers should have been. I didn't bother asking her what she would use for erasers because I knew she would give me that look—"I don't plan to make any mistakes"—but just in case, I was looking around for the erasers, when the mom behind us, a tanned, taut-bodied young woman with a perky blond ponytail and a designer tennis outfit with matching shoes (in contrast to my real mom look of pasty-white saggy skin, uncombed hair, stained khakis and a BUSH-QUAYLE 1988 T-shirt) says to me, "You were such a bitch on *Meet the Press* yesterday morning."

Emerson squeezed my hand. She knew. She was just six years old and she knew her mother could break bad at any moment. And I might have, if her knuckle smashing into my palm hadn't been so distracting. Instead, I came home and said to James, "I don't think I can raise my kids here."

After that, we started to talk about leaving.

JAMES

THIS IS A FACT that can never be disputed: the single most vicious and cruel specimen on Earth—and I'm including al-Qaeda recruits, great white sharks, king cobras, pit vipers, whatever else—is a seventh-grade girl. I've said this to audiences. I've talked about this with other parents. Nobody disagrees with me on this.

And to the seventh-grade girl, there's no more humiliating specimen than her daddy. It's a temporary phase, but it's a painful one. My daughters and I have always been close. Growing up, they always wanted to do stuff with me and have their friends do stuff with me. I thought I was sort of like a cool dad.

But it was not like that during seventh grade. Not at all. I might as well have had the plague. It was all venom and attitude. I was only good for feeding them and clothing them and giving them rides to visit people they actually liked. Beyond that, my usefulness was extremely limited.

It's an evolution. Every age brings its own adventures.

MARY

JAMES ALWAYS TOOK MIDDLE school personally. It wasn't him; the girls were living in a world not unlike our worst campaigns and certainly nothing like our young years.

I did not like being a teenager. And I wasn't looking forward to my own girls' teen years. But I thought I'd be dealing with those issues when they were *actually* teens. Today's world of preteen and tween girls contains a kind of sophisticated cruelty akin to a maximum-security prison of hardened criminals. It's a world of bully girls and cliques and Facebook viciousness in training bras. It's even harder for older parents because we are literally from another paradigm.

5.

Sex When You're Old

MARY

I RESPECT ALL RELIGIONS (except those that promote violence); am open-minded about political views (except those that begin and end with demonizing demagoguery); am not particularly judgmental about consensual adult relationships (except those that are flagrantly and gratuitously paraded in my face). I try to be a good listener should a friend have a personal crisis of faith or politics, or a problem "in the bedroom," but in general, don't seek out those subjects on the grounds of, "it's none of my darn business."

Obviously, I cannot object to anyone questioning my politics; and I am always happy to evangelize—though not proselytize—when asked about my Catholicism. And, of course, I understand the days of Mary Tyler Moore and Dick Van Dyke sleeping in separate twin beds is *so yesterday*, but Lord Have Mercy . . . I have just never adjusted to the casualness and frequency of queries about the sex life of Mary Matalin and James Carville.

I cannot deny James and his boy pals obsess about sex like they are still sixteen, but even the sex-crazed Carville is reticent to talk about sex much in mixed company. So I am just not sure how our union manages to invite so much personal scrutiny.

JAMES

WHAT CAN I SAY? I'm a ravenous heterosexual.

I'm sixty-nine now, not sixteen, but sex is not an ancillary part of my life. It's central to who I am. It's like food or sleep. Just something you need to survive. I always thought everybody was like that. Apparently, some people are not, but I'm not one of them. Never will be as long as the parts work. I actually don't understand the big taboo about sex in this country. Maybe that's the New Orleans in me. But I'm actually amused by things like abstinence programs. I find it almost laughable that anybody thinks you can stop this kind of thing.

It's human nature. Why would we pretend it's not?

MARY

FROM THE BEGINNING we were always asked, "How do you do it?" but that question was directed at our divergent political views. Today, we are asked more frequently than you would imagine, and by people you would never imagine, "How do you do *it?*" . . . and they aren't talking about our political life.

How could you sleep with her/him? Is he/she great in bed because there is no other possible explanation for being with him/her? Do you have great make-up sex? Do you have political fights just to have great make-up sex? Do you do politics rather than sex? Do you stop to have sex during a campaign? Who is better in bed, Republicans or Democrats? Do Republicans keep their socks on during sex? Does your pillow talk include exchanging politics secrets? Have you been to a D.C. orgy? Doesn't everyone in politics cheat on their spouse? Do you cheat on each other? Did you stop having sex after you had your kids? Did you have sex more than the two times that produced your daughters? Are your kids adopted? How often do you have sex? Do you still have sex? Aren't you too old for sex?

Seriously people? Here's your answer: *none of your darn business*.

6.

ADHD

MARY

MY FATHER, MY HERO, whom I always strove to emulate, was superintense and had limitless curiosity and countless projects. My brother was always really hyper, which my mother attributed to a special trait she called the St. Vitus Dance. He endlessly entertained all of us with his nonstop antics—or maybe he just entertained me, since I was often a coconspirator. As for me, I was a courteous kid, but rambunctious, and as a teen, I ran with a never-still gang. More than once we had to be bailed out.

My earliest boyfriends all had many disparate interests (sometimes this trait manifested itself in being interested in many girls at the same time). My college buds and beaus always had multiple shifting majors and excelled at all of them.

From bartending to campaign toiling, my adult life was one parade after another of over-the-top, outside-the-box adventures and characters.

Campaigns attract the most energetic, adventurous, curious and original cast of eccentrics, and I loved them all, all the time. I was especially blessed with great bosses in my first "real" political jobs—

incomparable, inimitable forces of nature, like the poker-playing card-sharp Rich Bond to the guitar-picking Lee Atwater. Even when he was dying, Lee Atwater could not sit still for a minute.

I never even thought about it. All I knew was there were only two things I just could *not* deal with: boring jobs and boring people.

So meeting James Carville in middle age seemed par for the course. But little did I know that he was a quantum leap in energy and eccentricity.

Back in those days, nobody talked about ADD or ADHD. We were swimming in a sea of high-energy megatalents. And since most of our dating years were spent in separate cities, whenever we managed to get together, we were both crazy hyper and crazy for each other so who noticed?

For years, everyone around him, especially his mom and five sisters, worshiped and adored him. And his steady stream of lovelies who had preceded me had simply adjusted to him, bent to him. Because James was just James. Growing up, he had been a wild boy-child, an episodic LSU student, a gung-ho marine, and all the other things he became, while being so gifted and compelling that everybody just accepted his oddities. Plus he was the oldest of eight raised in a part of the world that is still renowned for being the last bastion of the authentic eccentric.

But once he and I hit real postdating life, I couldn't help but notice that James wasn't just unique. He was a challenge to coexist with.

I remember one night when we were having dinner at our restaurant, West 24—it had been one of our mutual lifelong dreams to own a restaurant—when I finally lost it. We were with my close friend Ann Devroy, but James couldn't stay seated in the booth. He kept jumping up, almost frantically, and talking to everybody who walked in. When he'd sit down for a couple seconds, his legs would be jumping under the table as if he was already trying to run away. I mean, there was no freaking point in even trying to hold a civilized conversation with this guy.

This was hardly unusual behavior for James. And like everyone else, Ann was totally chill with him. And, in fact, like everyone else, she told me to chill out.

I snapped and became totally enraged.

"I can't stand this anymore!" I yelled, quickly apologizing to Ann. She just laughed and said, "Oh, what's the problem? He's just being James."

Exactly. The problem was James being James. But not for her; she wasn't married to him.

After that, *snap crackle pop*, almost everything about him set me off. When I could get him to the movies, my favorite kind of date, he got up and left after thirty minutes to make phone calls in the lobby or his car. He couldn't sit through Mass or dinner or a TV show. He couldn't sit period. He couldn't listen either. We had precious little time for random conversation, and every time I would start one, he would pick up the phone or a book.

Though I was certain my inborn impatience or new-mom insecurity was the problem, I was always trying to change him, get him to settle down. Trying to get him to *pay attention to me, listen to me*.

There was a lot of fussing and fretting and crying and door slamming, hurt feelings and harsh words. In rational moments, I was always trying to communicate my irritation in a way that I thought was crystal clear.

Like most women, I'm hypersensitive to the unspoken—to body language and various social cues, both incoming and outgoing. If I do say so myself, I'm overly gifted that way. Though not everyone thinks it's a gift, being able to intuitively read a person or a whole room of people can be a helpful life skill.

James didn't offer himself up easily to being judged, studied, intuited, read or flat-out comprehended. In his defense, what seemed crystal clear to me was a nightmare of unfathomable passive aggression to him. When I thought I was transmitting the signal, *Hello! Earth to James, please sit down/pay attention to me,* he was receiving . . . nothing. Nada. At most, he might offer up a blank stare.

Forget the intimate communication of marriage. His every waking moment became an irritation, another reminder that we weren't meant to coexist. In order to control his own ADHD, and bring order to his life and lifestyle, he had instinctively constructed a rigid routine for himself, a way of living, hour by hour, that had worked for decades for him.

James is early to bed, early to rise, and every day he runs at three p.m. He believes in discipline, moderation, punctuality and every meal being eaten as close to the same time every day as possible. And if he varies that schedule, like when he's traveling, he becomes miserable.

My preference is 180 degrees from that. I am antiroutine, antischedule. This is how I hold on to sanity. For me, every day should be a new day—and I want it to be different. I live episodically, and I like bouts of fun-loving immoderation. I like to stay up all night, linger at parties and prolong quiet dinner conversations to marathon yak-a-thons. Whatever I'm doing in life, I do 100 percent with obnoxious focus and drive—whether it's a craft project, my critters, reading books or studying art. I forget to eat. Even something as commonplace as listening to music is only gratifying to me if it's loud and long, and no one interrupts me. I love watching eight movies in a row (and often do), and more than once I watched episodes of *24* for twenty-four hours nonstop.

To James, this is insanity or worse. Sometimes, in those early days, he would give me a look that said, "I knew there was a reason I never wanted to get married." He just can't live the way I do. Any more than I can live tethered to a clock and a routine.

But after five years of marriage, we were at an impossible impasse. We loved each other desperately, but we couldn't stand each other's guts.

Then Matty started school. She enchanted her teachers, wowed them with her advanced verbal skills, imagination and vast repertoire of jokes.

She had lots of friends and was kind and thoughtful to everyone, and unusually sensitive and especially protective of kids who got picked on. We were beaming at our first parent-teacher conference as the teacher described the Matty we knew and loved. Then she lowered the boom.

Matty couldn't read. She couldn't add. She couldn't do the most basic stuff. Suddenly, the girl being described didn't comport with the perfect Matty who had just been lavished with praise.

My first reaction was to tell the teacher she was an idiot, but that was not an option, as Mrs. Ryan was the best teacher and person ever and I knew she adored Matty. More importantly, she went on to ask about something that suddenly explained a few of my baby's inexplicable home behaviors. Could Matty have vision problems? *Hmmmm*, I thought. This might be why she couldn't ride a bike, hit a Wiffle ball or roller-skate. And why she stood smack-dab in front of the TV to watch it, or put her face almost in her food when she was eating.

Her vision impairment, undiagnosed from birth, contributed to various developmental anomalies. And correcting it went a long way in helping Matty at school, as you might expect, but it didn't fix her basic skill issues. So she had the full battery of tests. My sister, Renie, who has multiple degrees in teaching learning-disabled kids and in teaching LD teachers how to teach LD kids, swooped in and enlightened us with ideas and advice. I read everything I could get my hands on. I *devoured* books on the subject of ADHD and every related processing issue, talked to every expert I could reach, every parent who would share, pored over every study I could find.

Finally a lightbulb went on, luminous and bright and miraculous. In my quest to resolve Matty's issues, I stumbled over the solution to my marital issue.

I insisted James go to a specialist to get tested.

I realized that he was an *ADHD poster child.*

You think I would have gotten a clue when even total strangers, random doctors in airports who'd seen him on TV, would be constantly stopping me, offering in absentia diagnoses, "You know your husband has ADHD." I mean any professional could literally spot him a mile away. But for years we all said, it was just James being James.

I was relieved to tears. Maybe I wasn't a shrew wife; maybe he wasn't a blockhead husband. Maybe it was just who James was as a person and part of his magic.

You hear in church that there's a lot to learn from the little children. I learned from my daughters, and from helping them—because they both have processing issues, which are completely different and require completely different correctives. I never for one second stopped unconditionally loving them and never had a solitary thought of wanting to change a single hair on their beautiful heads.

And in the wonderful way God works, I got a bonus lesson. I instantly felt the same way about their father. I didn't want to change a single hair on his beautiful head either, and not just because he has only a few hairs to begin with.

Almost overnight, his irksome ability to literally talk on the phone, work at his computer, watch ESPN and hear every word I'm saying and repeat it back to me verbatim stopped making me want to punch him in the face. His ADHD brain works on three levels of chess playing at one time. He sees the world through a different prism, his own prism, and often it's a kaleidoscope. Definitely not boring.

He begrudgingly went with me to a specialist and—*what a surprise!*—he got an official ADHD diagnosis and was offered medication to focus and live a little more "normally." To his credit—and for which I pledge my undying love— he said, "No way, José. I like who I am and this is how I know how to think."

On this point, we are in aggressive agreement.

JAMES

FOR YEARS, it had been a strain on our relationship.

Mary spent a lot of time feeling frustrated with me, though I wasn't always sure why. She'd accuse me of ignoring her or not listening because I'd be doing five other things while she talked. Sometimes I'd change topics in the middle of a sentence. She'd say, "You're not listening to a word I'm saying." But I was, and I'd recite back to her everything she'd just said. That would piss her off even more.

She'd accuse me of being rude if I got up and left the table. She thought I was angry at something. I wasn't angry, and I never intended to be rude. I was finished so I'd leave. What was the big deal?

Over time, it became a big issue for Mary. She told me I was too impulsive. She took it upon herself to make an appointment with a specialist. This was about ten years ago. We went together to see the guy at his fancy office up on Connecticut Avenue in Washington. He did all this diagnostic testing and evaluation. We had to fill out pages and pages of questionnaires. Ultimately, he diagnosed me with ADHD.

The doctor started saying he could put me on this medication or that medication. He detailed this whole regimen that he said could help me rein in the ADHD. I said, "Look, to tell you the truth, I don't want to be on a drug. I like the way I am." I meant it. It would be a whole new reality to get used to. I didn't know whether I'd be changing from a reality I liked into one I didn't.

Mary actually seemed okay with that. After she understood the basic reasons I behave the way I do, and that my idiosyncrasies aren't intended to insult her, she felt much better. "Now that I know what's wrong with you, I know how to deal with it," she said. After that, she became much more accepting and supportive.

You come to learn the things you can do and the things you can't, because the things that you can't do, you *really* can't do. The key for me is not to do work that requires long-term concentration. Political campaigns offered a perfect outlet. High intensity, a defined time horizon. I'm good at short bursts of intense focus. But I'd be terrible at something that requires an actual attention span.

I went with my daughter recently to help her open her first checking account. I remember sitting there thinking that if I had to work as a teller at the bank all day long, stuck in one place at one window, I literally couldn't do it. I would have a nervous breakdown. If I had to be an airplane pilot, sitting patiently in a confined cockpit for hours managing systems, I'd lose my mind. It's not that I don't have respect for those jobs. It's not that they aren't important. I just literally could not do them.

I practiced law early in my career, long before anybody even talked about ADHD, and it was an awful fit for me. Being a good lawyer is hard-ass work to begin with, and it's especially hard for somebody like me because you've got to pore over and rewrite contracts. You have to read through court documents, take long depositions. You've got to maintain your focus the whole time, and I simply can't do that.

My mother used to tell people I was like a toaster. The boy can't sit still for long before he pops. It's always been part of my nature. In my life, I've never slept in. Once I'm awake, I never sit still. I never nap. I don't like to sit out at the beach. Five minutes, and I'm up and walking. Probably half the movies I go see I end up walking out of. I never just hang out around the house. I can't stand it. I hate stillness.

Mary couldn't be more different. Whatever is the opposite of ADHD, that's her condition. She doesn't share my need for routine and consistency. She would sit and watch twenty-four hours of TV straight if it involves a show she likes. She'll stay up all night reading a good book. Not me. It's lights out by ten p.m. I could be watching the final scenes of *The Godfather*. I could be finishing the last two chapters of the *The Day of the Jackal*. Doesn't matter. I'll turn the light out and go to sleep simply because it's time.

Oddly enough, I'm way more punctual than she is. When I'm ready to head out the door, I head out the door. And when I'm ready to come home, I'm ready to come home. Mary's like Bill Clinton; neither one of them can leave anything. One of my expressions is "The only way to leave is to leave." Thank whomever and say good night. So a lot of times, when we're out with friends, I'll just say good night and head home. I'm not mad, not at all. I'm not trying to be rude. But I'm going home. She's welcome to stay.

That used to cause a lot of problems between us. Now she understands. Over time, you get to know each other as a couple and you respect each other's differences. You accept the reality of who your spouse is. You make adjustments. You carry on.

MARY

THE ADHD + JAMES epiphany gave me a new lease on our married life and I'm sure that was a great relief to his sister Gail, whom I used to call about every ten minutes for ten years and ask, "Is this normal?" and she'd answer, "Well, sister, *it's normal for James.*"

Though they never said anything, I am pretty sure James's family couldn't really fathom why I was always griping about "normal." By their estimation, for me to talk about normal was the very definition of the pot calling the kettle black. Nonetheless, I thank Gail for her decades of patience.

Every day there are big and little adjustments to make for his ADHD. Some days I am not as good as I'd like to be, but there is no more screaming like a banshee and door slamming followed by couch sleeping.

But there is one thing I will never accept: that these processing issues are *disorders* or *disabilities* or anything whatsoever to lament. Lamentations invite self-pity and the whole victim pathology. People who process outside of the norm, which is nothing more than the median, which is often *at best* mediocre, should be considered gifted not victimized. Seeing a gray world through kaleidoscope lenses is a beautiful thing.

I am sure it's painful for him because he thinks the girls inherited his processing issues and that it's a troublesome thing. He's always whimpering, "Oh, my poor little girls." Which annoys me so. Poor little girls? Are you kidding me? There is no aspect of their existence that wants for anything. There's nothing they cannot do, and everything they do they do exceptionally well. Which he ought to know because he is forever bragging about them way beyond the bounds of acceptable parent pride.

I can't help but think there is an instinctive political element buried in this pain. And nothing bugs me as much as a liberal's ability to see victims around every corner. "They aren't victims!" I scream. Can't help myself. "And Lord have mercy, neither are you!"

Do you know any exceptional person who doesn't process the world through their own unique prism? To me, the disorder is in trying to fit everyone into the same sorry, boring box. Instead, we should nurture, reward, regale and glorify thinking outside the box. And I suppose we do, but not enough. These people are writers, artists, thinkers, risk takers, inventors, innovators, entertainers, mystics, visionaries—people who shoot the moon.

I know James knows this and believes it, victim instincts aside. And he has spent a lot of time and effort working with ADD and ADHD kids; he is a real inspiration to them.

As it turns out, processing issues usually manifest differently in girls and boys. Girls tend to internalize when they have attention issues and can go supercreative or dangerously negative. Boys, because they tend to externalize, can dangerously "self-medicate" with recreational inebriation to slow the world down. On the more positive side, they often become the class clowns, *look at me, look at me*. They're intense and hilarious and adventurous and off-the-chain creative. They act like James. They act like Vince Vaughn. And I am the first to admit that those are the boys who always made me swoon. And still do.

JAMES

THE EASIEST WAY TO explain my ADHD is this: I am an utter and total creature of habit. Anybody I've ever worked with, anybody I've ever lived with, they absolutely understand this. One of the main ways I deal with the whole situation is to create structure and routine.

Take my typical day when I'm home in New Orleans. By design, it rarely changes. I have to run in the late afternoon. Everything else emanates from the run. I run the same four-mile route each day, twice around Audubon Park. Same route. Same direction. I run in the afternoon because I know I'm at my best in the morning for work. Any meeting with me, best to schedule it between nine a.m. and eleven a.m.

Most mornings, I'm up by six a.m. I go downstairs and grab the newspapers. The *New York Times*. The *Wall Street Journal*. The New Orleans paper comes three days a week, and the Baton Rouge paper every day. I go through each paper, one by one.

Whatever fruit is in season, I'll scarf down a bunch of that. I have a few hole-in-the-wall breakfast joints I like, so sometimes I'll stop by one of those places. I'll glance at the computer, maybe take a quick look at e-mail, then start making phone calls. People usually are calling me by seven a.m., anyway. Many of them are on the East Coast, so they're an hour ahead and they know I'm up anyway.

I talk to the same six or eight people every single day. George Stephanopoulos, Al Hunt, Stan Greenberg, Paul Begala, Rahm Emanuel. A few others. Most days, I also talk to my brother in Baton Rouge. With all of them, it can be five minutes. It can be twenty or twenty-five minutes. But we talk.

I usually try to get a lot done in the mornings and head to lunch around eleven-thirty a.m. I never wait until noon. Growing up, my uncle was a farmer, and we ate what we called dinner at eleven a.m. Dinner was the big meal of the day. Supper meant leftovers or something small in the evenings. In the summertime, you'd get up at four-thirty or five a.m., work for a couple hours before it got too hot and come back in for a quick breakfast. And then it was back to work until lunch at eleven. I still like it that way.

Most days, I'll go to one of my usual spots around town. I like to get out of the house. More often than not, I eat lunch by myself. It's not that I'm averse to eating with other people. But I like to sit and read the paper or watch sports while I eat. I like to have a beer, usually an Abita Amber. And I like to eat quickly. When I'm ready to leave, I leave.

I usually run a few errands each afternoon. I compulsively like to get the car washed. I'll drop the kids off somewhere. Run to the grocery store. By then it's time for the afternoon run. Same route. Same distance.

In the evenings, I'll head back out again for dinner with Mary and the girls if they're around, or by myself if they're not. There are probably five or six restaurants in New Orleans I go to 80 percent of the time. Mr. John's down on St. Charles and Clancy's over on Annunciation Street, for example. I go to this great little roadhouse called Mosca's over in Avondale. I often stop by Eleven 79 down in the Lower Garden District.

Certain nights I eat at certain places. Every Sunday, without fail, I eat dinner at the same Italian restaurant in Uptown New Orleans. Jews eat Chinese food on Sunday; I eat at Vincent's on Sunday. Mary and the kids usually like to stay home that day. So I go by myself. I love going in the fall because they always have the football game on. I always sit at the bar and talk to the same bartender.

I always have a Maker's Mark at dinner, usually topped off by a glass of red wine. I'm back home by eight-thirty, nine o'clock. If there's a good ball game on TV, I'll stick around and watch for a while. But I'm sound asleep by ten o'clock.

Of course, sometimes my carefully crafted schedule gets altered for me. I'm on the road a lot, across the country and all over the world. Traveling definitely throws a kink in the routine, but I've learned to game the system pretty well.

For instance, I know all the airports. Very seldom do I end up in an airport I've never visited. I plan ahead of time where I'm going to eat and what I'm going to eat. Take O'Hare in Chicago. There are two Wolfgang Puck restaurants there, in Terminal 1 and Terminal 3. I like their pizza. If I'm in Houston or Dallas, I'd head to any of the Pappas chain restaurants. There's Pappasito's Cantina and Pappadeaux Seafood Kitchen. I probably could tell you what and where I would eat at almost every airport in the country.

And when I get to where I'm going, I find a way to run. I build trips around making sure I have time for the daily run. It's nonnegotiable. I've taken the afternoon run in cities from Athens to Abuja.

I crave that kind of predictability. I need some element of certainty in daily life. When I get away from the normal routine, I get irritable. I can't think straight. I make errors. So I stick to it. I have no desire to alter it.

I don't mention all this because I think people give a crap where I eat or how I travel or when I get in my daily run. But I hope it illustrates the larger issues that so many families have to wrestle with when a loved one suffers from ADHD. My case was so obvious that a doctor came up to me in an airport and told me he could tell I had ADHD just by watching me from afar, and that I really needed to get checked for it.

But every case isn't so clear-cut. Left undiagnosed, it can lead to long years of misunderstandings, frustration, resentment and potentially unhappy endings. Mary and I know firsthand about those first few, but thankfully we figured it out in time to avoid that last fate.

7

The Dark Ages

MARY

ON THE HIERARCHY OF our connubial contretemps, as James and I have both repeatedly noted, politics is actually pretty low in the pecking order. For us, it's unrewarding and almost too easy. We aren't low-hanging-fruit eaters. We like to make everything worth the effort. And if we are going to use our finely honed fighting skills, we'd rather have skirmishes in a new territory, not the one we spend all day working in. Or, as James likes to say, "If you are a plumber by day, you don't want to come home and fix your own toilet at night."

By the time of the Florida recount in 2000, we hadn't really fought about politics for years, aside from some unpleasantness during the impeachment hearings in 1998. Matty, who was two, wanted to know "who is this *Mokina Loo-whisky* anyway?" since all the voices on the radio and all the faces on TV never stopped yakking about her. (Matty even went through a brief beret phase.)

I averted my eyes on the Clinton marriage issue. (Judge not, I say, since I wish everyone would quit judging my marriage.) And while the lying under oath part ground on me in the worst way—in my defense, I was in postpartum meltdown with a colicky infant—my rage was focused on how James was lied to by President Clinton, who then proceeded to relentlessly carpet bomb the airwaves with that mendacious message.

James's response to my complaints was: "If I did something that stupid with someone that young, I'd lie about it too." To my mind, not the best explanation for any wife, let alone a postpartum one.

So we managed to get all the way to Election Day in 2000—seven years of bliss, or our version of it—without much marital stressing over politics. Ironically, our relative marital harmony was aided by the otherwise worthless Al Gore, who wasn't high on James's favorite-people list, particularly after he launched his diss-Clinton charade, hypocritically distancing himself from the guy who brought him to the dance in the first place.

I was working at CNN in those days. Quietly, off-the-record and only episodically, I was in touch with the Dick Cheney political operation via his daughter, Liz, whom I admired but didn't really know well. The entire Cheney family—both daughters, Mary and Liz, as well as Mrs. Lynne Cheney—were laboring on the campaign for him, as they had for all his congressional runs in Wyoming.

Not that I knew Dick Cheney that well either, but I had been a Cheney groupie since way back in the Poppy Bush days. And I supported his short-lived 1996 presidential consideration.

Mostly Liz wanted a sounding board. First it was about whether or not her father could or should run for president himself, and then it was about being Junior's running mate. (Since we'd been office mates and had become friends on his father's campaign in 1988, I had always called George W. Bush "Junior." But after Governor Bush got into his presidential consideration mode in 1998–99, and I continued to reference him by his lifelong nickname, I was pointedly asked by his top man—in no uncertain terms—to cease and desist. Then I immediately felt like a fool. What president wants to be called Junior?)

By convention time, Liz and I were daily phone chatters. She'd share the campaign trail comings and goings. And when preparing to go on the air, I'd often check in with her. She knew she could trust me. I never repeat things I'm not supposed to repeat. And what I didn't want to repeat were talking points, which the airwaves were replete with; I hate talking points. And so did Liz.

It was pretty calm and quiet in the Matalin-Carville world (meaning that James was his version of sane) until Election Night. Then—in warp speed, which is his MO—he devolved into an anti-Bush Beelzebub, making a simple household or parenting exchange with him almost impossible. So I stopped trying.

During the recount, every day of our lives was terrible, a precipitous decent into political hell on the home front. Every day, every hour, his mounting anger manifested itself in hideous and frequent muttering-to-himself rampages. After years of a home truce on politics, it was truly miserable.

We had never once talked about getting a divorce. It was never an option for us—even before I was a Catholic. And I have never *not* loved James. But now I was having unrelentingly days of not liking him and my confidence in our continued marital status was disintegrating. He echoed all the crap and lies that the Gore people were putting out, all the supercilious spin the heads were spouting on TV, and every prima facie false allegation he'd ever heard of, read or imagined.

It's nice to be married to a confidently energetic person. And that had always been part of our mutual attraction. But suddenly life with James was like living with a caged animal. I'd like to think I was more measured in my affection for the Bush-Cheney team, but apparently—if he is to be believed (ha)—I was equally annoying.

For the entire duration of the recount, we were like two nuclear silos waiting for a button to be pushed. The tension in our house was worse than the Cold War, except I was pulling for mutually assured destruction. That seemed the only path to peace.

The recount itself—the management and legal argument—was headed up by a group of people I had worked with on many a campaign and for whom I cared deeply. The legendary James A. Baker III and his longtime deputy, the inimitable force of nature, Margaret Tutwiler, deployed to Florida and set up shop with their customary DEFCON 1 focus. My beloved Maria Cino, who had headed up the political effort for the campaign, did a whirling dervish version of her specialty, operations, and mobilized everybody who was anybody, catapulting them onto waiting Sunshine State–bound planes and making sure they were housed, fed and provided for. (We all knew it would be a heinous experience, as recounts always are. Little did we anticipate a political Bataan Death March.)

Even my former boyfriend, Michael Carvin, one of the most brilliant legal minds in D.C. or anywhere else, not to mention he's the wonderful person who taught me Federalism from the ground up, plus many more necessities of life (and certainly did not deserve the psycho female BFF that I turned out to be), was arguing the Bush legal case in state court. Michael's stunning televised arguments made me slap myself on an hourly basis. What cruel fate destined me to be incarcerated with a madman instead of hanging out with all my favorite people in the universe?

So in short, everybody I knew and had ever loved in politics and life was suddenly in Florida, while I was stuck in D.C., incubating in a petri dish of political mutation.

Truth be told . . . which is the point of this book . . . I have to admit I wasn't *all that* broken up about not being there, as I had suffered through too many cuckoo recounts in my life, and I, in any event, was lactating away, still breast-feeding little Emerson, our adorable baby. Plus, I was still in dumbstruck love with her big sister, Matty, then five years old. Both provided far greater *mature* interactions than my husband-from-hell, in his ever-escalating state of frenzy and outrage.

If there is anything more joyful than holding babies in your arms and marveling at their porcelain skin and little appendages, I haven't experienced it in this life. I have great memories of those sweet moments of motherhood. But even that God-given gift was tempered by the ugliness at home because Sweet Daddy James had reverted to that odious James

Carville Serpenthead. When I could get a word in edgewise with all his spewing to himself, I always asked the same easy question, "James, why are you fighting me tooth and nail over a chump you yourself cannot deny is a stone-cold loser? Have you forgotten his diss-Clinton campaign? Are you insane?" (Rhetorical question, of course.)

When the final decision came down in December—more than a month after Election Night—I watched from the tiny TV in our kitchen, heaving with slobbery weeps of relief and happiness.

For a nanosecond, things seemed a little better, for me at least. James is always more articulate at explaining the jarring feeling we both have when our side is victorious—because as happy as we are, we know that our spouse is suffering and will probably be miserable to live with for a while. This is the tension of our relationship: the yin and yang of self-joy and partner pain. Now that W had won—yes, won; *elected NOT selected*—I could afford to feel more sympathy and compassion for my husband, Sweet Daddy James, again.

Liz Cheney called the very next day. After we exchanged a few celebratory pleasantries, she said, "Mary, my father wants to talk to you."

JAMES

SHE WAS NO PEACH to live with herself. We had two little kids at home, so we were both running on fumes as it was. We'd weathered election victories and losses before, not to mention the Clinton impeachment and plenty of other partisan battles in Washington. But during the recount, we were fighting about politics in a way we hadn't for years. It felt personal.

Feelings were running pretty hot throughout the country. But I guarantee you they were running even hotter in our house because we knew the stakes, we knew the people involved and we each felt so strongly that our side should win.

I remember the Sunday after Election Day, when it was clear everything was going to be stuck in limbo for a while, Mary and I went on *Meet the Press* together with Tim Russert. She was already ranting and raving, regurgitating the Republican line about Democratic "party hacks" down in Florida trying to divine the will of the people by looking at hanging chads and calling the whole recount "a parody of democracy."

I thought the recount was a good thing. I thought it actually resembled democracy in action, at least in the early days.

"I happen to think that all of this is pretty good . . . The American people have produced a very close election. You can't blame them. With close elections come recounts, come challenges, come all these things. That's the necessity of it," I said that morning on *Meet the Press.* "They're proceeding under Florida law . . . We'll never get a perfect count, but we can sure get a better count. And at the end of the day, if Governor Bush is elected president, as I said the other night on television, I believe I'll be the drum major in his inaugural parade if he wants me to. But there's no reason that we can't proceed under the existing statutes to get as accurate a count as we possibly can. I can't believe that anybody would object to that."

Mary didn't like that a bit. She kept howling like some GOP banshee about the recount somehow undermining democracy and how you can't "just keep counting and counting and counting until you get the result that you want." Which is exactly the opposite of what the Bush people were doing—trying *not* to count all the votes so that they could get the result they wanted.

It only grew worse in our house after that. The more tense things got in Florida, the more tense they got at home. I knew she was talking with a lot of the Bush people, including the ones running the show down in Florida. They were talking more than Mary and I were talking by then, that's for sure.

I got angrier and angrier as the process went on. If there had ever been an actual recount and Bush would have won, fine. I could have lived with it. But the way the Bush people and the Republicans in Florida used the judicial system to secure the election, it set my blood boiling.

What got to me the most was this bullshit narrative that began to develop, thanks to the Bush people (my wife included) pushing it and the press adopting it. The narrative held that the Supreme Court had stepped in and did what it had to do in *Bush v. Gore,* but that it didn't really matter because Bush was going to win anyway. The truth of it was that if there would have been a state-wide recount, Gore would've won easily. And the Florida Supreme Court was going to rule for a statewide recount until the Supreme Court decided it would rather decide the election.

I was in San Francisco when I got the word that the court had handed the election to Bush. I remember seething about it. I didn't want to see anybody or talk to anybody. I couldn't get over it. I'm not sure I ever really got over it. Even now, I'll never say we "lost" the election, because we didn't.

That election year actually turned out decently for the Democrats. We picked up four seats in the Senate. Gore won the popular election by half a million votes, and let's all be honest, he also won Florida. Or rather, would have won Florida if we'd have counted the votes like a true representative democracy.

The recount soured everything. It was a weird time in the country, and certainly a difficult time in our marriage. The worst part was that when it finally ended we couldn't just lick our wounds and move on, the way we always had in the past. I was still infuriated by the whole situation. And not only had my side just had an election victory pulled out from under it, I had a suspicion that I also was about to lose my wife to a new job in the White House for a president I sincerely didn't believe should be president.

MARY

SO WHEN LIZ CHENEY called and said, "My father wants to talk to you," I presumed it was an all-call to work on the transition from hell, so called because everyone knew it would be nothing but miserable. It was going to be a marathon at sprint speed—two-and-a-half months of work smooshed into an unfathomably few short weeks.

Usually a newly elected administration has from the day after their November election victory until Inauguration Day in January to get its act together. Actually, the official transition process starts way earlier, immediately following the official nomination by each party's respective national convention, when candidates for president and their senior staffs begin receiving daily briefings with info and intelligence accessible only to the president and his senior officeholders.

In a civil and mature world (which is neither mandatory nor automatic in national politics), an informal transition starts even earlier, as soon as the candidates mathematically secure the delegates necessary for their respective nominations. That's when incumbent administrations— if civil and mature—reach out to the unofficial candidates and their respective staffs to congratulate them and start an informal conversation, facilitating the later official one. It's the right thing to do for the country and for the candidates, one of whom, immediately following their two-year, nonstop, mind-numbing and exhausting-to-the-bone election campaign, will be walking into a man-eating buzz saw.

Digression for political newbies: you would be shocked at how little of the basic transition mechanics of a functioning democracy from one Leader of the Free World to another are taught in our very, very expensive public education system—or maybe you wouldn't be. *Anyway,* deprived students, above are the basics—and everything you need to know—despite the political media and punditocracy's endless attempts every four years to make the process unintelligible (yes, yes, guilty as charged, not proud of it) and more fraught with drama so the ratings (surprise!) climb as the whole not-so-confounding process unfolds.

Meanwhile, it turns out there *is* something worse than a transition hell that's smooshed into a few short weeks. And that is transitioning from an administration with a civility and maturity level lower than Animal House's, a comparison that is actually a compliment to the outgoing Clinton administration.

You think I'm being a partisan exaggerator? Well, would you call this mature and civil? Once into the White House, we found all the W's had been stripped from our computer keyboards and our desks were full of molding garbage, uneaten fast food and/or porno—and those were only the cute stunts. The vice president's offices were the worst because, as it turns out, Al Gore is not what you'd call graceful in defeat. Instead, he lived up to his reputation as a real loser.

But I'm getting ahead of myself.

As thrilled as I was to be presumably on Cheney's short list for transition assignments, I had to take stock of the situation. Okay, I've got a new baby, I told myself. And I hadn't experienced anything other than chronic fatigue for a long time. (FYI: a woman in her midforties does not "bounce back" right away after having a baby. My kids are leaving for college and I am still waiting for the bounce to happen.) Plus, I had a couple of years left on my CNN contract, a job that was lucrative and fit in well with all my overparenting tendencies. And then there was James. I had just lived through a couple of months with a rabid husband whose frothing didn't stop with the election's termination.

At the same time, I was mindful of the wretched years my campaign colleagues had just been through and figured it was my duty to make a volunteer contribution to the transition, to join my buddies in hell not for the first time. And, at the very least, I wanted to see the Cheneys and congratulate them in person.

Slightly nervous, but pumped up with victory adrenalin and joy in my heart for the Cheney family, I popped over to their town house in Virginia.

My first verification that this was truly transition hell was the fact that it appeared the Cheneys' town house *was* the transition. The vice president–elect, supported only by his immediate family and one landline—an ancient princess phone in their kitchen—was command central.

He and Lynne were sitting together in their family room very calmly. I'm not sure what I expected, but his greeting was a surprise too.

"We want you to come into the White House."

I'm not often speechless, but this left me breathless. I hope I said thank you, but all I remember wheezing out was something along the lines of "I have two babies at home. I have a family. A new house and an old husband."

Not your optimal White House staff profile, let alone one befitting the well-known Cheney high standard.

Lynne conveyed their rationale. She laid out the new administration's sentiment. "We want people who have families; we have to always think of family. We need people in government who understand what a family is and how policies impact them."

Presumably my breathing resumed, but I must have looked confused. She went on to explain what that had to do with me. "We need your perspective, Mary. We need the perspective of a mother," or words to that effect.

"And we need your skills," the vice president–elect chimed in.

This is a truncated version of a longer, more coherent meeting, but suffice to say, I was left trying to recall the last time my mind had been so totally blown—and began having flashbacks to high school experiments with altered states. Waking up from my daze, I realized—wait—I am a full-fledged adult now. With adult responsibilities. Many of them. How many directions could a person be pulled?

Nor had I any cravings for a White House job. The White House Power Job scene never held much allure for me. It is one around-the-clock, superserious, supercautious, by-the-books place. I am more cut out for seat-of-the-pants operations, high-adrenaline places with lots of all-nighters, like campaigns.

On the other hand, I wanted desperately to work with Dick Cheney. My admiration for him was immeasurably vast and deep. In a world with no shortage of butt kissers, backstabbers and dimwits, he was a man of impeccable integrity and incomparable depth.

Among other things, he had been a congressional leader, the youngest White House chief of staff in history as well as secretary of defense during the Gulf War. And while I can't remember working with him in those years, I did know what it was like to be in his vicinity, a place of Zen-like calm and timeless, principled wisdom and purpose.

He is a leader among men. I don't know how else to say it.

The only thing that could draw me to the White House was the chance to work for him. But it did vaguely occur to me that my years of disparate experiences, which seemed willy-nilly as they were unfolding (my father would always ask me, "When are you going to get a real job?"), might be uniquely useful to this administration.

On the other hand, I had no further career ambitions, loved my later-in-life unexpected motherhood and marriage, and I was just too old to be poverty-stricken by government wages again. While I was mentally ticking through the long list of reasons a White House job was simply not possible, the single-minded political me was becoming breathless with anticipation at the prospect.

And I knew right away what (low-pay, high-stress, husband-infuriating) job I wanted: to facilitate the integration of the vice president's office with the West Wing. George W. Bush had made it clear his central reason for choosing Cheney was because he was a seasoned, mature politician who didn't have his own agenda, and who could handle a big, important portfolio of issues. W wasn't setting up a political heir. He was looking to govern with a solid policy partner.

Integrating and "synergizing" the Office of the Vice President and the West Wing for maximum output and impact was an obviously logical but impossibly elusive undertaking. In all the previous White Houses I had interacted with, or watched over decades in Washington, those two power centers usually ended up detached to the point of being adversarial. It happened with Reagan and Bush. It happened with Bush and Quayle. It definitely happened with Clinton and Gore. Each started out connected at the hip with grand visions of brotherhood and good government, but, between the inevitable competing personal ambitions and policy agendas, the environment disintegrates into a miasma of counter-productivity.

It happens in ways big and small. Petty policy disagreements and minor acts of selfish personal positioning evolve into internecine political death matches. Longtime colleagues and foxhole buddies morph into the Capulets and the Montagues. The typical dynamic is a slow trickle of distrust following the first midterms that swells into a tsunami of paranoia and double-dealing by the second term walk-up to the next presidential election.

What I'm saying is that very quickly, for a host of different reasons, all well chronicled by White House gossips, the vice president's office can quickly become a no-man's-land.

George W. Bush had lived through it with his father on both the vice presidential and presidential sides and knew the waste and pitfalls. If anyone could force White House–wide synergy, it would be that man I'd seen bend reality to his will with his force-of-nature resolve. But for the offices to be truly integrated, we were going to have to make changes, both obvious and subtle.

Solving this kind of problem is totally in my preferred wheelhouse. What could it take? Six months, max?

I already knew that my lifesaver in this out-of-the-blue disruption of our whole family life would be Geneva Watkins, my Nee Nee, the incredible, loving, patient, wonderful caregiver who was devoted to both of my babies and to James and me. Even before Matty was born, we had found her through a nanny agency—but she was more than that. She was a master at mothering and teaching me how to do it. She knew a baby was going to cry and stopped it just by entering the room. She was magic. She was love. And she was my ticket to making this all work. Without Nee Nee, I am 100 percent certain I would never have even considered the White House job, dream spot or not.

Okay then. How do I break the news to James?

Most wives or spouses can say, "Oh, what an incredible opportunity! We have a big decision here—we will have to work together and come up with a solution and isn't it wonderful that we can!" My spousal option included that much, but then I would have to tack on something along the lines of "Taking the job will separate us for months, force more parenting responsibility on you, cut my income by 90 percent and preclude my active intervention between you and my critters you so loathe." *Hmmm.* Not much there to work with, so I figured I would conclude with a sweetener, "But, but, but . . . it will be only six months. What do you think, sweetheart?"

Sweet? Ha!

For one thing, we still weren't speaking since the searing recount experience. And, unlike me, he suspected I'd get a call and had preemptively, clearly and loudly made known his feelings about any possibility of any job other than the ones I already had. And they weren't positive feelings.

So why ask his opinion?

I don't remember how, or even if, we talked about it. But after that, I sure remember that we didn't speak again, in any substantial way, until Memorial Day 2001.

JAMES

THE RECOUNT AND ALL the bitter feelings that came with it made it that much tougher to accept Mary's talking about working in the Bush White House. Plus, it happened so quickly. *Bush v. Gore* got decided on December 12. By then, the Bush people already were moving fast to put everything in place.

So it's not like we had a bunch of time to talk about the job and really consider what it would mean for our family. Not that she was very interested in my advice, anyway. We were still hardly on speaking terms after the election.

We spent part of the Christmas holiday that year out at our farm in Virginia. It felt good to get out of Washington after the intensity of the past six weeks, but even the fresh air and the scenery of the Shenandoah Valley didn't do much to lift the tension.

I remember it as one of the harder times in our marriage. We had an awfully nice life before the election. We were spending a lot of time with our two young kids. We'd have these long weekends together out at the farm. Mary and I had carved out careers in public speaking and on television, and we were making a good living.

I didn't need anything different in my life. And I sure didn't need my wife working eighteen hours a day and taking a huge pay cut to do it. There were real costs involved for our family. Besides, I didn't really like these people who were going to be running the country, even though I knew she was close with the Bush crowd. I remember feeling just generally pissed off at the world in those days, and I didn't do much to hide it.

Mary kept saying it would last only a year at most. She promised she wouldn't stay longer than that. She also promised that she'd make it home for dinner most nights and be around as much as possible for the girls. Promises, promises. I didn't buy that shit for a moment. I knew what life was like in there. I didn't think the Bush White House would be much different than any other in that regard.

It's a grueling existence. I'd been through it myself and seen my friends endure it. You're up one day, down the next. They pay attention to you one day; they don't pay attention the next. You're in this meeting. You're not in that meeting. Blah, blah, blah. Also, I knew there wasn't any such thing as a normal workday in the White House. Maybe twelve-hour days, if you're lucky and the world isn't on fire. But you can bank on a lot of fourteen- and eighteen-hour days. And you can bank on not seeing much of your family. I knew all that.

One of the things that you learn in a marriage is that if your spouse wants to do something you've just got to get with the program. Mary really wanted to do this. She wasn't asking my permission. So I eventually just accepted it, even though I never pretended to like it. I got more accepting of it as the months went on, but I still missed our life the way it had been before.

MARY

MATTY WAS FIVE AND Emerson was two when I started my big, beautiful, exciting, White House dream job for two of the most honorable men and effective leaders I had ever known.

Every morning I cried in the predawn dark while I drove on the deserted highway into the city from our home in Old Town Alexandria. I cried while I hung my wet head of hair out the window to dry. I cried while I tried to put on makeup at the stoplights. I cried at the reflection of my exhausted, conflicted face in the rearview mirror. My unhappiness was exasperated by James's refusal to be even *fleetingly* happy for me— or remotely proud. Not even close. He was, in fact and in every deed, unsupportive and often downright unpleasant, when he wasn't totally ignoring me. So I decided to pump up myself instead, hence all the weeping, which was all I could come up with.

I'd finish blow-drying my hair inside my West Wing office, unsmear my mascara, buck up and head to the daily seven a.m. senior staff meeting, which was originally scheduled at six-thirty a.m. until President Bush pushed back the time of the meeting in the first week of the administration after Karen Hughes, on behalf of the informally organized women of the West Wing, appealed to his abundant common sense, and possibly compassionate conservatism. Working parents and all. Bush 43 wanted a family-friendly White House. They all did. We all did. And we meant it.

James came to my swearing in. It's a big deal to be an assistant to the president, a certified commissioned officer. We were all assembled in the front of the yellow-gold, magnificently appointed East Room—a handful of fellow travelers (in the good way) receiving that historic and coveted honorific, the Honorable, under the proud and awestruck gazes of our beaming families. The photo dogs were snapping away, chronicling our crowning achievement.

I didn't *ask* the perpetually pissed-off James if he'd like to come to the swearing in. I told him he had to come. I said, "This is the one thing that I want." I didn't throw it in his face how much I had suffered after Poppy's loss in 1992 and didn't bring up all the accolades and official events and award ceremonies that I had soldiered through for him, while adoring liberal sycophants cooed over him and elbowed each other out of the way just to be in the presence of the Ragin' Cajun, the political strategist and, in their estimation, possibly the Second Coming.

I just stated in that way that precludes negotiation: "You're coming."

But then, as I raised my hand to take the oath, I looked out at his miserable mug and saw him completely unable to share in the enthusiasm of my day and surrounded on all sides by a sea of uberconservatives, and I wished he hadn't come. Instead of reveling in the special day, I hated myself for being such a cruel and selfish psycho wife.

JAMES

I DID DRAG MYSELF over to the White House when Mary was sworn in as an assistant to the president. I knew it meant a lot to her and, frankly, it was just easier to shut up and go than to try to get out of it. So I went.

The truth is, George W. Bush is a personable guy. He knew that I was suffering. He could tell how miserable I was about the whole deal. So at one point during the swearing-in ceremony, he went out of his way to come over and greet me and talk for a few minutes. I'll give him credit for the kindness and compassion he showed that day. He tried to make a miserable situation a little less miserable.

MARY

I COULDN'T WAIT TO start working.

Six months. That's all. Trying to adhere to our messy marriage compromise, I had assured him it would be only six months. One football season. Heck, he could wait years for a good Rhône red to open up. Even though we both knew that was pure fiction, that was my story and I almost believed it myself.

So from the minute I started, the clock in his mind started running too. The countdown was on, and James is nothing if not a numbers junkie, which he learned from his legendary card-counting bridge-champion mother—and which accounted for his endless show-off victories at gin rummy, so much so that I considered it cheating.

And day in and day out, James was so unhappy, so distant, so down-right self-righteous that it was soul-sappingly god-awful for me. The only available recourse was to go into "partner mode," where the glue of love and affection is unnecessary to fulfilling daily obligations and duties—dealing with the kids, paying bills, attending to the shared-life stuff. It was the only way to continue. James had shifted into partner mode the day of W's election.

So we put love and affection away on the bottom shelf, and never let my job enter the house. There was never any mention of my jam-packed, stressful, mind-sapping days. What little physical and mental energy I could reserve was channeled into devotion to family and him. Which was doubly hard since he didn't want to have anything to do with his selfish psycho wife and the kids were mostly sound asleep by the time I got home.

I pleaded with him to stop sulking. "Look, just give me six months." And in an occasional nod to reality, I'd try to slip in a provision—"At the *worst* it will be until the midterms."

And I (sort of) meant it—about the six months—or I really meant to try to work toward it. The plan was to help the new incoming crew get settled, get organized, integrate the VP and West Wing offices and then Mama would be coming home. He knew I had no interest in working those kinds of hours, enduring that kind of relentless stress, earning those meager wages (which meant no retail therapy for me). He knew I wasn't tempted by the perks of the White House. Years before, I had even turned down an offer from my beloved Bush 41 to work there.

But there was nothing I could say, no deals I could strike, nothing in my bag of wifely tricks that would assuage his anger and his concerns. So, we just coasted along in partner mode and tried to stay in neutral gear, not talking for about eighteen hours of my day and pretending it wasn't happening. I like a good fantasy as much as the next guy, but he remained a hothead and I was one hot mess.

Mothers of kids that age—five and two—may be the only ones who really know what it means to leave your nest in the dark before dawn and not return until long after the dinner hour every night. Those are *babies* at home. Those are potty-training years, nursery school, preschool, Play-Doh, *Teletubbies, Scooby-Doo.* I took to sleeping with the girls every night, just to get a chance to breathe their sweet air in the same room.

And the normally insatiable James didn't even care. That hurt. That man can really put on some pain. When he decides on a strategy, he is nothing but discipline, a proud marine. His battle plan in this case: inflict maximum pain, grief and guilt, and exacerbate these with frequent really cool foreign campaign trips, like the ones that I had previously accompanied him on. He actually deserves his reputation as a kick-ass, take-no-mercy, in-it-to-win-it fighter. Semper fi, Corporal.

JAMES

HOW ELSE COULD SHE have expected me to act at the time? Should I have packed her a brown-bag lunch each morning and wished her good luck on cutting taxes for rich people on her way out the door? Should I have baked cookies when she came home and asked whether they made any progress drilling in the Arctic National Wildlife Refuge?

I was trying to remain civil and generally composed, and some days that was enough of a challenge by itself.

Mary would get up before dawn to head to work at the White House, and as often as not she'd come home well after dark. It wasn't like I was a single father or anything. She rushed home as soon as she could in the evenings, and when she had to work weekends, she'd usually take the girls to the White House with her. We had Geneva, who came during the day and helped out tremendously, especially when I was away giving speeches or working on foreign campaigns.

But a lot of times it was the girls and I at home together, which turned out to be a blessing of sorts. I've never exactly been Mr. Mom. Mary always changed most of the diapers. I would do it; it never bothered me. But if there were a hundred diapers, I might have done two. Mary didn't really trust me to do it right, so she'd say, "It's easier for me to do it." It never was that big of an issue.

So maybe it wasn't ideal for Mary to be away so much during the White House stint, but I don't remember it being a particularly stressful time with the kids. I might not have been the textbook stay-at-home dad, but we made it work. Often, I'd put the girls in one of those yuppie carts you see everywhere and take off running all over town. They liked it, and so did I. A lot of times, we'd walk down and get ice cream in Old Town Alexandria. You can never go wrong with ice cream. For some reason, I remember watching a lot of *Scooby-Doo* episodes with them. Always *Scooby-Doo*.

I loved taking the girls to school. We'd sing songs in the car, most of them stupid little tunes like the Barney theme song. "I love you, you love me . . ." But we'd also play a lot of old New Orleans music. We listened to a lot of Irma Thomas, the "Soul Queen of New Orleans." I taught them to appreciate that stuff from an early age.

As much as I wasn't thrilled about Mary working in the White House, I looked forward to that time together with the girls. It was our time. I'm not sure we would have had that if Mary had a more normal job.

MARY

AT LEAST I HAD the good sense to craft a rewarding job and a big dual title for myself at the White House. As anyone who's spent any time in Washington, D.C., knows, there are two basic kinds of people at the White House. There are the ones who don't care what job they have, but they want a big title just for vanity—and then sport their White House badges in restaurants. And there are people who have been around the block or were blessed with wise advisers, who knew they needed a big title to get anything done.

A big title was the ticket to the meetings where the action took place or where you could force action, where you got the information you needed to figure out action. At the White House, information and access are the only coins of the realm.

The first-class, full-fare ticket title was Assistant to the President, which designated positions entitling the bearer to unqualified access to all meetings. I knew I would have to attach that one to my already august title, Counselor to the Vice President, which would give me a dual-title, full-fare status as an Ambassador Without Portfolio, allowing me to stick my nose into any and all issues, whatever the VP was into.

To facilitate the White House model George W. Bush had requested, each presidential West Wing position had a commensurately skilled and titled counterpart in the Office of the Vice President (OVP). We had domestic-policy counterparts, legislative counterparts, national-security counterparts, administrative counterparts, etc. We all operated together, merging our work products and skill sets to produce a whole greater than the sum of its parts. Sure there were some distractions caused by mattress mice—what Cheney always called the people nipping at the crumbs of power, the people he was good at ignoring—but mostly, it really, really worked. And that was a good thing, because we hit the ground running.

JAMES

THE TWENTY-FIRST CENTURY was shaping up to be a bitch.

Mary and I had endured a long, angry month during the recount. And things hadn't gotten much better after the whole debacle had ended. It's always tough in our house when one person's candidate wins and the other's loses. If you've won, you feel simultaneously elated by the victory and sympathetic to your spouse's heartbreak. If you lose, you feel a sliver of happiness for your spouse along with overwhelming personal disappointment.

This was different. I was still pissed off and in a dark place. It's one thing to lose. It's another to feel wronged. I believed Gore had won, and so did most of the rest of the country. And now she was marching each morning to work in the Bush White House. I could have puked.

Needless to say, I didn't go to the Bush inauguration in January 2001. That would have been the last place I wanted to be that day. I don't even remember what I did instead. I could have been writing a speech. I might have gone to a movie. I could have been doing any number of things. But showing up at the Capitol wasn't going to be one of them.

It was a celebration for Republicans, which is all well and good. But I didn't feel much like celebrating. I felt about as miserable as the weather that day. It was hard enough to see Bill Clinton's time as president draw to a close after all the good he'd done for the country and all the hot coals we'd walked over together. On top of that, a guy I was pretty certain had lost the election was on the podium getting sworn in. I didn't need to be there to witness it.

In addition, my mother had been slipping away for the last several years, deeper and deeper into dementia, and by the time Bush took office, she was in awful shape. I was out in California giving a speech at the Hillcrest Country Club when my sister called to say my mother had died. It was a Thursday, February 15.

We all knew that day was coming, though that didn't do much to soften the blow. My sisters, saints that they are, had done an unbelievable job caring for her, especially my sister Mary Anne, who's an expert in home health care. The last four years, my mother couldn't leave the house and basically was bedridden, and never once did she have a bedsore. And neither did she have to go to a nursing home.

Ms. Nippy, as everybody called her, was quite a woman. While my dad ran the general store back in Carville, she went door-to-door selling encyclopedias. Together, they managed to send eight children to college. She wrote a popular cookbook full of Louisiana recipes. She didn't believe in calling people names or using racial slurs. She read her daily prayers. She had a wicked sense of humor, and she was a hell of a bridge player.

She also was an old-school Democrat. She was always pro-life, but she looked at life as a "seamless garment." She would say, "We are pro-life, but because we are, we have a heightened responsibility to the poor and less fortunate." She believed that if you were insisting children be brought into the world, society had a real responsibility to help any way it could once they arrived.

My mother had always been an ever-present force in my life. Whenever I worked on a campaign, she'd find a way to come visit. When I was working for Bob Casey in Pennsylvania, she'd show up and play cards and answer phones. During the Clinton campaign in 1992, she'd sit there and knit in the war room along with Virginia Kelley, Clinton's mother. She'd always been there cheering me on, and it was tough to imagine that she no longer would be.

I was saying good-bye to a lot of things in early 2001. Good-bye to the woman who never ceased being my biggest fan. Good-bye to the president I'd help to put in office. Good-bye in a sense to my wife, who I thought I would see very little of once she went to work in the White House. I'd had better years.

MARY

THOSE FIRST MONTHS WERE a blur of long hours. As the weeks passed, and the months unfolded, I noticed that our beloved Nee Nee wasn't her old self. Over the summer, she was getting thinner and thinner. Her skin began to have the awful pallor I'd seen too often before on sick people. She had always been right out of central casting—a big robust nanny, a big woman with a big hug. Now the weight was falling off of her.

I asked her if she was all right, and she said she was. I asked her again and again, and she insisted again and again she was fine.

I still worried, but I couldn't deploy my usual medical buttinski persona ("Mary Matalin, M.D.," as the kids call it) into the situation. Nee Nee wanted peace and privacy. And to be honest, my emotional tank was running on empty after that long cold winter. I was trying to enjoy what little passed for a stress-free life in those days.

I had adjusted to four or five hours of sleep a night and battering-ram days at the White House. The system we all worked out to coordinate the president's and vice president's offices was starting to work smoothly, or what passes for smooth in a roller-coaster world.

Things with the hubby were better. Everything is relative in a marriage, and in contrast to the first couple of White House months, his diminished pouting and the occasional conversation felt like a honeymoon to me. I'd like to think he might have come around to thinking I had done the right thing by taking the job, but his improved attitude was likely more attributable to anticipating that my tenure at the White House would be ending soon. Also, his forced Mr. Mom tenure wasn't as bad as he thought it was going to be; in fact, he was so good with the kids and having so much fun, I was jealous. By the end of the summer of 2001, everything seemed, if not totally right with the world and our marriage, at least not the pit of doom it had been.

One of the president's first executive orders called for the development of a modernized, comprehensive energy policy—which he assigned to the OVP. What did I know about energy?

I knew that James was always crabbing about my wasting it by opening all the windows when the air conditioner was on (I prefer fresh temperate air to his Southern obsession for recycled ice air). But I was determined to learn everything I could. I did my grind thing, became a student and fell in love with the subject. Energy became my obsession. While the whole Carville clan was clowning around at our Easter festivities, I was holed up with a white paper on pebble-bed reactors, then the latest in nuclear energy, which seemed not to be everyone's cup of tea. But I was in heaven. (It is a good thing I was so into the topic, because when it came time for the big public rollout event in Pennsylvania, the VP lost his voice and at the last minute it was decided I would have to make the presentation. I remember hoping my enthusiasm for energy reform would make up for my knowledge deficit.)

Today, the public—badly informed—associates Dick Cheney exclusively with foreign policy, but at the outset of the administration his tasks were on the domestic front. While the OVP hunkered down to develop a new energy policy to update our antiquated energy infrastructure, which was plaguing huge swaths of the country with rolling black- and brownouts, we were equally wrapped up in the president's economic reform policies, which were just as pressing since we had entered the White House on the front end of a recession (which everyone forgets).

Like everything else he was assigned, the VP was an instant whiz kid at economic policy and enjoyed it.

He would invite economists of all political stripes for regular brainstorming sessions in the Roosevelt Room. You might be surprised to know that economists are quite a lively and entertaining bunch, contrary to their reputation as dreary buzzkillers. For pure cranial delight, nothing beat Cheney going at it with a liberal economist.

Not that Cheney ever cared about his popularity, but his poll numbers were stratospheric, which unfortunately was overblown by the mainstream media so it appeared he might be overshadowing the president, which incited the mattress mice to unkind chatter. But Bush 43 truly wanted all his staff (and the VP is staff) to have ample and unquestioned authority; that way they could serve as force magnifiers for his agenda. The president also demanded the unvarnished truth and a deep analysis from all perspectives on all his proposals.

That was Cheney's sweet spot. His MO was to give POTUS a full analysis, then "salute smartly" and execute whatever course the president ultimately decided on.

The VP's other superpower was *spear catching*. He reveled in catching the flaming arrows of the always-on-the-attack Washington weasels. He therefore became the canary in the coal mine and took point on the most controversial issues. With such an expansive portfolio, unrivaled brains and guts, influence on the Hill and Ciceronian communication skills (the man always spoke in complete paragraphs without taking a breath or breaking a sweat), he was the undisputed champ of policy and political articulation on Capitol Hill, in the print press or on the tube. When he spoke, the chattering classes listened. Just his going out on an issue telegraphed *this is serious*.

A big part of my job was to make sure he was briefed with the necessary political and policy ammo whenever he went out. Which was pretty funny because the running joke of the whole OVP was, "Cheney is his best staffer," because at our marathon briefings, he would always end up knowing more than all of us put together.

I remember sitting—or rather, kneeling on the floor in my OEOB office at eleven on a Friday night, stretching out a pair of hateful panty hose and punching holes in piles of briefing materials that filled four three-inch, three-ring binders for one of his Tim Russert *Meet the Press* appearances. The scary thing was, by Sunday morning, he would have consumed every word, and in less time than it took me to assemble the voluminous briefing books.

A recurring thought on those late nights alone on my knees in the dark, was *What has my life come to?*

My hectic, nonstop workdays were regularly interrupted with frantic, dramatic phone communiqués from Mr. Mom. James was now speaking to me again, which wasn't always a good thing. He'd pull me out of meetings, interrupt conference calls, have my assistants track me down in the ladies' room with frenzied reports of some home-front terror, like the death of Matty's hamsters that he had unknowingly left in direct sunshine and heat (which every mother knows is a highly effective hamster killer). Even though I was a rat lover, in the scheme of things, that hardly constituted an emergency interruption, so I rolled with it, but still I hated missing anything in the kids' lives.

The only time I was happy at the White House was when I was in the room with the vice president. He always got instantly to the heart of any matter and was never distracted. When I was with him, I never felt like I was wasting my time or spinning my wheels, an occupational hazard in many White House jobs. His focus and mental clarity were infectious. And he wasn't like so many needy politician types who crave attention and affection. He just wanted to think clearly through problems and be effective.

That first summer, after we presented the president's new energy policy to the public and sent it up to the Hill to do their political Cuisinart slicing, dicing and pulverizing, we turned our focus from that cool issue to what was then called Homeland Defense, an interesting although *holy-shit* scary issue.

We reviewed and synthesized all the different blue ribbon commission reports, set up an in-house task force, hired a team of experts and scheduled September meetings with Senator Bob Graham, chair of the Senate Intelligence Committee, and the other Hill bosses of Homeland Defense.

It was a subject that deeply troubled the vice president. He knew what the threats were. He was an expert on "dark winter" and suitcase bombs. Earlier in the year, he and Scooter Libby had been to a number of simulation events, held by the Centers for Disease Control and Prevention, and learned more than you'd ever want to know about germ (bio) and gas (chem) warfare and all those other awful things that nobody likes to think about, especially mothers of young children.

I had to catch up on the subject myself, and was proud that by the time Judith Miller's book, *Germs: Biological Weapons and America's Secret War,* the first comprehensive mainstream book on the subject, came out that summer, there was nothing new in it for me, when just a few months prior, if you'd asked me about germ warfare, I would've said it was why God created hand sanitizers.

"What keeps you up at night?" the vice president was asked by Nick Lemann for a *New Yorker* article that also ran that summer, and Cheney said, "I think we have to be more concerned than we ever have about so-called homeland defense, the vulnerability of our system to different kinds of attacks. Some of it homegrown, like Oklahoma City. Some inspired by terrorists external to the United States—the World Trade Towers bombing, in New York. The threat of terrorist attack against the U.S., eventually, potentially, with weapons of mass destruction— bugs or gas, biological, or chemical agents, potentially even, someday, nuclear weapons."

But I relegated germs and gas to a distant cranny of my consciousness in August 2001, when James and I got all revved up to take our first time off together in forever, *without the kids,* on a romantic Black Sea cruise we couldn't afford. I got some rest, which I needed. He got some attention, which we both needed, interrupted by only one shore-to-ship call from David Gregory, which really kicked up a bad bout of sea sickness, since I presumed his calling had to be over something I didn't want to hear about or worse. It was about something really banal, though, and resulted in one of many Gregory-Matalin verbal fisticuffs. I do love that guy, but he can get on your last nerve.

I returned to duty after Labor Day, remarkably less laborious now, since our office was now a (mostly) well-oiled machine. The West Wing and the OVP were working well together. We all knew more or less what to expect. At home, James was not unhappy, which was maybe the most I could ask for. The girls were in their back-to-school groove. We had a crack caregiver, who was tired a lot, but she repeatedly insisted she was fine and would only speak of her love for us and especially for her "babies," Matty and Emerson. I set up a car to ferry her to and from her home every day, to make her life easier.

As for me, I had long ago adjusted to less sleep and more work hours, and after our restful vacation, even though I still looked like something the cat dragged in, I almost had a spring in my step. I worked Saturdays, but I did manage to keep Sundays mostly free, if you don't count my being on call 24/7. I had entered a chilled-out phase of worrying less about everything because nothing would last that much longer anyway.

I relied on my campaign seasoning, the comfort born of "you can do anything because you know there's an end to it." I was looking at the end-game already. In my mind—and in James's, per our agreement—we were almost there. There were natural breaks in the White House rhythm and I was about to jump off the merry-go-round at one of them.

Then that September, America was attacked. And in October, Nee Nee died.

JAMES

I WAS AT A BREAKFAST sponsored by the *Christian Science Monitor* that Tuesday morning inside the St. Regis Hotel, just a couple blocks from the White House.

It's one of these events where you go shoot the shit with a bunch of print reporters over coffee and scrambled eggs. It gives both sides a chance to have a longer discussion than the typical sound bite reporters usual have to settle for on deadline.

The breakfast started at eight a.m. Stan Greenberg, Bob Shrum and I had come to talk about the state of politics in general, but also about some polling Stan had done. In part, it showed that 43 percent of the people polled thought George W. Bush was already "in over his head" as president.

At one point, journalist Godfrey Sperling, Jr., who was moderating that day, asked us whether the Bush presidency was vulnerable, meaning could he lose at the polls next time around. Of course, I was already hoping that would be the case and said as much.

"I don't care if people like him or not, just so they don't vote for him and his party. That is all I care about. I hope he doesn't succeed, but I am a partisan Democrat," I told the group. "But the average person wants him to succeed. It is his country, his life or their lives. So he has that going for him."

Years later, I got accused by some conservatives of having said that I hoped Bush failed on the morning on 9/11. Well, I guess I did say I hoped he failed, but at the time nobody had an inkling about the hell that was coming that day. I was talking about his domestic and economic policies. I did want those to fail; they were bad policies. I wanted the Republicans to lose the midterms in 2002. I wanted a new president in 2004. That's what I was talking about that morning when I said I didn't want him to succeed. Terrorism? That was another story.

Toward the end of the breakfast, cell phones started buzzing. People started getting word that a plane had flown into one of the World Trade Center towers in New York. At first, it didn't make any sense. I'm a weather watcher, and I remember how it was a really beautiful, blue-sky September day in Washington and that the forecast was the same up and down the East Coast. Airplanes just don't fly into buildings on perfectly clear days.

Pretty soon, another plane hit the second tower. We all knew then, of course. And I knew instinctively that the political landscape we'd been discussing minutes before was about to look drastically different. Who gave a crap about poll numbers when the country was under attack?

"Disregard everything we just said," I told the reporters. "This changes everything."

And it did.

MARY

I GOT TO WORK at six-thirty in the morning on September 11, 2001, and, unlike my usual got-dressed-in-the-dark look, I was spiffed up for a meeting with union leaders (largely construction unions, who really do care about the jobs of the rank and file, as opposed to their own feathered beds). It was a big deal that they were supporting the White House on our new, seriously comprehensive energy policy, the first in a generation.

So I arrived at the White House in a fantastic royal purple Louis Féraud suit with an amazing tapered jacket and pencil skirt, accented with a red knit top. On my feet, I was wearing a pair of impossibly high but oh-so-fabulous Charles Jourdan black-and-red patent-leather spike heels, the height of which will become a factor later. My hair was not blown-dry via the car window that morning but looked a little more attended to. And I was wearing makeup applied while looking in an actual mirror, as opposed to blindly using sense memory.

I am elaborating on the ostensibly superficial details of my 9/11 attire because I don't want to leave you with the perception that one has time to deal with appearance in such a job. Working for the president may be the job of your dreams and the pinnacle of your political career, but, sadly, while you're doing it, you will never look more haggard, and that includes immediately after giving birth.

As the day wore on, though, I returned to haggard status quo. The photo record does show that with each passing hour I aged dramatically and my once-fantastic outfit became moist, rumpled and slept in. And while vanity was the farthest thing from my mind, I couldn't forget about those ridiculous designer shoes as long as they were on my feet. I

don't want to suggest that professional women should dress for the possibility of catastrophic events, but one should always keep a pair of portable ballet slippers in one's purse because you never know.

The first plane hit when I was in my small West Wing office—one
floor up and down the hall from Cheney's office. Like everybody else in
the White House, I had multiple televisions in my office, all going at the
same time. Morning shows. Morning news. By a weird sixth sense, the
kind of inescapable gut instinct I have no control over, I knew we had a
big problem before the disoriented reporters knew what to say. Suddenly
all three channels cut to it. *This is no accident. It can't be an accident.* I felt
certain of this immediately. I bolted up from my chair and raced down
the stairs—or raced as quickly as I could in those heels—straight to the
vice president's office.

I barged in. The vice president was in a meeting with John McConnell, our lovely, brilliant, universally adored speechwriter. But they, like
me, were already on high alert. The VP and John were staring disbeliev-
ingly at the tube. That's when the second plane hit.

With no words or hesitation, the VP sprung into action. The president was on the road so the VP proceeded through the response protocol: contact POTUS, contact the authorities in New York, starting with
Mayor Giuliani. Cheney didn't do an Al Haig panicked megalomania
thing, like when Reagan was shot in 1981, and declare himself in charge
of the country. He just did his calm-quiet-never-ruffled Cheney thing
and began issuing orders. "Do this . . ." "Get that . . ." "Find so-
and-so . . ." He was coolheaded and totally focused.

Within minutes, our chief of staff, Scooter Libby, a seasoned foreign-
policy and terrorism expert, bolted into the operating-at-high-gear con-
fab in the VP's office, and unlike the confounded John and me, he
understood the potential implications of the hit. He and the VP began
considering the possibilities, which although incomprehensible to us,
were immediately evident to them.

They spoke in shorthand, exchanged sentence fragments with each
other. I heard the words *Massoud* and *al-Qaeda*.

Massoud, aka the "Lion of Panjshir," had been assassinated by the Taliban just days before in a cave in Afghanistan. He was a renowned, fearless warrior in the millennial struggle over the landlocked east-west passage that was Afghanistan, which had been traversed by traders from the beginning of time. The Taliban were the agents of al-Qaeda. Scooter and the VP quickly surmised that al-Qaeda was likely the agent of this unspeakable and unimaginable terror.

There were communication problems in the White House right away. The VP had trouble getting a secure connection with POTUS on *Air Force One*. Cheney is never one to blow up, get angry or express his ire— but as the communication snafus continued, and became potentially very serious, he got impatient. He didn't need to express himself in more than a few words and eyebrow bounces, but there was no missing his sense of urgency or his unspoken message to "get on the connectivity problem!" It wasn't entirely the White House's fault. Securing POTUS required communication adjustments and nobody was able to reach Mayor Giuliani in New York that day, or efficiently for many days to follow.

Before we began to attend to the VP's communication concerns, he was ripped from our midst. Out of nowhere, a team of superfit, deadly serious, square-jawed, don't-mess-with-us professionals with skills you don't learn on a Wii barged through the VP's small office door (how those big guys got through that little space so gracefully is still a mystery to me) without so much as a cursory knock. As John and Scooter and I backed off lest we be thrown back, the team wrenched the vice president from behind his massive desk, whipped him off his feet by his belt and hoisted his formidable frame up and over like he was a feather pillow. They were decked out in nice suits, but they were operating like heavy furniture movers.

Even though we were already in a parallel universe, we weren't sure how to take the VP's surreal departure. I wasn't even sure the professional movers were real agents. Was the VP safe? Should I tackle the big guys? That last thought was an indication my mind wasn't working in the reality zone.

Not many words were exchanged—just your basic "Move it! Now!" etc.—but the VP seemed to know the drill, which assuaged my concerns for his safety. If you're having trouble imagining this, there's a stunningly good rendition in the White House movie, *Olympus Has Fallen*.

Once my baffled mind registered he was safe, I reverted to no presence of mind whatsoever. In one of my more unheroic moments on Earth, I thought, *Wait a second. What are we, chopped liver?*

Luckily, some primal survival instinct precluded my voicing this thought aloud, but my mouth had a mind of its own. It started firing off unanswerable questions to no one in particular, since the VP was way gone within seconds.

"I need to go with him," I said to no one. "What should we do, what should we do, *what should we do?*"

Every fiber in my being, an automatic response, was screaming to be with the VP—to go wherever he was going. Not just because I loved him, but because that was my job. It was disorienting to suddenly be separated from him and have no idea where he was. Were they putting him on *Marine One?* What was I supposed to do now?

Within moments, I got an answer. We were ordered to "evacuate *immediately!*" Everyone still remaining in the West Wing was shepherded to the White House Mess, where we were to await further instructions.

"I have to go to my office first," I said. "It's just one floor up."

"No, you aren't," a voice snapped. "You're going to the Mess. Move it—*now.*" ("Move it now" was clearly the phrase of the hour.)

So there we all were, the White House staff hanging out in the Mess with nary a soul having the slightest clue what we were to do there. Not that we had much time to ponder our situation or cluelessness. We were spared that brainteaser by another order issued before we could get comfy. In retrospect, it was delivered in a weirdly calm manner.

"Run for your lives. A plane is going to hit the White House."

It was absurd, ridiculous. I was thinking, *Run for your lives? Really? What drama queens are writing this script?* But even more absurd were the

Charles Jourdan red patent-leather five-inch spike-heel pumps that I thought the Teamsters would like.

Outside, people were indeed "running for their lives," fleeing the gates and grounds of the White House and heading down the street in every direction.

I had serious trouble walking in those pumps. No way could I join the stampeding crowd. Judiciously, in my best fashionista fashion, I opted to "walk for my life" instead.

Cars were stopped in the middle of the downtown streets, left deserted, their doors open. Terrified people were running away. No orders from military aides were necessary. Somehow everyone got the memo. A plane *was* coming—and one did—one that would eventually hit the Pentagon.

I didn't get very far before my cell phone rang. Which, in the middle of that chaos gave me a thrill of unexpected joy because the cell service had been down and I *needed* to find out where my kids were. But I never got the chance to find out.

"Where are you, ma'am? The vice president wants you."

I wanted to say, "Can I call you back after I check on Matty and Emerson?" but I said, "Wherever you want me," to which I stupidly appended, "Where is he?"

"Where are you?" was the smart retort. I gave my location to the serious voice coming out of my cell, and in what seemed like seconds, two uniformed guys—big guys with big guns—arrived to escort me back to the West Wing. There, I was taken to a top-secret elevator with heavy steel-reinforced walls, like the one in the opening credits of *Get Smart*, and we descended into the below-the-basement bowels of the White House. When the armored elevator doors opened, my military escorts led me through an underground labyrinth of hallways. A series of heavy steel doors opened onto a small airless room with a desk in the corner and a long conference table where Cheney was centrally positioned, in command and focused on the fallout of the terror attack. Three large screens overhead were playing two live newscasts without any sound.

JAMES

THE PLANE HIT THE Pentagon, and you could see the smoke rising up in the distance. Nobody had any idea what might come next, what the next target might be. People on the street were incredibly polite, almost eerily polite, but you could see the worry on their faces. I'm sure they could see the worry on mine.

I knew Mary was at the White House, but I didn't know what was going on with her and I doubted I could reach her even if I tried. To be honest, my first thought was that I had to get across the river back to Alexandria to get my girls. The youngest was at home with Geneva, but my oldest was at her school that day, six miles from downtown Washington.

It was not an easy thing to make those six miles on that morning. It might as well have been one hundred miles away. The roads were clogged and all of Washington was on high alert, but I would have swum the Potomac to get back to my daughters. It took a while, but I actually made it back and got Matty home from school before lunch.

MARY

THERE WE WERE, deep beneath the East Wing of the White House in a bunker designed to protect the president (and designated "protectees") in the event of an attack. Presumably it was also a "hard" target or impenetrable to all incoming "attack devices" with the probable exception of a nuclear blast. Its point of entry was a labyrinth-like series of corridors, interspersed at regular intervals with highly classified, reinforced steel doors and manned around the clock by Joint Service military staff.

If the big guys with big guns hadn't been leading me along as if I were a puppy on a leash, I'd still be wandering down there—even though, a couple weeks earlier, I had visited this underground dungeon for my top-level security clearance training, but I might as well have been blindfolded. No chance of my committing a security breach with my sense of direction.

I am using qualifying words such as *presumably* and *probable* because the Presidential Emergency Operations Center (PEOC) was originally constructed during World War II for President Franklin D. Roosevelt, and no one alive remembers using it for its intended purpose, which only drew our attention to the fact, once again, that this was a unique event in our nation's history. Not that anybody needed reminding.

Our connectivity system—apologies to readers who don't enjoy government-speak, but this is how people in the White House actually talk—was composed of a couple of big screens (which could be used to broadcast TV or to connect with other secure government facilities) and a couple of secure phones stationed on opposite ends of a small conference table (smaller than our seven a.m. senior staff meeting table). In the corners of the room, there were very small workstations.

The room had a low ceiling, bad lighting, and was pretty stuffy, as though it contained air dating back to World War II.

Maybe it was state-of-the-art in FDR's day, but it appeared eerily antiquated when I had a chance, finally, to catch my breath and survey our surroundings. Was this really *it?* Was this room adequately equipped to deal with an event of such enormity? My instinctual unease was validated almost immediately.

The equipment started choking right off the bat. Even when the big screens before us were connecting to something—TV or another government agency—they weren't functioning in any useful way. You could get sound or visual, but not both. You could get another government agency or TV, but not both side by side.

It had instilled so much confidence, the impressive speed with which the "mil aides" had collected and carried away the VP, then rounded up the requested list of his staff and National Security Agency top aides from the smoldering D.C. streets and delivered us to the stuffy PEOC. But as soon as we arrived, that confidence began to dissolve as we faced the reality of the internal mechanics.

It's hard to remember the days before iPads and reliable bandwidth, but since we had never had such modern wonders, we didn't miss them. But we did feel crippled without our desks, our desktop computers, our landlines and especially our secretaries. In those days, the secretaries were often the only ones who knew how to work the computers and phones.

The PEOC technology was inadequate, we were getting hotter and stuffier by the second, and no one knew for sure what was going on aboveground. But the ad hoc assemblage didn't miss a beat. The VP and Condi Rice sat together at the conference table, facing the screens, and for the most part, the senior staffers stood behind them, or kneeled next to them for direction. Transportation Secretary Norm Mineta sat across the table, thoroughly engaged in identifying any still-airborne civilian aircraft. The order to ground them had gone out immediately, but that's easier said than done. You can't just parallel park one thousand jumbo jets in midflight.

Meanwhile, POTUS had been evacuated from his No Child Left Behind event in Florida. He was *really* not happy that all the security experts insisted he not return to Washington immediately, an unhappiness that grew with each failed attempt to connect with us. His secure connection from *Air Force One* to Cheney in the PEOC kept dropping.

Secretary of Defense Donald Rumsfeld was literally incommunicado, unresponsive, his whereabouts unknown, despite the VP's repeated attempts to get through to the DOD and his old friend. We discovered later that he was pulling his injured and dead colleagues out from the smoke and debris of the Pentagon carnage.

Secretary of State Colin Powell was in transit from Lima, where he'd been meeting with the president of Peru, and he was hard to reach. The congressional leadership had their own security protocols, and they weren't so easy to connect with either.

Many minute-by-minute accounts or "ticktocks" of the whole long mind-blowing day have been published already. I don't need to add to them, except to say we should have been far more terrified than we were. In truth, I don't think we had the luxury or the time to be terrified.

But I could sense the VP's preternatural unflappability was still being strained by the escalating connectivity problems. As is always the case, he didn't need to raise his voice to make his frustration—and expectations—crystal clear. (I'm not sure I'd like to witness what DEFCON 1 Cheney looks like.)

"Fix it. *Now.*"

Later on, I saw a widely circulated photograph, which subsequently became one of the iconic freeze-frames of that horrific day. It captures the conference table in the PEOC at the moment our frenetic activity screeched to a halt. We were all stone-cold still, staring with disbelief at the big screens, aghast, wordless.

The World Trade Center towers—the instantly and universally recognized symbol of superpower accomplishment—were crumbling in a cloud of dust and disintegrating before our eyes.

No one said anything. What was there to say?

We just went back to work.

JAMES

I STILL DIDN'T KNOW anything about Mary. As long as I was able to focus on tracking down my daughters and making sure they were safe, I'd been able to keep my mind occupied. But once I got the girls home and flipped on the TV, that's when the real fear settled in. People were talking about putting tape over your windows and crazy stuff like that. There were rumors about more attacks, speculation that the White House was still a target. In the middle of all this, I had no idea where Mary was, what she was doing, who she was with and whether they were safe. I can't remember a time when I felt as uneasy and as helpless. There was nothing I could do.

Finally, the phone rang. There was a man on the other end, and he said, "Mr. Carville, this is lieutenant commander so-and-so . . ." I felt myself tense up. I had no idea what the rest of that sentence might hold, whether he was calling with good news or bad.

He said something like "I am authorized to tell you that your wife is safe and is in a secure location. Other than that, I can't tell you anything else."

That was it. That was all I really knew about Mary for days. As I recall, we might have gotten some clothes together for her and dropped them off at the White House. But I never heard a word from her and never got any more updates. It was massive uncertainty.

Four or five days later, she came home. She never did say exactly where she had been. I never asked. For all I know, she was holed up inside some fucking mountain in the middle of nowhere. I didn't really care. I was just relieved to see her walk through that door.

MARY

LAMENTING OUR TECHNICAL DEFICIENCIES was not an option. We pushed ahead, attending to the myriad critical tasks that were cascading on us nonstop, such as working through the proper orders and chains of command to take out any nonresponsive civilian aircraft, reaching global leaders to assure them—with authority and confidence—that the terrorists' objective to "decapitate" the U.S. government was unsuccessful, calming the financial markets.

From the get-go, overriding all the other issues, was the necessity to communicate with the American people.

Who goes out? Who should address the people? Obviously the first and best choice was the president, but his security was paramount. The VP, attending to the relentless incoming barrage of one crisis after another, couldn't leave the PEOC.

When? Obviously, ASAP; but we realized that we could make a very bad situation much worse by saying anything without verifiable facts.

Any incorrect information would have to be later "adjusted," which would undermine the confidence we were striving to project.

What venue? Our first choice to demonstrate the U.S. government was fully functional would be the White House briefing room, but the Secret Service gave us their version of a belly laugh to that proposal—that is to say, they just cold-stared at us. No press would be allowed in that unsecured area, nor would we be allowed in.

What words? This task was not as obvious as you might think. We couldn't believe what we were seeing ourselves, or conceive what might be coming next, or anticipate the president's orders in response to all of it. How could we comfort a nation likely more shocked than we were, since they had even less information than we did?

We were missing our best wordsmith, Karen Hughes, who could represent President Bush with unquestioned authority. She never, never, *ever* took time off. But that day, her wedding anniversary, she had taken an opportunity—afforded by the president's travel—to spend a few extra morning hours with her husband, a sensible Lone Star State man who was wishing he was anywhere on the globe but Washington, D.C., that year, or any year. Karen had been trying to make her way to the White House all morning through the traffic-choked streets. And connecting with us by telephone was near to impossible.

After many failed attempts to reach her—and many dropped calls to POTUS—the VP tasked Anna Perez, Condi's top aide, and me to draft a statement and to just *get it done*. I considered making the point that only Karen could speak for the president, but I determined that Cheney didn't need to consider why that was so.

The VP issued the broad concepts of what needed to be said in the statement, and Anna and I were to find the perfect words. That sounds easy, but the words are less an issue than the "voice." Since we had no idea who would be issuing the statement, it wasn't easy to come up with words to fit. Given a little more time, I would have had a massive insecurity attack over this—and it would have been an epic one—but miraculously, Karen appeared in the PEOC just in the nick of time.

She grabbed the seat where Anna and I had been pecking at the keyboard and, with lightning speed, cranked out the perfect combination of words to convey resolve, authority and comfort in a "voice" that sounded more like President Bush's than his own.

It wasn't the first or the last time that I thought, *Damn, that girl is good.*

Then we had to confront the issue of how to get the statement out.

Again, easier said than done, as there was no obvious *secure* broadcasting facility to assemble at and hook up with the media. We were absolute—and unanimous—in our conviction that we couldn't just issue a disembodied press statement. Once we discovered a secure site in the Justice Department, we had to figure out how to get there safely—without getting our media colleagues or ourselves blown to smithereens. Not that I was thinking that way.

The next thing I knew, Karen and I—heavily guarded—were escorted into an armored-to-the-teeth caravan and were careening through the desolate streets of D.C. And the next thing I remember was praying with Karen in a holding room adjoining the ad hoc press center in the DOJ. Or, to be more precise, she was praying and I was choking up.

She prayed for grace.

I was neither religious nor antireligious in those days. But I remember vividly how she expressed her faith in that moment. It has clarity to me, piercing sharpness in the midst of a blurry day. Before she went to speak to the entire world, Karen simply and humbly bowed her head and said, "Give me grace, give me grace."

It was an act of pure faith, something I was unfamiliar with then. I had seen acts of faith, I'm sure. Maybe I had seen them almost every day, but I hadn't really understood how faith works. Karen wasn't sappy or hysterical. She wasn't Tammy Faye Bakker or any of those corny images propagated about people who are "religious." She was simply strong and deeply faithful, and it was an inspiring moment for me. And it left an impression with subsequent significant consequences.

After praying, she lifted her head, walked to the podium and was 100 percent totally Karen Hughes, counselor to the president of the United States. No drama, no fireworks, just steady Karen. She gave the statement, took no shit, and left.

Much of the remainder of that day—which went long into the night—lacks clarity for me. It was a rush of responsiveness, of staying on top of my assigned duties and of focusing on the moment. And in truth, I haven't tried to recall it in detail.

Except for two things I can't forget, hard as I've tried.

One: I never called home. It was unthinkable to commandeer one of the few secure phones for a personal call. Nobody did.

But no matter how clogged up my brain was, I knew on a primal level—and didn't want to think about—that my kids were within spitting distance of the Pentagon, that James was across the river from them, that traffic wasn't moving, and that they all would be petrified about my whereabouts and safety. If I thought about those things, I got woozy.

The only way I could maintain some semblance of equilibrium was to compartmentalize and find sanity in my certain knowledge—on an equally primal, cellular level—that James would somehow get to the kids, keep them safe and be able to "feel" that his wife was okay.

It was hours later that I learned from an anonymous military aide that James had been located and assured that I was okay—and told that I may not be coming back anytime soon.

That was good enough for James. Neighbors told me later that they saw him running up and down the block in our neighborhood waving a beer in each hand and screaming, "Mary's safe! Mary's okay!" or some Cajun utterance to that effect.

To the thoughtful military aide whose name I never knew, thank you. Thank you. Thank you.

The other haunting memory that still closes off my throat more than a decade later was getting word from Haley Barbour that our dear mutual friend, Barbara Olson, was on the plane that was commandeered and crashed into the Pentagon.

Only a few short months earlier, I had been trying to talk Barbara into replacing me on *Crossfire*. In the PEOC, when we heard the news, nothing was said—quiet took over the room—but none of us could stop thinking about her husband, Ted Olson, the Solicitor General of the United States, our longtime colleague and friend. We were told Barbara called him from the plane just before it went down.

As the days unfolded, we and the rest of America learned of friends who were gravely injured or perished in either New York, Pennsylvania or the Pentagon. They were buried or burned alive, or they jumped from the burning buildings.

Most everybody in the country who was watching television that day probably has a memory of either Karen giving that first White House statement—announcing that the president was in an undisclosed secure location and holding a National Security Council meeting by phone—or they remember watching the smoky holes in the ground that had been, only minutes before, the very epitome of financial and military might.

But my memories of 9/11 are very different. I become reticent when the topic of 9/11 comes up—because I didn't see what the rest of the country saw in real time until one year later. On the first anniversary of the attacks, I lay on Maria Cino's TV room floor with my girls and wept.

In some ways, it still hasn't sunk in.

On our way back to the White House, I ditched security and snuck up to my West Wing office to get my running shoes, and without thinking I grabbed the little pottery animals my girls had made me, which I kept on my desk (and still do). Then I ran into Karen's office down the hall and grabbed the first family token I saw—a framed photo of her son and husband. As far as I knew, it would be days before we'd see our beloved peeps again.

It all started moving quickly after that. My next distinct memory, a touchstone that delineated day from night, was the president's return to the White House and the gathering of his political/communications staff outside the Oval Office—Karen, Dan Bartlett, Karl Rove and I. Each of us bolted there with our notes, things we thought the president might want to say, things we'd jotted down over the course of the long day on paper that was rumpled and stained with grease and barbecue sauce from the ribs and drumsticks we devoured, which had been left over from a congressional barbecue that had never taken place that day.

In his hands, the president had his own notes. We looked over his shoulder, and there we saw fragments of remarkably organized policy propositions he had assembled during his roller-coaster flights across the skies of the USA. He wanted to do a live Oval Office address to the nation as soon as it could be set that night.

Needless to say, I was not only impressed but I was also comforted by his coherence and clear vision—and humbled by my own shakiness. The president was light-years ahead: he already knew what he wanted to say and communicate.

The truth is, he didn't need us communicators. I am not saying this sycophantically—but honestly. I remember feeling overwhelmed (in a happy way) by what a clear grasp he had not only of the gravity of the threat we faced but of the response that was needed. He had the language and tone and voice already.

What he'd already wrapped his mind around were the contours of the Bush Doctrine: *if you harbor terrorists, we're going to treat you like a terrorist.* What he wanted us to think about was a template, a way to measure our progress as the struggle against terrorism unfolded that could be communicated to the country. Combating this enemy wouldn't look like the Gulf War or any war Americans had ever experienced. And our success or progress would happen in a way that people couldn't see—CNN wouldn't be there to record footage of the storming of beaches. It would happen in the "shadows," which the terrorists owned. How could we make it easier to chart progress so Americans would feel secure?

Disrupting financing routes, or gathering one thousand disparate bits of intelligence, or breaking up invisible terrorist cells—this was hardly the stuff of compelling visuals.

As it turned out, the public understood our plans (people are way smarter than policy nerds give them credit for). What was less clear were the terrorists themselves. Who was this shadowy enemy? What kind of soldier hides among civilians or dresses in women's clothes? How is a chain of command hiding in caves wreaking such havoc? What do people without a sovereign state want?

Addressing that ongoing information deficit is what later led to the formation of the White House Information Group (WHIG), which was much maligned by partisans and the press. One of the best ideas of WHIG (I think it was Dan Bartlett's idea, or maybe it was just lifted from the intel guys) was an FBI-like Most Wanted poster lining up head shots of the al-Qaeda hierarchy, with big X's over the photos of the ones we had captured or killed. Osama bin Laden meet Tony Soprano.

One problem with the al-Qaeda Most Wanted poster was, given the shadowy countenance preferred by terrorists, we didn't *have* a lot of their photos. It's not like there were libraries of high school senior photos or Facebook head shots sitting around. So many of the Most Wanteds were blank squares. And even when we did have photos, they all looked alike. Now don't go all PC on me. There is not a lot of sartorial variety with the kaffiyeh look.

After the Oval Office address to the nation, we reassembled in the small stuffy PEOC. Unlike the daytime "nation under attack" atmosphere, the combo of a couple of hours with no planes crashing into American symbols of power and having the president anchor the table infused the room with a sense of calm. This group possessed such vast institutional expertise and wisdom that if you were a Catholic you would have crossed yourself.

Which I did. And I wasn't even a Catholic at the time. But I was so grateful, so humbled, that I don't know how else to describe it.

Say what you want about establishment Washington, this was an assemblage of people who knew what to do. They had the expertise and guts to figure it out quickly, even though it was a whole new world (dis)order. There was a seamlessness in how it all came together, how we worked together in many ways more flawlessly than we did setting up the new administration in the first place.

Nobody faltered or hesitated. Sure, there were the to-be-expected differing views and the occasional shouting matches—which President Bush desired and inspired, actually. Our team was in place, and it was security smart, Washington savvy. The principals all knew each other, and their deputies knew each other. When there's a crisis, you don't want a bunch of jockeying newcomers in charge.

But there were some things you can't know until you go through them. And one of the things we learned by going through it was that the apparently hermetically sealed WWII-era PEOC was set up with an insufficient circulation and ventilation system. Or, at least, with a system that wasn't sufficient to support an overpopulated prolonged stay. As the room got hotter and hotter, stuffier and stuffier, we thought our dizziness was a result of a massive intake of our only PEOC food source, M&M's—and the subsequent blood sugar crash. Turned out, we were breathing our own expelled carbon dioxide, asphyxiating ourselves.

Another occasion that strained the VP's customary unflappability.

"Fresh air. *Now.*"

JAMES

AFTER 9/11, my attitude really changed. I was genuinely happy that Mary was at the White House, really proud that she was working there. I felt like our family was contributing in a concrete way. She worked all the time, probably more than ever. But suddenly, I was okay with it. I knew she was doing important work, and I totally supported it.

Hell, I found myself feeling a little envious, wishing I could help in some way. Like everybody, I was consumed with patriotism during that period. I was ready to put my two stripes back on and head off with the marines. I told people at the White House, "Look, whatever you need. I'll go to Pakistan and churn out press releases or whatever." It was a different time. It changed my whole outlook.

MARY

WHEN YOU ARE TRAVELING at warp speed, the edges of your life, anything peripheral, are a blur. The days following 9/11 were unlike any other days I could remember. It had something to do with the focus of our jobs. The way the White House had to pull together and concentrate on this one thing—and all the attendant repercussions of it. For me, it was the longest expanse of being in the moment I've ever experienced. It wasn't just days or weeks. I was in the moment for months at a time, and there wasn't any other option really. There were things to do, things to think about, serious business. I wasn't resentful. I wasn't emotional. And for the first time since I got to the White House, I wasn't even feeling guilty about my kids.

Above all, I knew I had to be disciplined. Like training for a marathon, which was what it turned out to be. I had to eat right, sleep right, and take better care of myself. Beyond that, there wasn't much time to dwell on myself, have emotions or even daydream about getting a pedicure or massage. Sometimes I was away for days at a time, shuttling from one undisclosed location to another.

I worried about Nee Nee, who seemed to be precipitously and progressively worse whenever I was able to see her. I begged her to let us help—to see another doctor or any doctor and to stop being so dignified and stoic and secretive. James would report that she seemed too weak to play with the kids, after feeding and dressing them. It got so bad she couldn't open a can.

But no matter how many times I tried to raise the subject with her, she wouldn't tell me what was wrong or how sick she really was.

"Nee Nee, let me have somebody help you," I begged her. And whatever it was, whatever was wrong with her, I asked her to stay with us—and we'd look after her. And she did stay—until her last day, one month after the attacks. In those days at the White House, I never left for any personal reasons. But for Nee Nee's funeral I never even said I was leaving. I closed my office door, turned off my cell phone and drove alone to the same Pentecostal church in D.C. where she used to take Matty, where they'd sing and sway—Matty loved it. Now that church was crammed full of Nee Nee's mourners, her friends and family and faith community, a raucous, loving and loud group. People stood up spontaneously during the service to tell a story about Nee Nee, or sing a song, say a prayer, or simply break down. I have never cried so hard in my life. I wept and wailed. It felt like we were burying the only mother my girls had really had—and my own mother too.

Nee Nee's send-off was the sweetest, most life-affirming event I ever attended in Washington. My only regret, as the years passed, was not taking Matty, who'd been Nee Nee's companion nearly every day of her little life. When I was growing up, my parents never allowed us kids to attend funerals. So I didn't give bringing Matty to Nee Nee's too much thought. I assumed she wasn't old enough to understand the ceremony without being haunted or disturbed by it. But I was wrong about that. Matty would have understood and loved it as much as I did.

JAMES

I REMEMBER GROWING UP during the Cold War, how we would obsess about what might happen next, no matter how farfetched. Would they bomb Baton Rouge? Would they send submarines up the Mississippi River?

After 9/11, the same sort of speculation and uncertainty ran rampant. Only it seemed scarier as an adult, perhaps because I had my two girls to look after, my wife was off in some undisclosed location and Washington undoubtedly was a target. We didn't know if there were sleeper cells. People were duct taping their windows and garage doors. The rumor mill was churning at full speed.

In the days after the attacks, I certainly wasn't talking to anyone about politics. First off, it wasn't an election year. But that hardly mattered. Smoke literally was still coming out of the Pentagon. You couldn't fly. Washington pretty much remained on lockdown.

I would walk down to my office in Old Town Alexandria to work the phones, or people would come by the house. Either way, we all were just trying to figure out what exactly had happened and what came next. No one talked about anything else. Everything was sober and quiet and uncertain.

I was always waiting to hear from Mary—or at least to hear more about Mary. The girls would ask about their mother, and I'd tell them everything I knew. She's fine. She's with the vice president.

They had friends at school whose parents were killed in the Pentagon and whose families were grieving. It was a strange time. A strange and sad time.

MARY

WE MADE OUR FIRST trip to Ground Zero about a month after the attacks. The vice president hadn't wanted to go to Ground Zero before that, for the same reason George W. Bush didn't go to New Orleans in the immediate aftermath of Katrina. The extra chaos of an official White House visit wasn't what the overworked and traumatized response team, or anybody else, needed. No gains from a high-level visit could justify the distraction.

It was Cheney's first public outing since the attacks—and timed to piggyback on the annual Al Smith dinner, where he was previously scheduled to speak. It meant triple security. It meant the commotion of choppers landing, a complicated security plan, armed escorts and coordinating with Mayor Rudy Giuliani to meet at the emotionally traumatizing site of the still-smoking hole of Ground Zero. I couldn't even fathom the cavity that was once the towers. And the smell was wretched.

But the vice president and staff agreed: if there was any comfort we could bring to New Yorkers at such a terrible time, it would be an appearance at their cherished Al Smith gathering, a premier annual event that attracted Catholics and politicos from all over the state and, at the same time, didn't discriminate on the basis of religion or party credo.

While the VP did the rounds of the dinner reception and appeared to be making a room of shell-shocked prominent New Yorkers feel better, a mad scramble was under way back at *Air Force Two*. We received incoming intel that a bio or chem attack was detected in the nation's Capitol. It wasn't the first such report, since the early versions of the detection devices regularly registered false positives. But all we were being told at the time was that we were not allowed to return to D.C. as an attack capable of wiping out the entire city and beyond had been detected.

What? We can't go home?

You'd think by then that we'd be used to this—not being able to go home or hearing false reports of total annihilation—but the craziness of the "new normal" was starting to unravel my nerves. It seemed there were far too many recurring opportunities to have crazier-than-usual conversations with myself, such as *Wow, it's a good thing I duct taped the garage* before I left! And aren't I an incredible mom for stocking that so-safe safe room with tons of canned goods!* But then my mind would wander uncontrollably to the tangential truth of the matter—that our miserable, dirty, germ- and bug-infested junk-filled mess of a garage was about as fit or safe for human habitation as a bio attack—and how I knew that someday we'd really fix it up and use it as a real garage in which to park an actual car. *Wait, isn't it actually fortuitous that I haven't gotten around to fixing up the garage yet, because, lucky us, since there's no car in there, the girls have more play space. But was it really okay that they were playing in that disgusting zone with all those broken toys?* Then I promised myself that

---

* The designated "safe room" in our house.

if by some miracle the whole neighborhood wasn't poisoned when I got back I'd get right over to Goodwill Industries and give those broken toys away.

Because, good God Almighty, my beloved miracle babies were about to bake alive in a pile of old junky toys and be charbroiled with the spiders! But wait, did I remember to leave them a can opener by the lifetime supply of Progresso soup cans?

Boom! *Snap out of it, girl!* Eventually, I got ahold of myself.

And pardon me if the above conversation with myself lessens your confidence in those on whom your safety and security depends. But your mind would wander too, I promise, if you thought you were never going to see your home and family again—or if you did, it would be like coming home to Charlton Heston in *The Omega Man* or to my go-to movie reference point and constant vision, *Mad Max*.

The world we lived in was constantly too bizarre to believe. It was not at all farfetched to think all of our families would be dead and that we were never going back home.

Meanwhile, back at the Waldorf, the vice president was still comforting the crowd and, despite all he knew—which was way more than we did—he never lost his focus. He and John McConnell had sweated bullets over what would become the VP's first major speech after 9/11, which was delivered to a room of heartbroken notables and worthies with full-on press coverage. The rest of the Office of the Vice President, who would usually butt in—vetting and editing Cheney's speeches (and essentially ruining John's perfectly assembled presentation)—were distracted when the germ/gas attack report came over the chatter waves.

Important as it was at the time, the speech seemed a tad secondary to impending mass murder and chemical warfare, but in the end, it was better for the lack of our interference.

And it opened with some really good jokes.

"It's nice, for a change, to be at a disclosed location . . ."

"And the Waldorf is a lot nicer than our cave."

The speech quickly pivoted to the moving, dramatic and really painful times we were all living through, and the incredible strength that the city of New York had shown in the face of tragedy. "We have to assume there will be more attacks," Cheney said, "that is the only safe way to proceed. And I want to assure each of you that in the face of these dangers we are doing everything we know how to do. For the first time ever, the country has a strategy of *homeland security* and a cabinet officer to carry it out."*

Our office had, in fact, been assigned the job of recommending to the president the best and most expeditious way of creating a domestic-security operation commensurate to the immediate threat. Even before the 9/11 attacks, after our energy policy assignment was completed, we'd been working in this area and recommending the right individual to run the new cabinet-level department.

Following the attacks on our own shores, securing the homeland obviously became a priority. The groundwork had to be done in just over a week, only days away, by September 20, when the president was scheduled to update the nation—and the world—in an address to a joint session of Congress. On the continuum of big deal speeches in the history of our country, this one was off the charts. And it would be the most serious and consequential speech of Bush's career after less than a year in office.

The new president had to assure the world that the United States was fully capable of and prepared to secure the nation, our allies and global freedom. With the whole world listening, he had to describe the measures being taken and the programs being established to "harden" the vulnerable target that America had unbelievably become. Our plans for retaliation and bringing justice to the evildoers had to be front and center. And while he was at it, he needed to comfort a stunned nation that hadn't been attacked on her own shores for more than a generation. He had to acknowledge the nation's grief and steel it to move on with resolve.

---

* Meaning cabinet-level department and officer, which was essential.

Speechwriting is always a collaborative undertaking at the White House, but in this case, the OVP, taking on the daunting task of adding flesh and bones and muscle and grit to the President's emotional speech on the evening of 9/11, had the singular task of contributing most of the Homeland Defense piece of it. Time was short, the situation urgent. And while we had been working on the concept of homeland defense for a few weeks prior to 9/11, we still hadn't officially consulted with all of the relevant congressional committees, subcommittees, chairmen and ranking members, which meant a multitude of governmental straphangers—who could make or break policy.

There was no time for multiple megameetings with all these people and entities. Not for the first time, I thanked God for the vice president's and Scooter's long familiarity and experience in this complex field, because when the rubber hit the road, the president knew he could rely on the vice president. So there we were, the three of us, the VP, Scooter and I, grouped around one desk, scrambling to put the finishing touches on a critical defense and security measure for the president to share with the world.

We went over names of individuals we thought could honcho Homeland Defense. Obviously it had to be a person of experience, credibility, gravitas, maturity, and someone with the right executive skills to know the way stuff works in government. Giuliani was first on our list, even though he was obviously completely taken up with the restoration of his city. We also instantly considered Tom Ridge, but I never thought he'd take the job in a million years; he was a sitting governor of a major state and he had small children at home. Nobody in that situation was likely to pick up and move to Washington, and then have to work 24/7 for who knows how long. But these were pressing times, and good people were called, and they came.

By necessity and philosophy, there was no desire to create a whole new department of government. And it's no state secret that the vice president was adamantly opposed to it. His guiding principle in life and politics was always "less is more." A new department would create more problems than it would solve. It would add another layer, take months to pull off, and produce chaos not security.

There were myriad structural and policy shortcomings that led to 9/11 that suddenly had to be corrected overnight—and not just for the purposes of the president's imminent speech, obviously. There was a whole pre-9/11 mind-set that now had to be overhauled. Intel fiefdoms built up over decades and turf battles seemingly as old as Sparta and Athens had to be wiped out. *Permanently*, if peace were to reign in the land.

And, if history was any guide, it would be mere moments before the unstoppable force of "politics abhorring a vacuum" would kick in. We needed a central clearinghouse with immediate and unfettered access to the president where disparate pieces of intelligence, offense and defense activities could be synthesized.

The vice president was trying to reconcile opposing strategies. How to find a place where "less is more" meets "weakness invites provocation," aka "peace through strength"?

During one brainstorming session with the vice president and Scooter Libby, I blurted out my sense that the words *homeland defense* sounded "kind of pre-9/11." It was more like a not-crazy conversation with myself than anything else. My mothering instincts rather than my political instincts were trying to get some clarity. *We have to telegraph a lot with minimal language*, I was thinking. *Every word has to count. And I don't want to feel* defensive. *I want to feel secure.*

The vice president and I had one of our many Jedi mind-meld moments—we were often on the same page without having to spell things out too much. Hence, without further discussion, the name Homeland Security was adopted. In the scheme of all the decisions made that day, that week, that month or year, it is almost too minor a contribution to mention. But I note it here because you'd be shocked how many things—big and small—happen like that, off the cuff, while making policy or history.

Or maybe you wouldn't.

Being an assistant to the president requires a top-level security clearance, and once you go through all the checks, oaths and such, and you are "cleared"—then you are declared, in the vernacular, "read in."

Being read in allowed me to see or read the hot, top-secret classified stuff. This level of access came with certain responsibilities, which are very serious and must be respected in all cases. So obviously there are some things I can't talk about to this day. There are other things I am free to discuss, such as the anthrax vaccination shots I was offered, which would keep the senior White House staff alive, theoretically, if there was an act of bioterrorism involving anthrax. The vaccination series took nine months in all, and was so awful, and hurt so much—you couldn't move your arms for days after a shot—I decided that I'd rather take my chances and just avoid opening mail. I stopped the regimen.

Another thing I declined, after a couple weeks of exposure, was the opportunity to continue availing myself of the "raw" overnight worldwide intelligence.

Every morning, after the senior staff meeting, I grabbed a cup of bad coffee from the West Wing Mess, crossed over to the OEOB and started my workday locked in the special room inside the office of our national security genius, Eric Edelman, and read these strange dispatches of raw data. At first, the stuff was utterly meaningless to me and I'd have to ask Eric what it meant. Eventually, I started getting a better sense of how to process it. But it was time consuming, and it felt like learning a new language. You didn't really know what you were hearing or seeing. It was a mosaic of ambiguous information, glimpses of things going on—or *possibly* going on, you never knew. It was like looking at shadows in a cave. You knew it was a reflection or a rendering of a reality of some kind. But you weren't sure what you were looking at, except that you knew it was dark and ugly.

Most of the conversations were in code. The bad guys were evil but they weren't stupid; it didn't require genius to figure out we were listening.

Even in this obscured form, pure evil was jumping off the pages. All

I could think about was the ending of *The Screwtape Letters* by C. S. Lewis, the devil's discourse against democracy.

The point of this listening exercise was to expose myself to the way the enemy thought, to inform my own thinking for the purpose of being able to communicate the nefarious and dangerous force we were confronting. For the same reasons, I went to in-depth intel briefings on germ warfare and other terrorist tradecraft—which is when I figured out that women are much more obsessed with germs than the many other unthinkable options for mass annihilation.

I don't even like scary movies. And growing up in the Midwest didn't exactly prepare me for tunneling inside the minds of America-hating terrorists, so it wasn't a bad idea in theory. I'd been on the political team for Gulf 1, so I thought I wasn't a complete newbie in terms of warfare and security threats, but this was different. I had never sat in a room *alone* before, getting inside the heads of barbaric mass murderers, while at the same time acutely aware of my kids at home, who were possibly not safe in their cozy little beds anymore.

Every morning, after unlocking myself from the special security room, I walked back to my office furious—totally enraged. And after about three weeks, I had to stop completely. I couldn't spare the time or the emotional energy. It was counterproductive.

Hoping to find a better way—more organized and less evil—to get informed, I began consuming everything I could about the history and culture of the long-troubled Middle East and increasingly extreme political Islamism. We all had to take every available opportunity to learn more. Karl Rove's shop set up in-house seminars with military historians and Middle East experts, such as Bernard Lewis and Victor Davis Hanson. I read all their books and more. And, of course, I was at the elbow of the greatest font of historical and practical knowledge, one Richard B. Cheney.

By the time we returned from our walk-up-to-the-war trip, visiting twelve Middle Eastern countries in ten days, I knew more than I wanted to. You don't go about your day in the same way after you've drenched yourself in this kind of stuff. But at the same time, I didn't want it to change me. I knew there must be a way to do my job well without getting all twisted up inside or corroding my naive, believe-in-the-basic-goodness-of-humanity mind-set for good.

The VP had multiple deep intel briefings every day. Eventually, I knew I could learn everything (and more than I ever wanted to know) from them. Security and conferring with the president about possible threats to the country was the VP's major task. But unlike the way he's been portrayed in the media, supposedly cherry-picking intelligence to make a case for invading Iraq, the opposite was true. Cheney was skeptical, more likely than not to disbelieve the chatter—and he spent a lot of time at the various intel agencies at every level, asking questions, following up with the people who were on the front lines gathering the raw intelligence in real time. Because, by the time the intel made its way up the chain of command, it was often diluted and distorted. Cheney knew this firsthand from his experience with the faulty intelligence during the buildup to the first Gulf War. How the raw intelligence is gathered, and by whom, was critical in determining its reliability.

Intelligence isn't a science. It's more like guessing how a puzzle is going to look when you have only a fraction of puzzle pieces on the board. Experienced and trained professionals can make amazingly coherent deductions and solid assumptions from disparate and fragmentary pieces of microdata. Decisions and policies have to be made on the basis of these probabilities. There are no surefire strategies. Yes, it is much more than random guessing—and the efforts to verify, augment and refine are ongoing and endless. Still, by necessity, at some point you must go with "guesstimates." Believe me, no one *but no one* wants to be wrong about these things. At the same time, there is no certainty. The absurd accusations that we were making these decisions and policies using some political calculus still makes me sick to my stomach. Though I have to confess some gratifying schadenfreude while recently watching President Obama and Secretary Kerry labor and squirm their way through the same stupid accusations they once hurled at us.

JAMES

IN A STRANGE WAY, 9/11 was good for me and Mary too. I hate to say 9/11 was good for anybody, of course, because it was such an awful experience for so many people. But we had been so at odds for so much of the past year, and that terrible event brought us together again. It obliterated a lot of the tension that had been there, hovering in the house for months and months. It gave us perspective.

MARY

EVERYONE YOU CAN TRUST on a campaign or in the White House is a foxhole buddy. You need each other. You've got each other's backs. Focusing on gender is not something you have time to do—or, at least, it's not something that women do, because it would be way too girly and a huge waste of time. You don't need to talk, you just *get it*. Female foxhole buddies get each other's complicated lives, tethered to the push and pull of the personal versus the professional, and therefore how crucial it is to get stuff done quickly and well without dragging your fat ego into every meeting.

Unlike in real life, women in a high-stress and fast-paced work environment preen and posture less than men do. In the natural order of things, the male species gets to have striking plumage, but since political males are denied any fun colors or cuckoo getups—being restricted to a bland uniform of gray slacks or khakis, navy jacket, button-down shirt and striped rep ties—the only outlet for their unremitting peacock instinct becomes *the meeting*.

This strikingly male behavior, also known as prolong-the-meeting-so-every-person-of-the-male-persuasion-can-strut-his-stuff, is not peculiar to the political business. It just seems far more pronounced and problematic in government, given the endless nonstop urgency of every minute of every day.

In fairness, the Bush White House was way better than most on this front, owing to the fact that George W. Bush was a meeting speed demon and notoriously disdainful of time wasters.

But in our early White House months, pre-9/11, there was an excruciating number of meetings. We had lost important transition weeks during the recount and had to scramble to set things up. There were meetings about infrastructure, substance, personnel—all critical—but there were far more meetings about what kind of meetings to have and who should/could attend them (really important because if you are not invited to the right meetings, you have no White House whack). Then we had follow-up meetings to make sure something actually got done. And, of course, there were meetings to ensure that credit for getting anything done was assigned appropriately.

I am not being critical. This is simply the law of the political jungle. One giant saving grace was we were all issued brand-new BlackBerries and everyone, including the men, did their real work on them while attending the right meetings. Impressive facility with a BlackBerry is actually the one area where men truly exceed women in multitasking. Karl Rove could work countless devices simultaneously while running a meeting and making lucid, often spot-on points and handing out orders.

Seating is the next all-important pecking-order revealer in a meeting. Some of this is set by protocol—some by habit. But after six months of sorting this out like a pack of dogs, the White House became a well-oiled meeting machine, which everyone assumes is an inborn Republican trait. But then the terrorist attack pushed us to retool again.

On the morning after 9/11, we went back to basics, starting with a roundup of the political girl-squad. For the 101st time, I leaned once again on my friendship with Maria Cino, my old grunt-gal roommate from the Reagan-era days who was, perfectly enough, now the deputy secretary for the Department of Transportation, which gave her dominion over water evacuation in the event of an attack. (I admit that I thought of this immediately, as my family—my girls—lived right on the banks of the Potomac.) Maria was essentially doing for Norman Mineta, the transportation secretary, a version of what I was doing for Cheney. And there was Torie Clarke, another longtime close friend from the Bush 41 days. She was at the Pentagon, doing another version of the same job, as deputy for Secretary of Defense Rumsfeld.

Condi Rice of the Bush 41 days was now National Security honcho; Margaret Tutwiler, going back to the Ford days, was now (the first female) ambassador to Morocco (yikes, in a 9/11 world); and Karen Hughes, longtime superstar at media and everything else, was not just the Queen of Queen Bees, but the Master of the Universe for the Grand Pooh-Bah.

It felt like everybody I loved, girlfriendwise, was attached to principals who were largely longtime friends, and the deputies were all old friends. This is one of the things that people outside of Washington criticize—the insiders' game. And while there are downsides—mostly the kvetching of the chattering class, who are themselves the most cloistered of incestuous insiders—when planes are flying into American institutions and there are big guys with big guns across the street in Lafayette Park and vigilant snipers on the roof of your place of employment, you tend to put a premium on getting things accomplished a lot faster, which is greatly enhanced when you know whom to call, how to reach the right deputy, and when you can quickly assemble a team of people who worked together before. Like *The Avengers*, it's especially useful for fighting evil. One of my lasting remembrances of 9/11 was the sense of coherence and focus among those gathered in or communicating with the PEOC. And much of this had to do with the personal relationships between the individuals.

The women of the White House doubled as my workout buddies. Months before, in the spring, after so many meetings and sitting in chairs, we realized that we had totally different rhythms from the guys. For one thing, they all went to lunch every day. We ate at our desks. They went out to dinner at night, obligated to conduct various important meetings in various restaurants around town. We stayed in the office until it was time to go home.

We wanted some kind of outlet. And there was something else. All that chair time causes unfortunate changes to one's shape. Our rumps were expanding.

We needed exercise. And we needed a break from all those endless meetings and our increasingly painful carpal tunnel syndrome from BlackBerry overuse. One day we just said, "What the hell? It's bad enough we're not having lunch. Why can't we get a workout in?" We were all kind of physical. Karen Hughes is a real athlete and a dedicated swimmer. Condoleeza Rice is an athlete and a lifelong runner. I can't remember what (the domestic policy genius) Margaret Spellings's sport was, officially, but you know all these Texans are physical people. They ride. They hunt. They clear brush and build bonfires.

I have always needed exercise, but unlike James, I hate running. B.O.R.I.N.G. Nothing is worse for me than grinding it out on the street, getting into the flow, and then running into people I know. How are you supposed to keep your heart rate up with the constant distraction of political gossip? I like a good basic sweaty workout and have been going to the gym since I was a little girl, when I made my dad, a total health nut, drag me along. He taught me how to lift weights, work various muscle groups and enjoy a good sweat and a relaxing steam afterward.

Once we decided to turn our office frustrations into physical fitness, it occurred to us that Mrs. Bush had a trainer, the preternaturally toned cardio goddess Trish, who came every day to the White House to work out with her. In fact, she'd moved up from Texas with the Bushes, so we figured she might be looking for more to do.

We tried an after-office-hours kind of thing, but it didn't work. Too hard to coordinate, and at the end of the day, we were too wiped out. So we tried midday, lunch hour workouts together, doing lunges down the hall in the OEOB and running up and down the long circular marble staircases in our work clothes and pantyhose and gym shoes. But it wound up being kind of dangerous, not to mention all the mean looks and slammed doors we got from our distracted colleagues who were working and the sweaty clothes we had to wear the rest of the afternoon.

That's when we decided to pick an hour, three times a week, and do a full-fledged workout in the senior staff gym in the OEOB, changing into gym clothes and doing it right. Obviously, there were days we cut it short or abandoned it totally. But we often got in a full hour of strength and cardio—lots of weights, lots of endurance, really working the machines and finishing up with some cool-down yoga stretches—then we took a slam-bam shower. If we ran out of time, we just splashed water on the critical areas, what my mom called a "futsky bath," and then we'd run back to our offices. Refreshed, strong, and guilt-free about the extra LUNA bar that was our lunch.

We followed basic gym etiquette. You didn't talk to your fellow gym rats unless they wanted to talk. But as our commitment increased and our workouts became consistent, our group signed up for a gym hour when we'd be alone; and while we were working out, we had fun and even laughed—a rare occurrence at the White House. Unlike a campaign, it's a much more serious environment. But in the gym with my gal pals, we guffawed, gossiped, got our endorphins going. We'd go back to our offices feeling renewed at the cellular level.

And we started looking better too—without dieting, which we'd all been compelled to constantly do just to compensate for the chair time and its less than enchanting effect on our behinds. Trish was violently antidiet (easy for a twenty-something who weighs eighty pounds soaking wet) and would regularly admonish us forty-somethings whose use of spandex was the only thing keeping all the loose flesh from flapping in a strong breeze: "Forget all of that dieting. Just follow this exercise routine for six weeks and I guarantee you'll lose inches. Your clothes are going to fit better."

And she was right. Trish worked us so hard that we couldn't even sit down to go to the bathroom because our quads hurt so bad; we couldn't raise our hands to get attention in the meetings dominated by men because our triceps were paralyzed in pain. I mean, she killed us. It was boot camp. Just when we were about to give into the pain, we were all wearing clothes that hadn't fit in forever—able to sliver into frocks that had been reduced to an almost permanent status in the skinny section of our closets, quite separate from the bloat-days section and the flat-out-fat sections.

Overall, of course, I was still basically a mess—with ever-present one-inch roots belying my attempt to appear devoid of ever-increasing gray streaks and a makeup regime that consisted solely of ChapStick— but the difference was, I felt really good. And when you feel good, you look better and work better. It's true. It wasn't a vanity thing. It was a sanity thing.

An equally unexpected but more important by-product was how much we accomplished workwise while we were lifting weights and running on the treadmill. What started out as a reprieve and relief from work turned into our most productive and clearheaded hours. We shared information and ideas. We saw ways to help each other solve problems and think through things, and developed economies of scale and divisions of labor strategies.

We got to know each other better too. Karen's the most amazing, talented, faithful person I've ever worked with. She taught me by her example how to apply the principles and values of faith to one's work. And despite a schedule from hell, she always took time for reflection and prayer and gratitude.

I didn't know Margaret Spellings when we started, but it turned out we were basically the same person (except she is a natural blond). And I loved Condi Rice, always stately in the gym or even with sponge rollers in her hair, which we shared as occasional bunkmates at Camp David after 9/11. Despite our girl chitchat and attempts at normalcy, post-9/11 Camp David was hardly a gals' sleepover kind of thing.

One day, our private White House boot camp in the gym was interrupted by a call to an emergency meeting, aka "an uncalled meeting" in the West Wing. So we ran, sweaty in our workout duds, from the OEOB across the hot parking lot and up the stairs to the West Wing Oval Office, which I'm proud to say we could do now without panting and wheezing. An inviolate POTUS 43 law was being on time to meetings, even ones you didn't know about—he demanded punctuality in all things, small and large—so we arrived in our running shoes and weight-lifting gloves.

The president, who had a wonderful habit of siding with the women in the morning staff meetings, glanced up and quickly said, in his droll Texas deadpan, "Hey, it's the chicks with mitts. Glad you could make it!" That got a big laugh.

In meetings after that, he'd sometimes say to us, "Flex!" or "Show these puny boys some bicep action!"

Our arms were incredible. They were rock hard and impressive (in a forty-plus way). So impressive, we got special dispensation from the jackets-must-be-worn-in-the-West-Wing-24/7 rule and were allowed to wear sleeveless dresses and tops, which was very cool, because in the spring and summer D.C. is very hot. (And even in the winter, the old West Wing was horribly overheated.) When the mood struck him, which was frequent, the president would ask the guys to remove their jackets and show their bare arms—and "flex!"

What an embarrassment for them. The White House men had no tone or definition at all. It was like the scene in *Popeye*—only a gender-reverse version—when spindly Olive Oyl pulls out her stick arm and a tiny muscle appears at the top of her upper arm, then wobbles and falls, appearing underneath. Oh, the president loved that.

JAMES

I WAS RIGHT ABOUT what I said that morning when the planes hit the twin towers: it did change everything. At least for a while.

I didn't know exactly how, but it was clear that the contours of American politics were going to be altered for the foreseeable future. Its immediate effect was pretty dramatic. The conversation, what people thought about and talked about, it all changed. You seemed trite if you were talking about environmental concerns or income inequality or schools or whatever. National security was foremost in everyone's mind.

Politically, that change was favorable to Bush and the Republicans, no doubt about it. It conferred on them an aura of competence. As in, you may not like what they do. They may be kind of personally arrogant. But, man, they know how to get things done. They might not represent everything you believe in, but they are serious, strong, capable, hard-ass people.

I recall friends of mine at the time saying stuff like, "I'm glad Bush is in charge." I heard Democrats say, "It's better this way. They can do this better." It was a pretty persuasive feeling at the time. That effect lasted for a few years. Bush's numbers went up. Republicans had two good elections in a row, in 2002 and 2004, which hadn't happened since 1978 and 1980.

Several things happened by 2005 that exposed just how incompetent Bush and the Republicans actually were. The White House and congressional Republicans intervened in the Terri Schiavo case in Florida, which was infuriating and offensive. Not too long afterward came the bungled Hurricane Katrina response, which along with the ongoing Iraq War debacle opened the eyes of anyone who wasn't already a skeptic of the Bush administration.

Until all that happened, some people really thought there was a fundamental change taking place in American politics after 9/11. Ultimately, it turned out to be a temporary phenomenon. It didn't permanently change everything, but it temporarily changed a lot.

MARY

I LOVED MY HUSBAND before the Christmas of 2001, but then a moment came—one of those sudden illuminations when you see your spouse in sharp, clear light—and I decided I loved him more than I ever had. I loved him madly, truly and deeply.

I had been traveling almost all of that fall, drifting in Cheney world from one undisclosed secure location to another. It didn't make much difference where we were—the living room of the vice president's residence, a cabin at Camp David or flying around in *Air Force Two*. Whether you're two miles from your house or two thousand, being away from your family, totally incommunicado and not knowing where you'll be tomorrow, is tough.

I didn't have to go on all the trips, and when I did, it was mostly to try to keep the West Wing and the vice president's office integrated, connected and working as seamlessly as possible together, despite the fact that the two principals could not be in the same city and then later, when things relaxed, couldn't be in the same building. When I traveled with the vice president, having the top-level clearance I did required that I not tell James—or anybody else—where or when I was going or when I'd return. This wasn't too good for a compulsively structured guy.

Somehow he got used to that, or he just never complained. That alone should have shown me something about his character, but I was living and breathing work in those weeks, an absent parent—barely a drive-by mother—and I was not able to focus on much in my home or personal life.

I came home when I came home—and spent as much time with the girls as I could. Maria Cino would always be there too, and we'd open a bottle of wine, never uttering a word of politics, and the girls would do dance recitals and put on various shows for us, usually while wearing their fluffy tutus and falling all over the floor. Reyes and Buck-Buck, our high-spirited spaniels, would do their high-pitched yapping while circling the girls and jumping around their feet. Our chocolate Lab puppy, Paws—so named for his yellow feet—would attack them with all his knife-edged puppy teeth, diving for the ruffle of Matty's tutu and hanging on for dear life, while Matty spun around and around, lifting Paws into the air, forcing him to orbit our family room, with all his yellow paws akimbo, like some kind of gravity-defying dog. We had moved down the street from Maria (not for the first time), who religiously checked in with the girls during my frequent and extended absences, with or without dance performances. She was their second mother. God knows they needed one. To this day, we all call her "the Good Mother" while I remain "Monster Mom."

The "read-in" (lingo for a top-level security clearance) senior staff would trade off doing travel duty, Chief of Staff Scooter Libby, counselor David Addington or foreign policy expert Eric Edelman—all longtime Cheney vets from his Defense and Hill days and way more useful to the VP than I was. It was an ad hoc rotation, just as horrible for them because they had families too. What we tried to do was keep the travel equitable, not forcing one senior staff member to log too many miles, or do back-to-back trips. But the boys got the brunt of the work, punishment for their extraordinary expertise, while I was rewarded with a stay-at-home base for being a worthless roadie.

Sometimes we would go together, a mobile feel-your-pain consortium. Halloween was brutal—and a wake-up call for me. It's my favorite kid holiday—well, really, with or without kids, an all-around favorite celebration of mine. Every year, I dressed up as Tigger and Matty was Pooh. Emerson was not a Winnie type and would don nothing except a princess outfit even though one year she was Marilyn Monroe.

We went trick-or-treating around our Old Town neighborhood together, the girls toting their orange plastic candy-collecting pumpkins, me with my sippy cup full of red wine. (One year I *accidently* filled my sippy with vintage Château Latour from James's secret special stash, which really ticked him off, because, as he said, it should never touch plastic or be aerated through a plastic sippy straw.) Every house was open and decorated, replete with scary witches and ghost sounds. The Old Town streets were filled with kids, adults in the best costumes sat on porches, and John Warner, the governor then, had the best open house of all, drawing hordes of young goblins and an equal number of adults, all old enough to know better but still outrageously costumed in lace bustiers and pirate garb.

When Halloween 2001 came around, I tried not to think that much about our sacred Halloween tradition—of course I'd be working and of course that's what I was supposed to be doing. And sure enough, I found myself that Halloween in a not unpleasant but nonetheless undisclosed secure location, unable to even call my family. There were some kids with us, Cheney grandkids mostly, who dressed in their costumes, trying to enjoy the night. We even put on a tiny two-house trick-or-treat thing, pretending we were normal, but when Scooter and I closed the door and said good-bye to the last of the intrepid trick-or-treaters, we just looked at each other mournfully, deriving no comfort in feeling each other's pain. I wanted so much to call my own kids and just say hello. I tried conjuring up a good mood by imagining how they were doing on Lee Street, and the fun they were having in their little Pooh and princess costumes. But that night I cried myself to sleep.

Christmas approached. The vice president usually spent the holiday in Jackson Hole, Wyoming, with his extended family. There could be no lapse in our post-9/11 work so our amazing take-care-of-all-things office maven, Claire O'Donnell, somehow procured a one-floor condo in Jackson Hole for our whole family to stay for a couple of weeks. We weren't alone by any means; a good number of Cheney staff, by now our extended family of sorts, would be enjoying a pretend Christmas too.

James had been noticeably quiet about the prospect of a Christmas away from home, barely uttering a moan or sigh of complaint, even though he hates cold weather, hates snow, hates icy roads and hates the mountains in winter more than almost anything. Nothing puts that son of Louisiana in a worse state than a white Christmas.

To keep him from descending into a rotten holiday mood we had tried our best over the years to head south to warmer climes in December after a visit to see my dad in Indiana, where he had moved and remarried. My father's new wife, Barb, adored him and he always said how God had blessed him with two spectacular wives. A veritable Christmas queen like I was, Barb had four sons and loved pulling out all the tchotchke stops at Christmas. Then we'd be off to Christmas with the Carville clan (who literally filled half the pews and all of the standing-room-only in the back of their church in St. Gabriel, Louisiana, at Christmas Mass). The Carvilles really know how to put the merry into Merry Christmas, complete with old-school Southern comfort of many varieties, including the traditional Christmas singing contest, which I always lost, even when my rousing rendition of "White Christmas" one year was clearly the best. (Maybe the whole anti–white Christmas thing was in their genes.) In any case, none of that was possible this year.

So I went into Miss Christmas overdrive, determined to produce a holiday so festive nobody could complain. All would be merry . . . *or else*. I overloaded several giant plastic crates with our homemade ornaments, our lights, our stockings, our family Christmas bric-a-brac—from a global Santa collection to various *Sesame Street* characters in holiday hats—plus all the presents for Emma and Matty. I had the crates delivered to *Air Force Two* along with our luggage.

The overcompensating continued when I called ahead to ask if the unfailingly fine Cheney advance staff in Wyoming could please, *please*, *pretty please* pick out a Christmas tree for us as a special favor and stand it in the living room of our rented condo. My Christmas queen idea was that we'd arrive with all our ornaments and a beautiful tree to decorate, and the girls would barely notice that they weren't at home. And, of course, brilliant Santa Claus would know exactly where we were—and deliver all their presents down the condo chimney! It wouldn't be a horrible working Christmas away from home after all. It would a *super-duper winter wonderland adventure*!

You guessed it. We arrived to a condo that was so small we had to walk single file from one room to the only other room. And the Christmas tree wasn't a tree so much as a spindly shrub with a few errant branches, a very small version of a freaking Charlie Brown tree. To make things infinitely worse, our teeny condo, smothered under fourteen feet of freezing, hard-packed snow, was indistinguishable from the hundreds of other condos around it, all of their chimneys barely visible under tons of frozen white stuff. This seriously reduced the girls' confidence in an accurate Santa delivery.

Meanwhile, I took a hard look at that horrible tree—it didn't even look like an authentic *plant*— and cried out, "Are you kidding me?" (Actually I said, right in front of the children, "Are you *f–ing* kidding me?" and promptly fell apart.)

I was in a puddle of self-pity, not even able to apologize to the girls, who were tsk-tsking me for my potty mouth. While James, the ultimate bah-humbug hater of white Christmases, had started to croak out Christmas tunes, cocking his head as if hearing reindeer hooves on the roof. He was joyful. He was merry. And, quite impossibly, James had suddenly become the epitome of holiday spirit. *What was up with him?*

"Come on, Mary," he said, pointing at the shrub, "I think it's kind of cute, in a pathetic kind of way. Isn't it, girls? Let's have some Maker's Mark and start some merriment, darlin'!"

In the weeks preceding our departure for Wyoming, I had wondered how James would fit in with my office mates—and presumed it would be kind of socially weird to be in a homey holiday together. Later on, we spent so much time together that James became friendly with Cheney's staff and with the Cheneys themselves, but that first winter, I was sure he would be regarded as evil incarnate. Almost any workplace has its own culture and cultish aspects. It's almost impossible to avoid coming down with a case of Stockholm syndrome of some kind. But a political job creates a more extreme version of this, because the us-and-them mentality is very strong. And just as I was surely evil incarnate to the Clinton White House staff in the 1990s—and somebody they'd rather not see or speak to or be reminded of, if humanly possible—they never failed to hiss at me when I had to do a forced appearance at a bipartisan gathering—I was certain James wouldn't be a particularly desirable sight in Cheney World.

But some mystical, magical combination of Southern charm, Christmas cheer and Maker's Mark created a whole new Stockholm syndrome. Before the night was up, he was holding court and swapping sports stories, telling jokes and bartending; he commandeered the miniature kitchen and was whipping up Cajun treats for one and all. He inspired great merriment in Cheney World, made many new friends and converted our cramped, ice-covered condo into Christmas central. Joy radiated from him. The girls were in their glory.

James was so good—*so* ridiculously and painfully good.

The night before Christmas, I looked out the window and little fluffy snowflakes were falling outside, so poignantly fragile and small. And there was James in the kitchen—I am getting a love burst just remembering the moment. I knew every nanosecond of existence away from his routine and schedules, and even the warm sun, was misery for him. And I knew that he knew that he should have been persona non grata in Cheney World. He was not with his people, by any stretch of the imagination. And yet, here he was, being pleasant, being sweet, being kind and selfless, and endlessly entertaining.

It was all for the girls. He loves them with all his heart. And maybe, maybe, maybe a little bit of it was for me too.

JAMES

MARY REMEMBERS THAT CHRISTMAS in Wyoming as some kind of traumatic event. I had a fine time.

It's a beautiful part of the world. It's gorgeous, although I do remember it being frickin' cold, like twenty below. They say it's a dry cold. I don't know what the hell that's supposed to mean. It's just cold.

It's true that I don't like spending Christmas—or any time, really—in freezing climates. My general policy is not to pay money to be cold. But my wife was working for the vice president. She had to go out there. She was the one who had to staff it. Given my druthers, it's not where I'd want to spend my Christmas. But that's work. That's life.

We flew out there with the vice president on *Air Force Two*. Sure, the tree was kind of puny, in a comical way. We were surrounded by Republicans. But I had plenty of Maker's Mark and a good kitchen where I could cook, and I had my girls. I even found a gym, which made me happy because it was too damn cold to run outside.

What more could a Louisiana guy stranded in Wyoming want? It was merry enough for me.

MARY

You might assume that an august and austere White House title such as "assistant to the president" or "counselor to the vice president" would absolve the bearer from the job of dealing with the press. But no White House worker can avoid this dreaded job. Not only that, like many things in Washington, the bigger the title, the more shit-shoveling the job entailed.

Not that dealing with the press is akin to a barnyard task—at least, well, not always.

Another bit of counterintuitive job titling is the use of "media relations" as a job description. This means you are very likely a lousy source. Media relations peeps are restricted to dispensing the worst, the most detested and the most ridiculed thing of all: talking points. (Oddly enough, the people who are absolutely forbidden to talk to the press under penalty of infocastration are invariably the best sources.)

And then there was the White House caste that I fell into—the one restricted to dispensing talking points only but required to make them sound like they aren't talking points at all. In other words, it was up to you to make processed canned food taste garden fresh. There's an art to this. But it's not fun and the press girls and boys are totally onto the scam.

In a way, you can almost forgive members of the media for their regular hissy fits and their standard distrusting, adversarial, distracting and shallow ways. Unless, that is, your primary function is dealing with them day in, day out. Then you will not be able to find forgiveness. You just want to throw them into a meat grinder, turn it on high and leave the premises, like Ellstin Limehouse in *Justified*.

So while I was roaming around looking for trouble to shoot, there was always some press situation to deal with, which included trying to suss out where they were getting their most primo info. It was like a game of hide-and-seek. Other times, it was like whack-a-leaker.

Bush 43's Texas Mafia were a notoriously closedmouthed bunch, always on message and never leaking. They wouldn't give anybody the time of day without authorization. By the time the campaign press got to the White House, they were a pack of starving, ravenous animals. They hadn't had a decent meal in months. And the new guys, including me, were fresh meat.

I had spent time in that lion's den, to be sure, but not for almost ten years. Ironically, my years out of politics were spent on political TV, which seems to give normal people the impression that I'm a "journalist." And while those years gave me a greater insight into the frustrating world of political news gathering, I was never a journalist and could never fathom being one. I have little patience for observing and am too drawn to the thrill of doing. Also, my ass-kissing skills are limited to only what is absolutely required to get something done. And then there's the sworn duty of professional journalists: resolute objectivity. Sorry, that's not my scene.

Despite our mutual distrust, I understood the reporters' job and they understood mine. Except for some routine screaming matches (and one slapping match that I'm not proud of), we generally got along just fine. I actually like journalists. They come with built-in insatiable curiosity and the best ones don't let their institutions and ambition grind it out of them. I've had many a less-than-sober late-night conversation with members of the Fourth Estate who lament the scumbaggery often required of them to do a good job, or their bosses' idea of a good job.

Dealing with the media requires institutional knowledge. You can't treat everybody the same. Like people in every profession the world over, there are good guys and assholes. And some circumstances make a good guy go bad, but I've never seen an asshole turn good (pardon my language, just sharing the vernacular jargon). So the wisest thing is to take it one person and one situation at a time.

Problem was, by the time I had reentered the dance, the music had changed. The ethics and ethos of the media universe seemed to be spinning on its axis. There were lots of new faces, who rotated often, and very few individuals with serious political interest or experience. Gratuitous burning was commonplace, and once-regular adversarial relationships had become like Sunni-Shia battlegrounds.

It took me a while to get my sea legs. Covering the White House used to be the pinnacle of a career. Sure, over the decades the White House pressroom has housed more than a few kooks. But mostly it was a collection of professional journalists who had risen to the White House beat because they had talent and brains and a kind of healthy shrewdness.

One of my very best friends, before she died, was Ann Devroy, the *Washington Post* reporter extraordinaire who covered the White House in the Reagan and Bush 41 days. Ann was universally considered one of the media's most astute political minds. She was a piercingly insightful writer with impeccable integrity, and she certainly didn't regard her White House job as a stepping stone to riches, fame and fortune—or a gig as a talking head. And she never, ever in a million years would have rotated into the administration of any party. She thought of her profession as the great responsibility that it was and brought enormous intelligence and skill to everything she did. Her stories in the newspaper were unremittingly tough and, loyal to Poppy Bush as I am, it could be painful to read them sometimes. But I had to respect Ann's reporting, her ability to figure out what was really going on, to see through the weeds to the big picture. She used to call it "gathering threads" and had sources behind every bush and under every stone, kind of like Mike Allen of *Politico* today. Like Mike, she was kind and never snarky, even when institutional loyalty demanded it. Her untimely passing, like Tim Russert's, was paradigm shifting in the world of political journalism.

Although there would never be another Ann in the White House Press Room (or in my heart)—and I didn't expect to find any—I was thrown way off-balance by the younger generation of reporters. I had to start from almost scratch to get a trusted band of press partners to play ball with. Of course, Fox and most of the economic reporters were trustworthy straight shooters, but given the fat portfolio of the VP's office, I had to expand my reach. Some of them aren't conservative favorites today, but they were always fair to me. I am not sharing their surnames, because they might not want it known they were decent to a knuckle dragger (except for Don Imus, ironically a non-journalist who always produced the most fun and maximum coverage): John, Paul, Mathew and Mark (no kidding); John, Ron and Jon; David, Dan, Candy, Maggie, Sally and Sandy; Lloyd, Leslie and Lois; Mikey, Michael, Mike; Brian, Byron; Bill, Will and Wolf. And George. You know them all and might be surprised to know there are *many more*.

Even more important than developing a reliable outsource operation was figuring out who the assholes were—I am not going to name them here; I won't give them the satisfaction—but you know who they are too.

What was saddening though, despite the number of truly good political journalists remaining, was that a passion for the craft and subject matter or a sense of history seemed missing in the general atmosphere, in the stories as they were conceived and assigned. They might as well have been covering a baseball game. Much of this had to do with their command–and-control editors or the new warp speed of the Information Age. But a fair amount was due to a changed culture in their ranks.

I thought I had it mostly sorted out by the time the vice president embarked on a twelve-country ten-day trip to the Middle East, the walk up to the Iraq operation. Cheney began the trip doing daily readouts for our traveling press (i.e., debriefs from his meetings with foreign leaders or context for whatever country we were in). He wasn't trying to manipulate them, but for a host of other reasons, Cheney would start each readout saying, "This is on deep background" or "This is off the record." Those were the rules that he knew, I knew, the press knew, and the rules that had long been the standard of the road, so to speak. If a reporter needed to put background info into "for attribution" mode, he or she wrote "according to a source close to Cheney" or a similarly oblique version of that. This was not meant to obscure the source or the info, but most of the time, the "for attribution" stories were for the president to disclose and detail. We were the prep-work crew.

But that was so yesterday, because on this particular trip a network

James, jazz great Peter Fountain, (from whom the Carvilles purchased post-Katrina property in Bay St. Louis, Mississippi) and Father Kevin Wildes, S.J., at Loyola.

Mitch Landrieu, mayor of New Orleans,
at a fundraiser at the Carvilles' Louisiana home.

After another long day, James and Mary (and baby Matty) are lights out in the back of their SUV.

reporter announced right off, "We don't do deep background. We only take information that's on the record."

Those may sound like words of integrity. But the reality is that the vice president was respecting the intelligence of the press corps traveling with him by assuming it would be truly interested in acquiring a deep understanding of a sensitive and complicated moment in history rather than obtaining say-nothing quotes to plug into a formula story. "We only take information if it's on the record" is not the path of integrity. It is the path to zero understanding and cut-and-paste work.

The upshot is the public doesn't get information nuanced with shading and depth. It's more like one of those sticker books you give your kids when they are too young to actually draw. You punch out the sticker of the cartoon insect and put it on the outline of the insect body, and when all the stickers are punched out and pasted in, it isn't a book you ever want to look at again (or find interesting in the first place).

Or maybe they just didn't trust us and weren't interested in finding out if they could. Whatever, it came out to the same place.

Cheney continued to share his formidable knowledge and insights, but the sessions got increasingly immature so eventually we just gave up. We figured there was no way to talk to most of these meatheads en masse. We gave the group the stale readout with say-nothing quotes they could use for their formula stories.

I honestly felt for the guys who wanted to get to the heart of a story and portray a textured understanding for their audiences, and I tried to give them more "color," but it was not easy to quietly slip them intel in such close quarters. If you go back and look at those pieces, you can see who was reporting and who was just playing reporter.

JAMES

I'D BEEN AGAINST MARY taking the White House job in the very beginning. Then I'd been on board with it after 9/11, even when she worked all the time and traveled constantly and hardly ever came home during the day-light.

But the months leading up to the Iraq War in 2003 soured me all over again. I really was against the whole undertaking from the start. Vehemently against it, and Mary knew that.

That was one topic we really never talked about at home. We just didn't. It's not like I could wait up for her to get back after another eighteen-hour work-day and say, "What the fuck are you guys doing?" It's never worked like that with us, no matter which of our guys was in the White House.

Besides, bringing it up at home only would have led to a fight of epic pro-portions. And for what? She knew exactly how I felt. I was out criticizing the Bush administration's push for war on *Crossfire* and any other chance I got. I knew she was working for one of the main proponents of invading Iraq. What were we going to say to each other to change any of that?

So we generally kept the peace at home during that period. But it was an uneasy peace.

MARY

HE REMEMBERS IT ONE way—the wrong way. He remembers not being for the war from the start. But James is conflating time. He mushes to-gether the reelection, or "reelect" to use the political jargon, which got poisonously ugly—politics being politics—and forgets how it really was, how he felt at the time, how scary the threats and the possibility of weapons of mass destruction were. Of course, James is not alone. A whole raft of his liberal colleagues, from Hillary on down, voted for the war and uttered their supportive words and made statements. These are a matter of record.

I am not going to rehash the Iraq War or our effort to further democ-racy in the Mideast. Such matters are now the province of partisan pol-itics not policy reality. The enduring but demonstrably false "narrative" is *Bush lied and people died*. The irrefutable truth of the Obama administration's mendacity and incompetence in the Mideast from Egypt to Benghazi to Syria seems to escape such scathing narratives.

Today, the *smart people* have deemed Iraq the "dumb war." At the time, we certainly were cognizant of the age-old war dynamic: a battle plan is only good till the boots hit the ground. Iraq was then, as Iran is today, a closed society and near impenetrable to intel gathering. We had to plan for what we knew, for what we knew we didn't know and what we didn't know we didn't know, as Secretary Rumsfeld so eloquently put it.

We had some decent but not 100 percent intel, which is the very nature of intel; the world community was in general concurrence with the intel we shared; we had confirmation and support from the regional leaders for eradicating the growing threat of Saddam; we had the 100 percent historical record, which included his use of WMD; we knew for a fact from intercepted correspondence that al-Qaeda, in response to our efforts, was moving its front from Afghanistan to Iraq.

We didn't know the extent of the physical and psychic degradation wrought by decades of Saddam's tyrannical rule, which made standing up a democratic government more difficult. We didn't know the extent of stockpiled WMD, but we did know from defectors and inspectors, the means to produce more was largely intact, which made erring on the side of security. We did know the extrication of Saddam was not "Mission Accomplished."

As the Obama administration is now seeing, protecting our nation's strategic interests is not a textbook endeavor. I often wonder if they don't regret their venomous politicizing of national security.

And this seems important to remember: *The Iraq War made sense to the sensible until politics took over.* It wasn't until reelection politics entered into it that we began our epic battles. But when James goes political, all sense goes out the door. It didn't take much time or exposure to his uninformed, knee-jerk partisan blaspheming to make my teeth hurt and my head bang. Pretty quickly, he'd say one little stupid thing—actually, everything he said was stupid—about the war and I'd go crazy.

I was bone tired.

All our conversations became reduced to one topic, and not the one topic we should have dwelled on, since we had just *finally* patched up our acrimony from the last election and recount. Instead, we went at each other again. Everything he said made me nuts—and caught me in a perfect nexus of loyalty and policy, two things I care deeply about. His criticism concerned both my job as adviser to the president and vice president, as well as my own sense of devotion to Cheney, who was catching spears for the president while my husband was on TV every week as one of the misled, know-nothing spear throwers.

I will give it to him that he was careful not to directly attack Cheney. He knew that would be wrong. Or maybe he just knew it would be a divorceable offense.

Usually James is acutely aware of what he doesn't know—and he doesn't pretend to know things. But in this case, he was on the radio and TV, speaking with authority about things he knew nothing about. Meanwhile, I knew all this classified stuff that I couldn't talk about, and knew what was really going on. He was all curveball and yellow cake, very opinionated but with no facts. He was pulling it out of his ass. And since I had to guess that he knew that he didn't really know—and I did—it made me suspect that he was just trying to piss me off.

JAMES

THEY WANTED TO INVADE Iraq from the get-go. They came in wanting to do this. They were looking for any excuse to do it. And 9/11 gave them the excuse. In that sense, 9/11 was directly connected to the Iraq War. It created the atmosphere that allowed them to begin the march toward war.

Even all these years later, the whole weapons of mass destruction debate about Iraq still drives me crazy. It wasn't just that George W. Bush and Donald Rumsfeld and Dick Cheney and Paul Wolfowitz beat the drums of war. It was that a lot of people went along with it. And the standard excuse is "Look, a lot of people thought there were weapons of mass destruction; the CIA thought there were weapons of mass destruction, even Hillary Clinton thought there were weapons of mass destruction. In retrospect, we know there was flawed intelligence, but we didn't know that."

That is a very clever lie. It's clever. But it's still a lie.

All you need to do is look back at the timeline. The CIA initially believed there might be weapons of mass destruction in Iraq. Okay, fine. So Congress votes in October 2002 to authorize the president to use military force in Iraq.

What the apologists don't mention is what happened after that. The United Nations inspectors spend months in Iraq, and Hans Blix tells the world that his inspectors haven't found any "smoking guns." On the eve of war, Walter Pincus wrote two stories in the *Washington Post* saying the White House had exaggerated intelligence in its fervor for war and lacked hard evidence for the existence of weapons of mass destruction, but those stories got buried deep in the A section.

By the time the Bush administration went to war in March 2003, a lot of people were dubious of the justification. It's like the conventional wisdom that everybody thought the world was flat when Columbus sailed. Well, no, the whole educated world believed the world was round. By the time that we went to war in Iraq, many educated analysts thought it was doubtful that there were weapons of mass destruction.

We kicked out the UN inspectors. They said, "Give us another sixty days and we'll be through," and the White House said, "No, no, no, we've got to start now."

So now, when I hear editorial writers or even some of the moderate or liberal supporters of the war say, "You know, we were duped like everybody else," it drives me nuts. You were only duped because you didn't read the paper and you didn't think deeply enough about it. When somebody uses that excuse, it irritates the hell out of me. They act as if nothing happened between October 2002 and March 2003. And it's a really annoying and dishonest view of the world.

That's part of why the Iraq War still really bothers me. It was such a colossal mistake. It's easy to blame Bush, and, boy, does he deserve the blame. I'm glad to heap it on him. But a lot of people who should have known better went along with it.

MARY

IRAQ EVENTUALLY BECAME SUCH an ugly topic in our house that James, all on his own, just stopped fighting me about it. He said, "It takes two to have a fight" and withdrew.

JAMES

WE'VE HAD PLENTY OF ups and downs over the years, like in any marriage. We've fought about things at home the way any couple has. We'd go through periods of a week or more without talking, both of us just sulking over one thing or another.

But divorce? Throwing in the towel? That's not for me.

That's just not what's going to happen, from my vantage point. I can't do anything about what she believes, politically or personally. In fact, I've tried to understand it. And I can understand some of the things, but most of it I'll never understand.

It doesn't matter. When I got married, at forty-nine, I meant it. Cutting bait and running would be the easiest thing when the ride gets bumpy. Sticking around is the tougher choice, but also the better one.

MARY

NOT FIGHTING ABOUT IRAQ had repercussions on our marriage dynamic. Suddenly we weren't having it out—weren't fighting about anything. That might sound peaceful. But it's not a good thing. It's not healthy. And it messed with the basic foundations of our life and emotions. And our disagreements about Iraq, which seemed irreconcilable, would culminate in problems down the road when the reelection came. By then, politics had taken over and everybody on the left had total and complete amnesia about the war. *They were never for it.* And we were suddenly the dummies who'd been misled about WMD. Man, that was unspeakably awful, so maybe it's a good thing we weren't speaking.

And I don't mean to get too far ahead of our story, but the bad feelings about the war, and the weird aspect of James's not fighting anymore, culminated in his telling me that I couldn't become an assistant secretary of state for Condi Rice a couple years later, in the second Bush term, resulting in my huffily taking to the guest room. He claimed that the only reason I wanted to accept Condi's offer of a job at State was ego. That still infuriates me.

JAMES

NO ONE WANTED TO BE WRONG. That's my basic theory on how the Iraq blunder happened. People are afraid to be wrong. Unfortunately, that's not an uncommon occurrence in Washington, or inside almost any White House. People too often simply go along with something rather than airing their reservations, because it's tough to go against the crowd and it feels risky to be wrong.

Iraq ultimately was the Bush administration's failure. But it also was an enormous failure of leaving your skepticism at the door. That goes for people in the White House, people in the press. A lot of friends of ours supported it. Or more accurately, didn't actively oppose it. They just went along.

These people had no idea what they were getting into. And in many ways, I think the president and others got talked into it by this small group of people—Cheney and Scooter Libby and Paul Wolfowitz—who were dead set on invading Iraq. They had been since 1991. It was like an academic who has an idea and goes to the ends of the earth to test it out in a real-world setting. I think they all truly thought this was going to work. It turned out to be a colossal, massive screwup.

The whole debacle underscores another truth about Washington, which a lot of people in politics don't often acknowledge: almost all of the time, a fuck-up is just a fuckup. A cigar is just a cigar.

Most times, people do something because they actually think it's going to work out. Most times, they are not evil people trying to undermine America. Most times, there's not some underlying conspiracy or motive. In Iraq, it's true that there was war profiteering. It's true that there was a lot of oil there, which made it a strategically important place. But that doesn't mean those are the actual reasons we decided to go to war. We went to war because people in power actually believed it was a good idea. They were dead-ass wrong, but I don't doubt that they believed it.

It's not that you can't find instances where there is underlying criminality within Washington institutions. I mean, Watergate taught us that. It does happen. But in my experience, it's the exception, not the rule. There's a great tendency to overestimate conspiracies and underestimate stupidity. Iraq is a perfect case study of that.

And by the way, stupidity is a really good reason to vote somebody out of office. If you're massively wrong about a massively big thing, it really doesn't matter much that your motives were pure and that it fit with your political philosophy. That all might be true. But you blew it, partner. Time to go. That's what the American people should have said to Bush after his first term.

MARY

THE MONTHS PASSED, my *absolute* six-month marker came and went with no one even complaining since it was never realistic. Then a year went by. My work kept me endlessly active, lots of ups and downs—a front-row seat to history, as they say—but no memory stands out more than my total exhaustion and unremitting fatigue. I loved my boss, my colleagues and most of the work. Other than the silent Cold War over the Iraq War that was going on at home, there was a semblance of a routine. But I was burning out.

Things that used to tickle me became painful. For instance, most workdays started on the phone with an energetic battle of wits with David Gregory. He and his wife were planning a family, and we spent as much time on kid conversations as we did on policy and political ones. David made me laugh; he made me scream. And for a long while, it was a great way to start the day.

Then, suddenly, one morning when I was driving in the dark to work (as always), an unbidden thought came to my mind: *if I have to listen to one more syllable from David Gregory, I am going to slaughter myself with a stapler.* Suicide by stapler didn't scare me as much as having negative feelings for no reason about a guy I knew I adored. My patience and my mind were all crashing, my priorities disintegrating.

The one consistently coherent recurring thought was that I had to leave. A departure date called to me like the green light on Daisy's dock in *The Great Gatsby*. I couldn't look away, but I couldn't focus either. After the events of 9/11, a succession of tough new issues kept on pushing my possible departure date further and further out of reach. Corporate scandals, recessionary dips, it kept going on and on. Every day was a barrel of monkeys in the usual White House way. Before I snapped completely and stapled myself to death, or just stapled Gregory's mouth shut, I knew I had to tender a departure notice. Even if the date was still murky, I had to lay down a marker.

Karen Hughes decided she wanted out too. Her son didn't like Washington and wanted to leave. Her husband didn't like it either. All of them wanted to go back home to Texas.

Clearly, it wasn't a good idea for Karen and me to depart at the same time. Our jobs overlapped too much, and all the accumulated institutional memory and experience between us would be lost in one blast. And on a totally shallow level—which we cared much less about—we knew it would become "a story" if Karen and I resigned at the same time. *Mothers flee family-friendly White House in droves.*

Karen and I weren't fighting over who got to leave first, but let's just say a decision couldn't be reached because no one had a superior claim on misery. So we consulted the all-knowing, all-wise Margaret Tutwiler, our girlfriend consigliere who was the ambassador to Morocco at the time, a job that was hardly a picnic. We were kind of embarrassed to even approach her. We were miserable; she was on the firing line. After she heard both of our sides of the story, she pronounced her verdict: *Karen gets to go first because she did the 2000 campaign and you didn't, so she has suffered longer.*

I considered appealing on the grounds of *younger children at home*, but I wasn't sure if *teenage boy* wasn't the greater defense, and in any event, there wasn't an appellate process, so I accepted my sentence—but I did petition for a time-served reprieve that would spring me at the 2002 midterms. But then, after the midterms, a technical glitch delayed my release. I needed to remain through the State of the Union in January for reasons not worth breaking the flow of the story to describe.

I hate saying good-bye—or having parties or send-offs thrown in my honor. I kissed my great staff, packed up my kid tchotchkes and snuck out. This spared me the obligatory exaggerated accolades about how indispensable I was to the leaders of the free world. And I never got to raise a toast of my own and thank the president and vice president for their faith in me. The honor was all mine.

In any case, it was bittersweet for me, but maybe the happiest day of James's life.

JAMES

IT WAS A HAPPY DAY INDEED. When Mary started out at the White House, it was going to be for six months, but I always imagined that really meant a year. Fine. Then 9/11 came, and that one year turned into two. She always wanted to work at the White House. I guess I'm glad that she did. But I was also glad when she left.

Looking back, it was a good thing that she got to fulfill that goal. I'm happy she had a chance to do it, and I'm happy it lasted only two years and not four.

The rest of 2003 brought a mixture of sadness and happiness.

We'd planned a big get-together over the Fourth of July at our farm out in the Shenandoah Valley in rural Virginia. A lot of friends and family were coming up, including my youngest brother, Bill.

Bill hadn't always had the easiest life, but he was about as good a soul as you could find. Here was a guy who spent time in the army during Vietnam and came home with the mental baggage that so many other guys like him brought back from that god-awful war.

As was too often the case, he slipped into drinking too much and got mixed up with other substances. I think more than anything that it was a way of coping or trying to forget about some of the things he'd seen over there. He really struggled for years. My mother used to worry about him incessantly. All of us siblings worried about him. He was always a topic of conversation when we'd get together. Everybody would ask, "How's Bill doing? What's the latest with Bill?"

But by 2003, Bill really had gotten his life back on the right track. He'd stopped drinking. He'd just gotten married to a lovely woman from a wonderful family. They'd started to make a life for themselves. He'd really turned things around. For the first time, Bill wasn't the central topic of conversation in our family. He was doing well, and we'd started to worry less and instead began feeling happy for him that things finally were working out.

Bill and his wife were driving up to our farm to celebrate the Fourth of July with us that year. In Wytheville, Virginia, just a few hours away from the farm, he died of a heart attack. He was fifty-three years old. It was awful. It ripped our hearts out.

Bill had worked so hard to get his life in order, and just when things were looking good, *boom*. He was a good man who deserved better.

We buried Bill in the cemetery of the Catholic church in St. Gabriel, a couple miles from where we'd all grown up, and a stone's throw from the Mississippi River. Seven siblings gathered around to say good-bye to one of their own. It's hard to say if Bill's death deepened my urge to come back home again. But I do know it reminded me, in the most personal kind of way, that life is utterly unpredictable and too often unfair, and you might as well take a few chances, because you never know what lies around the next bend in the road.

Mary and I also were figuring out what lay around the next bend for us at the time. We'd been through a pretty slippery patch during the past few years.

On top of all that, I'd lost my mother and brother. And we were raising two small girls, who we adored but who also required constant attention and took up what little downtime we otherwise might have had during those tumultuous years. Needless to say, our marriage often took a backseat to other priorities.

I'm not the sort of guy to make grand romantic gestures. But I felt like I needed to do something to show her how much I still loved and appreciated her, even though we so often felt like two ships passing in the night and even though I'd spent much of the past few years generally pissed off and irritable about having Bush in the White House and my wife there working for him.

Our tenth wedding anniversary was coming up that Thanksgiving of 2003, and I got this idea to throw a party out at the farm. Unbeknownst to Mary, I called up her dad and also her best friend from high school, and they helped me plan a big shindig. We invited some of the people who were at our wedding a decade earlier in New Orleans. We even did a reenactment ceremony and let eight-year-old Matty preside over it. At one point she said, "By the power invested in me . . . Actually, I don't really have any power." Everybody cracked up.

It was a great night, a great Thanksgiving, a great anniversary. It was a moment in our marriage when the timing was just right. We needed something like that right about then.

For whatever reason, it helped us out a lot and gave us a fresh start. The future seemed wide open.

8.

Remarriage

MARY

HOW MANY TIMES HAVE I married James? Aside from Liz Taylor and Richard Burton, we might be the most remarried couple in history. We've managed to walk down the aisle three times already (and counting). The only difference is that we never bothered to get a divorce in between. Not that it was all bliss.

We survived the Florida recount.

We survived the Iraq War.

We survived the death of our parents and a sibling.

We survived teenage girls. (So far.)

You would think, after all those traumas, we could peacefully get through the day-to-day stuff.

But James has a verbal tic, which has caused a similar affliction in me. It goes that like this:

"Is that new?"

"Seriously? That has been in five houses of ours already and this is the fiftieth time you've asked me if it was new."

Or "Seriously? Do you know how many times I've worn this?"

Or "I traded for it."

"And how much did that cost?"

"What?"

"That."

"Got it on sale." Or "I forgot." Or "Two hundred dollars."

"What's this table here for?"

"That's a center hall table."

"I got that. It's flat-damn in the center of the hall."

"It's where people gather, and where they put their drinks when they are standing around at a party."

"I don't like it."

"Okay, honey. Let's just give it a chance. See how it works at the next party." (Patient smiley face.)

"I been holdin' my own damn drinks all my life. Who needs a table flat-damn in the middle of the hall to put a drink on? Who puts their drinks down anyway?"

"It's just a polite thing. Some people like the option."

"None of my people."

"Point taken. If you still don't like it in a week, out she goes. Promise."

Then a week later—wait for it—we have the exact same conversation.

But here's the kicker. I overheard James at our last party telling one of his people, *"This is for puttin' your drink on. Go ahead! Put your drink down! Nobody gonna take it. Mary got it on sale. It'll make her happy."*

So who wouldn't want to marry that guy three times?

The first time we got married was in 1993, in glorious beautiful New Orleans, a place we both agreed upon and loved. It was a bipartisan extravaganza, but there were no political confrontations because most of the guests couldn't figure out if it was a wedding or hootenanny. As Louisiana/Carville tradition dictates, weddings are celebrations to be remembered. Except the celebration aspect often works at cross-purposes with the remembering part.

James's sister Pat attended her husband's aunt's funeral the morning after the reception and announced upon her return to the day-after lunch (which was just an uninterrupted extension of the night before), "Sparky's aunt looked better than me." And no one disagreed.

In 2003, the year I'd left the White House, on our tenth anniversary, we did marriage number two. What started out as a small quiet renewal of our vows turned into a rockin' near repeat of 1993. The best part was, unlike our first wedding, which I labored over for months, I had nothing to do with this one. In fact, I didn't even *know* about this one. James pulled it off—the only good surprise of my life (I don't like surprises)—somehow assembling all my cherished loved ones from my college roommate to my whole family. I was so overwhelmed by James's thoughtfulness (and, to tell the truth, his organizational skills, which heretofore had not been in evidence) that much of that great day at our farm is a blur, though I distinctly remember Tucker Carlson and my usually civilized father raucously belting out show tunes at the piano.

Our best buds and the girls' godparents, Maria Cino and Paul Begala, read the beautiful and funny tributes they'd composed, and Matty "performed" the ceremony, witnessed by her "assistant," Emerson, each outfitted in matching black velvet girl gowns. I wore my Vera Wang pencil gown from wedding number one, which, to my mind, was as great an accomplishment as making it through ten years and two kids.

Much merriment ensued, most of which is unrecountable to protect the innocent, but I cried, I laughed, and whatever James was trying to pull off with this lovely stunt certainly worked. No man would have gone to that much trouble if he didn't mean it, I had to figure. Any lingering residue of the last couple of not-so-blissful years evaporated.

And guess what? We got married another time. At this point, you are thinking, *What is wrong with these lunatics?* or *Can't they can't come up with another party theme?*

We weren't trying to do a "third time's the charm" thing; we were getting truly married. During my RCIA (Rite of Christian Initiation for Adults) work toward my conversion to Catholicism in 2010, my wonderful by-the-book priest, Monsignor Nalty, informed me my marriage of seventeen years was not valid. My cradle Catholic nonhusband and I had been living in sin. I didn't bother asking what this made our daughters.

So, on Holy Saturday, in the beautiful New Orleans St. Stephen's candlelit church, the day before Easter, along with being received into the Church, James and I received the sacrament of marriage.

It was the only quiet marriage of the three, but by far the most memorable.

We were a bit sorry that we couldn't take our vows at the church where James's grandparents were married in New Orleans, which we believed was Mater Dolorosa.

JAMES

MARY HAD BEEN MARRIED BEFORE. So when we got married in New Orleans back in 1993, we didn't bother trying to get hitched in the Catholic Church, which can be pretty stingy about such things. Instead, we got married by the chief justice of the Louisiana Supreme Court inside the Royal Orleans hotel. Married was married in my book.

But after we moved back in 2008, Mary got very involved in the Catholic Church. She started taking religious instruction. She became a regular fixture at Masses, much more than I ever was. She decided she wanted to convert to Catholicism.

We figured maybe we ought to have a proper church wedding—renew our vows, reaffirm our commitment to our new city, have a priest bless this crazy union of ours.

So, after the Easter Vigil Mass that Saturday evening in April 2010, we got married all over again at St. Stephen's Catholic Church on Napoleon Avenue.

Some of my sisters and cousins came down, along with a few friends, but it was a low-key ceremony. We said our vows, grabbed a bite to eat and came on home.

About two days later, I get a call from one of my sisters, who's pretty dramatic anyway, and she says, "My God, you're not going to believe this." She'd been going through some old papers, and she found our grandparents' marriage certificate. "They were married in April of 1910, at St. Stephen's," she said.

My jaw dropped. Without having the slightest clue, we had gotten married—or remarried, I suppose—in the same church, at the same altar, one hundred years to the month after my grandparents. Unbelievable.

I knew that my grandmother, Pearl Slangerup (who everyone called Lala), had grown up in the Carrollton neighborhood of New Orleans, not too far from Palmer Park. I'd always assumed she and my grandfather, Louis Arthur Carville (known as Pa), got married at Mater Dolorosa, the Catholic church right around the corner from her house. St. Stephen's was several miles away.

I don't know how to explain exactly what it meant that Mary and I came along a century later and said our vows at that same altar. But I know it sent shivers down our spines, and I know it reminded me once again just how friggin' deep my roots run here.

MARY

FOR MY BIRTHDAY the year of Marriage Three, Monsignor Nalty presented me with a work of his own handicraft, among my most cherished gifts of all time. He mounted and framed our marriage certificate side by side with James's grandparent's. Before I even had a chance to hang Monsignor's masterpiece, James absconded with it and hung it prominently in *his* office! Events such as these make me say almost every day now, "There are no coincidences."

JAMES

IN MY OFFICE AT HOME, I now have two framed marriage certificates hanging side by side, both from St. Stephen's Catholic Church.

Louis Arthur Carville & Pearl Slangerup, April 1910.
James Carville & Mary Matalin, April 2010.

9.

Changes in Washington, and What Never Does

JAMES

I READ MARK LEIBOVICH'S BOOK, *This Town*, which focuses on what an incestuous, opportunistic place official Washington can be. It's a fair critique, and probably a book that needed to be written.

But many of the people he focuses on aren't the people who are really at the center of what's wrong with Washington. The Bob Barnetts and Tammy Haddads and Mike Allens might contribute to the inbred, superficial nature of Washington, but they aren't harming the country.

The real obstructionists, the people doing the real harm, are the ones whose names never show up in the society pages. They're the lobbyists and other deal makers who are helping to write bad legislation that helps the rich get richer or who are helping to kill efforts that might hurt the bottom line of corporate America while actually helping normal people. So much of it comes down to the god-awful amount of money that is spent by special interests in Washington.

I don't know who the top three lobbyists are at the American Petroleum Institute. Or the top three lobbyists at the Financial Services Roundtable. I don't necessarily know who is in the room when they're writing stuff alongside congressional staffers or when they're meeting with people at various government agencies. And that's the point. These are the people who are actually running the country.

MARY

THE POLITICAL CLICHÉ "If you want a friend in Washington, get a dog" has survived the decades for good reason, and the acts of betrayal and disappointment in Washington are numerous, notorious and even evil. These make for good stories, juicy takedowns in the media, and perpetuate an image that Washington largely deserves (and which I've discussed at length, maybe too much, in the why-the-hell-did-we-want-to-move explanation earlier in the book). But what you don't hear—almost ever—are that political friends can be among the most generous and loyal. These consistent (and not random) acts of kindness rarely get remarked upon or are lost in the quagmire of negativity.

Sometimes politicos will even request that you not publicly share some generous act of theirs—for fear it may tarnish the badass reputation they are trying so diligently to cultivate and nurture. Another reason they may not want selflessness and service to others to be made publicly known is that it's so easy for that to look self-promotional and personally aggrandizing.

There is no one who appears by name in this book who hasn't been the giver of thoughtful gifts, kindnesses and support in times of need, usually unsolicited. And there are plenty more unnamed.

You don't hear or read about the private visits to sick or depressed friends, or the support to the families of lost colleagues or all-night vigils with colleagues in crisis for whatever reason. You don't hear about the job and career help, food and board when friends are down and out, or loans exchanged during the many campaign droughts, which no one ever expects will be repaid and would be offended if they were. This sort of thing happens interparty, intraparty, cross party and even between the adversarial politico and media types. These are the gestures, the ties, the acts of true friendship between people that you hear least about—and that keep the whole crazy culture glued together.

And while I am a fan of Mark Leibovich personally and professionally, and confess to being as titillated as everyone else with his takedowns, one of the things I didn't like about *This Town* is how it makes all kindness and true connection between Washington friends look suspect—as if there were no such thing. *This Town* is an extraordinarily insightful presentation of the ugly side of that town, but the place is not as completely one-dimensional as you might have been led to believe. I am pretty sure Mark knows this, because he is a genuinely good guy and understands the sometimes unattractive accommodations necessitated by the rough-and-tumble of politics. People enter public service and politics for many reasons—and quite a lot of them are good. And the friendships created in D.C. are not *all* transactional. They can be real, and true and of pure motive.

JAMES

STARTING OUT, most people who run for president or Congress have a well-placed contempt for Washington and its ways. It doesn't really matter if you're on the right or the left. You run for office because you have a grievance or a long list of grievances that probably are pretty well founded.

That clearly was true with George W. Bush and Barack Obama. They never really liked Washington. They never really embraced it. But by the same token, they were both defeated by Washington in a lot of ways. They both got some of the things they wanted done. Bush got his tax cuts. Obama got health care. But they also both encountered massive opposition to any meaningful change.

The real distinction between Obama and Hillary Clinton during the 2008 campaign was not on the issues. If you took any ten issues, they basically agreed on at least nine of them. The main difference was the argument each made for getting elected. Hillary's message was "I've been around this place.

I know it. I can work the system and cut through a lot of the crap. Maybe I'm not all warm and fuzzy, but I'm the kind of person you need in there to deal with tough things." Obama's message was "I'm going to transcend Washington. I'm going to change the culture of Washington." So you had this classic confrontation between somebody who says, "I can work within the system to get things done," and somebody who says, "I can fly above the system. I can alter it."

If I heard this two times, I must have heard it a thousand times. Even good friends of mine would say, "James, I'm a Democrat. I like Bill Clinton. I was for him both times. I think Hillary's great. But we're not going to get anything done if she's elected because they're just going to drag up the same old fights. Obama is going to be fresh, and he's going to be able to work with people and is not going to have all of that baggage." And I was like: Do you really believe that shit? Am I really hearing this from you? They'd say, "We just have to turn the page."

Smart, well-meaning, patriotic people would say that stuff, and it was like you were an asshole if you argued with them. You wanted to say: How exactly is this guy going to come here and change anything? You think that all these Republicans are going to change? You think these lobbyists and all the other interests are going to stop fighting you tooth and nail? You think groups like the NRA are going to change one whit?

It became pretty clear right after Obama got into office that he wasn't going to change shit, and neither is anybody else. Not because of the individual. Not because Obama was dishonest about it or that he didn't really think that he could. I think he and the people around him really thought they could change Washington and genuinely wanted to, but when they realized that wasn't going to happen, they failed to engage it on its own terms.

I think it was naïveté. You get into office and you realize the sheer number and the sheer strength of all the barriers that are in place. Congress is a real force. You can't pass anything unless you go through this committee chairman or that Speaker of the House. And that same guy—because the place is basically run by special-interest groups—is really cautious about not pissing off the lobbyists he's going to go make a gazillion dollars for when he gets out of office. The incentives are screwed up in all kinds of ways, but that's the reality that a president has to confront. It's a fact of life.

Listen, I sympathize with Obama. He's saved the auto industry. He's gotten us out of these cockamamie wars. He killed bin Laden. And still, total and utter gridlock. He can't get any legislation passed. Virtually none of his appointments get confirmed. A lot of people on Capitol Hill exist solely to see him fail. But that's also a fact of life as president.

I remember back in the spring of 1993, when Clinton had just taken office and was trying to get an economic stimulus package through Congress, and it was kind of languishing in partisan gridlock on Capitol Hill. I remember Cokie Roberts going on air one day and being asked if Bill Clinton could end "business as usual" in Washington. She said something along the lines of "There's only one way that business is conducted in Washington, and that is 'as usual.'"

I remember thinking, *Goddamn. She's exactly right.* Because she'd seen it, again and again and again.

It's sad. It's depressing. But it's true. On some level, every president has tried. They come into office, and they're going to show Washington how to operate, and it lasts all of about a day. The difference is, unlike Bush or Obama, Bill Clinton adapted to it. He took the time to learn the system and try to game it.

I do believe that you can effectuate change. When Bill Clinton left Washington, you could hardly think of something in the country that wasn't better in January of 2001 than it was in January of 1993. But the one thing he didn't do was change the culture of Washington. He dealt with the culture the way it was. Sometimes you can game it, sometimes you can negotiate with it, sometimes you can do an end run around it.

But you cannot change it.

MARY

IN *ALL'S FAIR*, I breathlessly recounted how cutting-edge the 1992 campaign was, with our amazing "blast" fax machine that could reach one hundred supporters simultaneously. The campaign's *one* twenty-pound cell phone was another wonder of the modern age, and which James likes to remember as being bigger than George Stephanopoulos (inarguably the most handsome man in modern politics, which was a fundamental change at the time).

Twenty years later, nothing has changed. It is another universally unquestioned scripture of political gospel that Information Age technology has been a game changer when, in truth, technology has only made the game faster and more expensive.

Sure, an exponentially greater number of activists can scream and screech 24/7, but they are bellowing about the same stuff, if a darker version. There is arguably more political disinformation than policy truth speeding through the vapors.

The one thing that really did alter the political landscape, a truly transformative game changer, was ushered in by the most antiquated of twentieth-century information technologies: the radio.

Before Rush Limbaugh, there was no conservative sound system. There were erudite magazines and a handful of unusually gifted political orators who could be informative and influential, but their reach was infinitesimal compared to El Rushbo's.

His example spawned legions of common-sense talkers and transformed both the radio industry and political broadcasting in general. His daily enlightenment—making the incomprehensible clear and exposing political posturing and fraud with brilliance and hilarity—informed and empowered a citizenry that would have otherwise lost their grip on reality. Not to mention their constitutional rights.

Rush was my personal sanity ground zero in 1992. Almost single-handedly, he ushered in the first GOP House majority in half a century in 1994, and kept conservatives from mass suicide in 1996. He continues to inspire and move political mountains. I don't know how it is possible, but he is even smarter and funnier and more fearless today than he was when he brought us conservatives back from the precipice of extinction and out of a political desert.

No technology, no computerized algorithms, no crowd sourcing, no microtargeting, no fleeting political flavor of the day could do or has done what this amazing American has to save this great country from the desperate aspirations of the loony left. And no one gives the far-left lunatics more gas pains. Day after day. Year after year.

JAMES

THE REPUBLICAN PARTY HAS really changed in recent years. It has moved decidedly and decisively to the right. It's a different party from the one Bill Clinton faced. The Newt Gingriches who were involved in the Republican "revolution" back in the 1990s are nothing compared to these guys today.

At every juncture, the party has moved further and further and further to the right. There's no doubt about that. The transformation has picked up speed, if anything, in the last few years in Washington. The center of gravity has moved way off-kilter.

I've used this analogy before, but it's like Lester Maddox once famously said, "The problem with the Georgia prisons is the quality of the inmates. If we could just get some better inmates."

There seems to be this idea that if only Republicans had better statesmen, better leaders, everything would be fine. The problem is the people who vote in the Republican primaries. They're not looking for a statesman. They don't want to send somebody to Washington to transcend the partisan divide. Fifty-nine percent of the Republicans who say their party is going off on the wrong track think it's not conservative *enough*. This idea that small-minded, dug-in, ideological, fanatical Republican politicians are leading the party down a bad path is not the whole story. No. Small-minded, ideological-driven Republican voters are doing it.

Why can't we have leaders like we used to? Well, why can't we have voters like we used to?

The Republicans were pretty intransigent under Gingrich, but there were still people willing to deal and to govern. They didn't do too much dealing in

'95, and they didn't really start dealing until they screwed up on the government shutdown and Clinton had the upper hand, and he basically got most everything that he wanted. But even Gingrich came to the realization that votes are votes and they didn't have enough of them.

Not now. The current Republicans in Congress have to be against anything the Democrats are trying to do. If they actually agreed with Obama on anything, they'd all lose in their next primary. You see it happen again and again and again. And there's no evidence that they're going to change. Take last fall's government shutdown, for instance. They decided they would close down the federal government for the first time in seventeen years and furlough 800,000 public servants—for what? Because they simply didn't like a law that tries to extend health insurance to millions of uninsured Americans. A law, by the way, that was passed by Congress, signed by the president and upheld by the Supreme Court. All three branches of government signed off on it, and the country reelected the president who championed it. But because a handful of Republicans decided they didn't like it, they'd rather burn the whole house down.

I think 80 percent of what's wrong in the country is all contained in the Republican Party. I really do. And I don't say that because I'm a Democrat. I wouldn't be surprised if some average Republicans actually agree with me. The 1 percent is becoming more and more powerful economically and politically. I mean, they're really running the country now, and that's not a good thing.

If you go back to the start of the century, conservatives have been massively wrong about almost everything. There's something about the conservative mind that the more wrong they are, the harder they dig in. You can see it on the question of quantitative easing or the Obama stimulus package. You can see it on tax cuts and the deficit, on "global cooling" and any number of other issues.

If you still argue that invading Iraq was a good idea, or that quantitative easing in a depressed economy is going to cause high interest rates or that cutting taxes for rich people helps Joe the Plumber, you're beyond reason.

For whatever reasons, conservatives these days also take great pride in never reading anything from liberal media outlets—or, for that matter, straightforward, down-the-middle media outlets. It's part of their culture.

If I bragged to one of my liberal friends that I'd never listened to Rush Limbaugh or watched Fox News, or that I never read the *Wall Street Journal* editorial page, that would not be cool. The first question would be "Aren't you curious to see what they're saying over there?" Similarly, if you were at a liberal or progressive party and someone said something like that, the natural response would be "What are you afraid of?" I'll argue with certainty that liberals tend to read way more conservative literature than conservatives will ever read of liberal literature.

They view it as some sort of weakness to be exposed to another viewpoint, like you're going to be corrupted if you have to listen to other people's views. I do have a theory on this. I believe conservatives view their principles as the "Truth." There is a truth. They've figured it out. And it can't be diluted or questioned or compromised. But their "truth" so often turns out to be false.

Liberals are much more nuanced than that, sometimes painfully so. We can see six sides to the Pentagon. But that's preferable to being so dogmatic that you wear blinders. Like John Maynard Keynes said, "When the facts change, I change my mind."

Progressives would say that there is one economic policy that you pursue at a given time in a business cycle, and a different approach under different circumstances. We're more able to say when we're wrong and evolve over time. We don't view being inflexible and doctrinal as a virtue. For example, being soft on crime was not very smart. We pretty much abandoned that position. Busing was well-intentioned, but I'm not sure it was a very big success.

Look, every country that I've ever worked in has some version of a traditionalist, government-skeptical, pro-business, mercantilist, nationalistic party. And, honestly, that's not an unattractive kind of thing to rally around. Can you have too many taxes? Sure. Can there be too much regulation? Of course. Some of it can be mind-bogglingly stupid. Should a party revere the country, its traditions, its past? Absolutely. Is it better for people to grow up in stable, two-parent families? Yes. Is there sort of a correlation between some of this and church attendance? Yeah, I think so. Is there reason to be skeptical of academics proposing radical change? Yes.

But the stuff that they're wrong about—and it's an ever-growing list—they're never able to admit. They are the party that can't ever find the courage to say, "We screwed up."

What certainly has changed over time is how politicians get themselves sent to Washington, especially those trying to become president. Campaigns change over time. That's just the business. A lot of the basic principles remain, but the methods and the technology evolve.

The night before Bill Clinton's election in 1992—this was captured in the documentary *The War Room*—I gave a teary-eyed speech to a roomful of staffers and told them that we had changed the way campaigns are run. "Used to be, there was a hierarchy," I said that night. "If you were on one floor, you didn't go to another floor. If you were somewhere on an organizational chart, there was no room for you [anywhere else]. Everybody was compartmentalized."

I was proud then of how we had shaken up the old way people did things. I'm even more proud of it now because I see how that approach has endured over the years. I hope that part of my legacy in politics will be that I had the wisdom to recognize that within a political campaign, as within almost any organization, the very smartest and best ideas should rise to the top, not just the ideas of certain "important" people.

From the time I began working on campaigns, long before Clinton came along, I had one hallmark: I never wanted an office. Mainly, it was because I didn't want to have meetings. They're usually a waste of time. They're unproductive. So I always had my desk out in the open. If you were on the campaign and you wanted to ask me something, you could come over and ask me.

My theory always was, if you're part of a campaign, whether you're the deputy campaign manager or the guy opening the mail, I'm going to tell you exactly what's going on because what we do here is not a secret. We're actually in the business of disseminating information. It's not supposed to be secret. I'll tell you what our polls are showing; I'll tell you how I think we're doing.

And if you have something to say to me or an idea to pitch, come tell me. Anybody is welcome to listen in; anybody can have his voice heard. If I can't trust the people in that room, then who can I trust?

For so long, campaigns were run like big, lumbering corporations. There was a floor for the financial people, a floor for the strategists, a floor for the advance team. The real power might be concentrated on the sixth floor, but maybe you worked down on the fourth floor and your ideas never got heard. What bullshit. A campaign should not work like an insurance company. We really changed all that during the Clinton campaign. We flattened out the hierarchy and the infrastructure. And what we learned was that people can be trusted. You don't need to hide things from people working for you. Also, a good idea can emanate from any direction. To pretend that only a few top people have all the knowledge in any organization is a failure of imagination and leadership.

I've watched plenty of campaigns come and go since then. Some have taken that approach to heart more than others. Some have maybe even done better at it than we did. But they have all recognized the value of it on some level.

MARY

LIGHT-YEARS AGO IN terms of politics—in the 1980s and most of the 1990s—the media covering Washington really went crazy when they were called "liberal" or "conservative." Those labels were the exclusive provinces of opinion columnists. Today, it seems almost quaint when you hear journalists protest accusations of partisanship. Some political reporters still make a big to-do about not voting at all, or they volunteer their independent leanings, or they give disproportionate coverage to "no-label" or any bipartisan policy or political effort that ends up, more often than not, producing an inconsequential impact.

In truth, there actually are a handful of truly nonpartisan reporters, but it's a dying breed.

I'll never forget the first time I saw a poll on the media that quantified what I already knew by living with them. Eighty-nine percent of journalists self-identified as liberal. I was surprised. Who were the 11 percent who confessed to not being liberal?

As annoying as it is to the public, I much prefer today's open partisanship of the media. Nothing produced more hair pulling, breast thumping and chain-smoking in GOP camps than reporters professing no bias while reporting like Democratic operatives. Now at least, the Chris Matthews ilk just let their freak flags fly and I don't have to pretend like they're not crazy. It's kind of irksome that conservative media keep trying to be fair and balanced. Do you ever see even a *scintilla* of fair and balanced reporting on MSNBC (with the possible exception of Joe Scarborough on some topics)?

Anyway, the topic of "bias in the media" has been so hashed over, it's too boring to even think about anymore. But what continues to make me wish I still chain-smoked is the unremitting double standard, how the media swarmed on the Dan Quayle "potatoe" incident or the glee with which it hashed over Sarah Palin's geographic proximity to Russia. Yet, Barack Obama can repeatedly pronounce the "p" in Marine Corps—or redraw the map of the USA with South Carolina, Georgia and Jacksonville, Florida, in the Gulf of Mexico—and he's applauded for his brilliant insights.

Maybe it's not a double standard; maybe it's just a reflection of the disintegrating state of our education system.

The press will counter they put President and Hillary Clinton through their media meat grinder, but without the existence of some irresistible, salacious details, the Clintons wouldn't have gotten any of the treatment Republicans expect as standard operating procedure.

And in any event, the Clintons now enjoy a star treatment that you wouldn't want to hold your breath waiting for Bush or Cheney to get. A variation on the theme is the media's portraying Biden's dufus-osity as the lovable John Belushi and Cheney as the demonic Darth Vader.

Along with political bias, agenda bias is increasing at the same velocity. How often do you sit around the dinner table talking about reproductive rights or global warming, to pick just two recurring media all-time hits? And how much better would it be for your family, and the country, if equal attention was paid to public pension fund fraud or the irrefutable mandatory entitlement spending death spiral?

The good thing is—and in all things, per my mother, there always is a silver lining—the bias got so blatant and obnoxious and detached from reality, it produced two tectonic shifts in political reportage. The public lost trust in the mainstream media while conservatives and other inhabitants of "Realville" (where Rush Limbaugh reigns as mayor) broke out of their own parallel universe.

The advent of Information Age technology accelerated the public's ability to get some real and true and relevant info. It is no longer completely impossible to get a grip on what's really going on. And find some ideas about what to do about it. Or get connected to like-minded sane people. How is this so awful? It isn't. It's not clear our media environment is what he had in mind, but I hold with Thomas Jefferson's "Where the press is free and every man able to read, all is safe."

This new, almost-even playing field spawned a new generation of political and public information entrepreneurs. With Drudge and Rush blazing the trail, the route to practical truth quickly expanded. Now the *Daily Caller, Redstate, NRO, Transom, Instapundit*, and a plethora of online common-sense policy experts are giving normal people regular access to normal information, that is, info relevant to their daily lives and critical to preparing for their futures. They can now also rediscover our history, long lost to the revisions, distortions and/or denial by progressives (who truly believe they know best and are oh-so-smarter than you), from fearless patriots like Glenn Beck and Mark Levin.

For you liberals and lefty bloggers who live to demonize, can you identify one time, just one, when your rendition of a conservative utterance wasn't taken out of context or flat-out fabricated?

Have you ever found the covey of racist Tea "Baggers" that populates your ugly fantasy world?

Have you ever considered for a nanosecond that the female, black, Hispanic, gay—or any other conservative Americans you artificially hyphenate—aren't all sellout toadies?

I will never forget in the mid-1980s being asked by a media maven if I had "ever met an *evangelical*." She had the same tone you'd use if you were asking a person if they'd been exposed to the Ebola virus. You'd think that twenty years would be enough time to get over this kind of thing, but I was just as disgusted when a reporter in the first Obama midterm cycle asked, in the same creepy tone, if I had "ever met anyone from the Tea Party."

I'm sure these observations just reinforce the notion that I am hopelessly biased myself. So let me clarify my perspective: there are plenty of good people in journalism and bad people in political activism. There are fine Democrats and goofy Republicans. Just as there are good cops and bad cops; a handful of sick priests sprinkled among a legion of decent men of faith; hardworking public servants and trough-sucking government parasites; authentic discrimination fighters and money-grubbing victim hustlers; life-enhancing investors and Bernie Madoffs.

Therein lies the essential beauty of conservatism: you are obliged to judge each person on individual merit. So rather than gripe about generic, generalized "ugly partisanship," I prefer to expend my emotional outrage on individual jerks.

JAMES

WHAT DOESN'T CHANGE OFTEN enough is what happens when the election is over and the candidate is now the officeholder. What gets talked about most on the campaign trail seldom is what gets talked about most in Washington.

In short, Washington too often ignores the middle class. That's way more true for Republicans, of course, but both parties bear a measure of guilt.

During the 2012 election, like in almost any election, you heard a whole lot about the middle class. "I'm going to do this for the middle class; I'm going to do that for the middle class," the candidates said. It's all about the middle class.

Except that as soon as the election's over, what are the biggest issues that everybody talks about in Washington? Immigration, gay marriage, guns, NSA spying and on and on. I'm not saying they're not important to society. I have a position on all those topics; almost everybody does. To a certain number of people, each of those issues is incredibly important. But to the great masses of people in the country, those issues are ancillary to their daily lives.

Most people who have a gun don't own a thirty-round clip with it. They're law-abiding citizens who have no problem undergoing a background check. Most people are not directly impacted by gay marriage. They might have a gay cousin or a gay friend. I understand if you're gay and you want to get married, it's a huge deal—I'm totally with you. No one's for that more than I am. But it doesn't affect most people. Immigration? By and large, most Americans don't spend their days mulling over our immigration policy. In a macro sense, immigration affects wages and employment, but that's not what gets talked about when people discuss immigration.

I'm not saying that all these issues aren't significant, that they shouldn't be written about and debated. What I'm saying is that if you live somewhere in the middle of Ohio, for example, you're just not that affected by these things on a daily basis. These are not the topics that keep you up nights. So it's no wonder the debate in Washington feels so completely disconnected.

Most people spend a lot more time worrying about how to make ends meet, how to care for their families and hold on to their jobs. Too many folks have seen their incomes either fall or stay stuck in neutral, seen their net worth and retirement savings evaporate, seen their college-educated kids, unable to find work, move home again. If you're one of those people, nobody in power in Washington these days ever has anything to say to you about your life and about what's going to happen to people like you in the future.

That guy in Ohio—and millions and millions of people like him in the country—have had an absolutely gut-wrenching time in recent years, and they're not even part of the conversation in Washington. So you can understand the anger and frustration people feel in the wake of the financial crisis and why those feelings continue to linger.

The Wall Street bankers, they were irresponsible and greedy and reckless. Their actions directly hurt people and cost them their life savings. What they did knocked the shit out of that guy in Ohio. Just flattened him. It's like they took a big truck and ran right over him, and then said, "Wasn't our fault. Nothing to see here." If you're the guy who got run over, you feel like the only people who suffered were people like you, and there were no consequences for those actually responsible. And that's pretty much true.

As if that's not bad enough, a lot of what that same guy hears from Washington is about potentially cutting his Social Security, raising the retirement age, cutting his Medicare so that we can have a flatter tax on people who make more than a million dollars a year, and simplifying the corporate tax code. He's told over and over again that spending is out of control and we need to cut the budget. He's told that if you simplify corporate taxes and cut taxes on the rich his life is actually going to get better. Of course, he was told that in 1981. He was told that in 2001. And he's been lied to again and again. His life is not going to get better if you reduce his Social Security while cutting taxes on rich people.

Too often, the narrative in Washington is this: the United States has become an "entitlement state," and the country is on the way to going broke unless we deal with this crisis immediately. We are led to believe there are all these irresponsible people out there who don't pay in sufficiently and who take too much out, and if we don't do something about that, we're all doomed. That's the narrative, but it's not the truth. What about every fuckup that cost the country billions and billions of dollars, such as the Iraq War? Who's responsible for all that waste? Not the guy in Ohio.

Despite the messages they hear coming out of Washington, people in Middle America don't actually believe they're part of the problem, and they're right. Why would they think they're the problem when they see bankers loading up on 35-to-1 leverage? Why would they think they're the problem when they see their government sending their sons and daughters overseas with no idea how they're ever going to bring them back?

One way for Washington to win back public support is, first of all, to stop lying to people. Just level with them and say, "Look, we need to make some changes to Social Security to keep it on solid ground over the long haul. We might adjust the retirement age or tweak the benefits. But any money we save will go back into shoring up Social Security. It's not going to be used to pay for any war. It's not going to be used to pay for tax cuts. It's not going to be used to pay for anything else."

The net effect might be the same, but it would be communicating with people in a way that respects them and the lives they lead, as opposed to telling them that they're another taker in the entitlement state.

I sincerely believe that part of the problem is that so many of the people in positions of power in Washington truly, utterly, do not understand the struggles of average people. They literally can't wrap their minds around the battles ordinary people have to fight every single day, like finding child care for their kids or trying to hold on to their health care or living paycheck to paycheck because groceries and gas keep getting more expensive while wages haven't budged.

For years, we've conducted focus groups through Democracy Corps. We go throughout the country and talk to people about their lives and their finances and what's really affecting them. And you never do one where literally somebody doesn't break down crying.

It's always that times got so hard they had to move in with one of their kids, or one of their kids moved in with them. Or they're working two jobs just to scrape by. Or they're one disease away from bankruptcy. And maybe the most depressing part is when you poll these same people, they almost always say that they see no chance of things getting better in the next year. They don't see anyone in Washington who has an actual plan to improve their lives in the foreseeable future.

You look around, and you realize: these are people we all know. These are not whiners and complainers. These are decent, hardworking people. People you went to high school with. People you go to church with. People who made it through college and raised families. People who had real dreams, even very modest dreams, that have now mostly vanished. Maybe they were going to retire, head down to Florida and get a simple 1,200-square-foot condo two miles from the beach. And here they are, sixty years old, wrestling with heart trouble or diabetes or cancer, having lost a job or working double shifts. And that's it. That's their life. It's not just that they don't want the government to cut Social Security or Medicare, it's that, in many cases, this help is all that stands between them and the abyss.

After you sit there and hear these tales of genuine struggle, it makes your blood boil when you hear some Republican back in Washington saying, "Well, you know, some people in this world, they just don't work hard enough; they don't pull their weight," or "We're just going to have to make some hard choices."

Well, fuck you. Excuse me if I'm not all out in front on that deal. The hard choices we should be making are the ones to build and fund better schools, to put more money into community colleges, to create tons of new jobs rebuilding our roads and bridges and airports. Hard choices like not wasting billions of dollars and thousands of lives on stupid wars and unnecessary tax cuts. Our priorities are so screwed up as a nation.

The politicians and pundits in Washington—and I include myself in this—we too often live from event to event. This next vote on Capitol Hill. The next election. The latest stock market numbers. The latest scandal. The latest jobs report. The latest terrorist threat. Meanwhile, some very significant and very disturbing problems are unfolding in the country. The infrastructure's crumbling. Incomes are stagnant. The Earth's getting warmer. None of those things drive ratings like the crisis of the day. But it doesn't make them any less of a crisis.

The fragility of the middle class in America qualifies as a major crisis. But you wouldn't know that by the listening to a lot of the debate in Washington. To his credit, President Obama has talked about the woes of average Americans far more often than his predecessor did. He's tried to jump-start domestic manufacturing and put more money toward rebuilding our crumbling infra-structure. But the Republicans in Congress have blocked those efforts at nearly every turn, and the White House often gets distracted with other prior-ities and partisan battles.

We spend so much time and energy in Washington talking about fiscal re-sponsibility and the need to cut budgets and make "tough" decisions. Where's the federal Office of the Middle Class? Where's the think tank called the Insti-tute for Middle Class Studies? Where are the endowed professorships focused solely on the middle class?

In an election year, everybody talks a good game about helping the middle class. But after the polls close, there's no longer a sense of urgency. Washing-ton has a way of forgetting a lot of promises to a lot of people.

MARY

WHEN I STARTED OUT, campaign operatives and political junkies were a proud and motley crew of true believers. You labored on campaigns be-cause nothing mattered more than getting your candidates elected so they could enact polices reflecting your worldview. No one worked on campaigns or at the party committees to make money or launch a career. In fact, a lot of people populating campaigns interrupted their real ca-reers to pitch in.

Campaign operations provided neither a glamorous job nor an attrac-tive lifestyle. There wasn't much of a paycheck or many postcampaign employment prospects beyond another campaign, if you were lucky and so disposed and had proved yourself capable on the prior one. The world was pretty cloistered: everyone knew everyone else and no one in the normal world had a clue what went on inside a campaign bubble.

I laughed out loud watching the Richard Gere movie *Power* about a slick campaign guru in the 1980s. The expensive clothes, the private plane, the ubiquitous chicks. Okay, there is a fair amount of action on campaigns, but it's usually no more than fly-by relationships of convenience. But when I was in the trenches of politics in those days, nobody dressed like that, looked like that or lived that way.

Conversely, I was mesmerized by the realistic and surreal inside-the-bubble accounts of the 1972 campaign, *The Boys on the Bus* by Timothy Crouse and *Fear and Loathing: On the Campaign Trail '72* by Hunter S. Thompson. The best fly-on-the-wall campaign account, hands down, is Richard Ben Cramer's *What It Takes: The Way to the White House*, which gives the reader an almost hour-by-hour seat at the 1988 campaign. Amazing writing. Even better reporting. Sheer genius.

These wonderful works of journalism capture a paradigm shift in campaigns and the coverage of them, but there has been a subsequent cultural shift in campaigns that is just as dramatic.

What changed in politics is that it's now a full-time player in a media-driven culture of personality.

In the "old days," even though everyone was in the same bunker on the campaign trail, a staffer's name appearing in print was grounds for termination. Individuals who were suspected of unauthorized leaking were ostracized. The only way a person outside a campaign could know what really went on inside was to join a campaign and be there—or cover one. As revealing as Crouse's and Thompson's books were, much was left unreported.

Starting around the 1988 campaign, behind-the-scenes campaign stories started emerging not so much because they were relevant to the voter but because they were entertaining. And maybe because of the irresistibly colorful personalities involved, like Lee Atwater, or because a larger percentage of the political press and campaign honchos were of the same generation and they were all fascinated by each other, or maybe because a unique story line fulfilled some strategic imperative, such as demonstrating how modern your campaign was by parading all the women operatives in front of the press. This required a look behind the curtain, even if it was all staged.

By 1992, when Cramer's ultimate behind-the-scenes book appeared, a shift had taken place. Campaigns routinely provided stock footage for documentaries, and D. A. Pennebaker's *The War Room*, starring James and George Stephanopoulos, was nominated for an Academy Award.

And that's the norm now. Today, political dramas are the stuff of HBO specials, special-release Netflix series, feature films and countless books. And although so much of it is totally wrong and inauthentic, viewers think they know more about campaigns and the people who live them than they do about their neighbors and friends.

The upshot of politics becoming a made-for-TV endeavor in the Cult of Personality Era, like every other subject/person in this era, is both positive and negative. On the upside, campaigns and the antics of the offbeat people who populate them can be highly entertaining when authentically rendered. And the (overly) glamorized rendition of the field has attracted new blood to what had been a pretty insular business.

The influx of "professionals" and "specialists" into the political field that was until recently a cottage industry is now mega-BIG business. While improved professionalism can be a good thing, on the downside, politics pursued as a career rather than a passion has a mitigating impact on the ethic of loyalty and commitment to a candidate and/or cause that previously animated the field.

I was having a spur-of-the-moment dinner with a couple of political household names recently and as is always the case with longtime foxhole buddies, we got to telling old war stories. After we ran through our "classic" stories—some glorious, some devastating, many hilarious—we started comparing notes on the career trajectory of operatives today.

This was not a bunch of old fogies, lamenting a bygone era. But we couldn't help but be saddened by an increasing trend in our beloved field. While we would crawl over cut glass in rush hour for our candidates, today's operatives are like free agents in football. The animating motivation is less loyalty to a team than a personal career. There's nothing wrong with procuring super deals and salaries or even jumping teams, but putting your self-interest above your candidate's is not a good thing.

And it can often result in what used to be considered unethical, if not downright immoral, behaviors and activities.

Ultimately, the wheat is separated from the chaff. Good candidates and good operatives will find each other, but another fallout of Cult of Personality politics is truly destructive in the short and long term. Namely, way too much of the relentless, instant in-depth scrutiny and publicity politics and politicians receive in the Information Age is false, ugly, ignorant, uninformed and decontextualized. This kind of coverage—the reportorial proctology—repels many good people from actively engaging in politics. Solid citizens who have so much to contribute recoil from politics for fear some ancient youthful experience will become the narrative for their entire life; or that some overdramatized misstep will upend their own and their families' lives. The "Where do I go to get my reputation back?" syndrome is less difficult to deal with than it used to be, but it's always a disheartening, destructive and often expensive undertaking. Just observing good people unfairly getting the bejesus kicked out of them also repulses the kind of informed voters necessary for a flourishing and healthy democracy.

A less destructive but still negative consequence of politics-as-business is the institutionalization of perverse incentives. "Politics is showbiz for ugly people" used to be a funny truth; now it's frequently a repellent one. Gratuitous provocateurs and flat-out crazy people get more coverage than sensible, thoughtful, earnest policy makers. Vacuous cleverness trumps boring sincerity.

For good or ill, the other by-product of politics as entertainment is TV punditry. And yes, I can imagine how laughably hypocritical this might all seem—for me to comment on the plethora of TV pundits today, having supped at that table a time or two. Believe me, I'm laughing with you. And I am just trying to point out a change over the last two decades—to paraphrase my dear friend Donna Brazile—qualification for the opining business should be more than just having once voted!

JAMES

I DO THINK I'VE GOTTEN more conservative in some ways as I've gotten older.

I think it's much better that people get married and stay married. I think kids are far better off if there are two parents in the house. I'm persuaded by the argument that you can change things too fast, that society has to build on tradition to some extent. Certainly, the whole Iraq/Afghanistan adventure has made me much more skeptical of intervention than I used to be. I'm not all that keen about legalizing marijuana everywhere.

Maybe some of that is just a generational thing. Maybe it's having children. I don't know. Personally, I think about it as being more *traditionalist* than being conservative in any political sense.

I do think a valid critique of Democrats or liberals is that we seldom look at the world through the eyes of the dry cleaner or the guy with the lawn-mowing service. I'm not saying that we hate business or anything like that. It's just that this perspective doesn't enter into our debate that much.

If I were a Democrat running for office, I'd make sure to spend time inside small businesses—a limousine service, a deli, a lawn-mowing service, a software company—just to see how regulation affects them.

Not that the dry cleaner shouldn't have to follow environmental regulations. That's not what I'm suggesting at all. But it's a hard thing to do, to go out and set up a business. Maybe there's a way to make that person's life a little easier.

Don't get me wrong. Good regulation is essential. What kills me about Wall Street is that these guys blew up the whole world and they actually thought we'd bail them out and move on. Their attitude was how dare you come in and regulate us. Just keep giving us interest-free money and let's move on.

We need strong regulation. For banks, for airlines, for any number of industries.

I became a little more conservative politically when I realized that once something gets written into law, once it's in the bloodstream, it's really hard to undo it. You've got to be careful before making big changes. That applies to wars. It applies to tax cuts. It applies to expanded government programs. Once you start something in Washington, it ain't going away for a long time. Sometimes, it lives forever.

I'LL TELL YOU WHAT I'm really liberal on: birth control. I'm not just for Planned Parenthood. I'm for Planned Parenthood in the schools. I'm not just for teenagers having access to the morning-after pill. I'm for giving it away.

I'm not going to change on that. Not one iota. Because here's something about which I'm pretty certain. Every effort ever designed in the history of the world to keep people from having sex has failed. It ain't gonna work. We have thousands and thousands of years of human experience to teach us that. People are not going to stop fucking. I'm sorry.

The abstinence-only crowd cracks me up. What a surprise that it doesn't work. Did you ever think that it would? What in the human condition would suggest to you that abstinence would be an effective strategy?

Let's recognize that bad things happen. They happen more than anybody would want. Teenagers have sex. Girls get pregnant. It's not ideal, but it is inevitable. The important thing is to have in place the kind of infrastructure to deal with it. That's a hell of a lot more useful than living in some fantasy world where sex doesn't exist.

MARY

JAMES AND I SHARE AN APPRECIATION, indeed a delight, for young people who want to have a career in politics. Given the histrionic preponderance of reporting on cynicism and corruption in politics (not to mention the dearth of history teaching), it is a wonder anyone under the age of the Dwight Eisenhower era has any interest in, let alone respect for, the political process.

James and I are proud of our work in the political arena. And for us, politics is still an honorable, even noble, calling. James never fails to tell young people, "You can be a rainmaker or get rained on," meaning basically: you don't play, you will pay.

I tend to stress "With rights, come responsibilities." We are all obliged to be stewards of our freedoms, guardians of our republic.

When the girls were little, I always took them to vote with me and never failed to get choked up as I cast my single vote. I wanted to impress on them the glory and necessity not just of voting, but of actively participating as a citizen.

There are many ways to participate in the political process, but for those young people who have been asking us for over twenty years now how to break into the political arena, here are some insights:

Don't do it for money.
Don't give in to the cynicism.
Don't burn bridges.
Don't backstab.
Don't fear failure.
Don't expect a return on every favor or good deed.
Don't worry about your career, only the race you are on.
Never ever lie to colleagues or reporters.
Trust your gut.
Be loyal to a fault.
Play hurt.
Stay in it to win it.
Prepare for sleep deprivation.
Be equal parts grateful and humble for victories.
Be equal parts honest and earnest about learning from losses.
Seek mentors and protect/support them unconditionally.
Take care of the underlings and volunteers.
Revere your foxhole buddies.
Remember liars and promise breakers.

Learn every campaign skill set.

Go deep on at least one *policy area you like.*

Keep your ears open and your mouth shut before getting the lay of the land.

JAMES

THERE'S MORE TRUTH TO this than either side would care to admit: Republicans tend to love specific human beings, but they don't care as much for humanity as a whole. Democrats often don't have a particular affection for individual human beings, but they care deeply for humanity.

What do I mean by that? Take Mitt Romney, for example. During the 2012 campaign, there were all these stories about Romney's kindness to specific folks, how he used his wealth to help people he knew were in need. I don't doubt any of the stories. But the policies he proposed would have ravaged the middle class, discriminated against gay people and generally hurt the poor and elderly.

Now, a lot of Democrats I've encountered over the years can be a little prickly, person-to-person, too. Paul Wellstone, the late, very liberal senator from Minnesota, was not a backslapping kind of guy. But he had this enormous affection for humanity and the human condition.

I don't think Franklin D. Roosevelt was particularly prone to go visit the dying or the old. But he cared deeply about the suffering of the most vulnerable in society. The New Deal happened because he cared about those at the bottom, not just those at the top.

Lyndon Johnson could be a real son of a bitch. He manipulated people and coerced people. But he did have a streak of courage and a conviction to help the poor and the oppressed. The Civil Rights Act. The War on Poverty. He wasn't necessarily a likable guy, but he cared deeply about righting the ills of society.

MARY

NORMAL PEOPLE ARE OCCASIONALLY hesitant to ask James or me a personal question, such as "How can you two lunatics stand each other?" but everyone is inexplicably interested in the lives of people who work in politics. So instead they ask us about people we know or have worked for—political celebrities, which I guess is what the political arena has now become. They want to know what Bill Clinton is "really" like. They want to know about Bush 41's health. They ask if Dick Cheney is really Darth Vader and Dr. Strangelove. They want to know all about Karl Rove or Maureen Dowd.

More generally, they'll ask me: "Are there any liberals you love?" My answer to this question varies. Sometimes I'll use it as an opportunity to make a larger philosophical point. I will say: "None." I don't love any modern liberals because they have totally bastardized classic liberalism, which was all about encouraging freedom and individualism, and building a society that tolerates a diversity of opinions. This goes all the way back to Socrates, the ancient Greek philosopher who believed there were ultimate truths, although nobody has a personal claim on them. The only way to get to an objective truth is by observing, verifying, listening to and comparing verifiable facts. Unlike what passes for debate today—trashing your opponent and fictionalizing his argument—in ancient Greece those antics were reserved for the theater.

Many of the liberals I knew twenty years ago embraced this idea. They talked *and* listened. They were open-minded, liberal in the best sense. But today's "progressive" liberals are different. They have no interest in debate. They're closed to any ideas beyond the hard left–sanctioned ones, which they've turned into a purity litmus test. There is only one point of view—theirs—and they will lay waste to anyone who disagrees with them, who doesn't frog-march in perfect unison to their principle-free and provably preposterous policies and programs. It's their way or the highway. I guess to their credit, they are straightforward about their political strategy: utter, complete and unrecoverable destruction. Their go-to tactic is to brand everyone who opposes them as haters and bigots.

Obvious to anyone beyond third grade, liberals have finely honed the tactic of emotionally attacking messengers rather than logically debating messages because it's easier to emote than explain. Of course, *there is no explanation* for pursuing and expanding policies and programs that have been exposed as demonstrable failures.

Failed outcomes are irrelevant to progressives; their template for success is good intent, *their* good intent. But what really cranks me up even more than the vile, stupid things progressives say and do is their habit of never subjecting themselves or their families to the destructive policies they foist on normal Americans. They wouldn't think of having their kids ground up and ill taught in the pubic school system they wrecked; and you won't see them wading through the incomprehensible Obamacare hustle they devised for their own health care.

I could go on, but you get the drift.

Sometimes I give a more personal answer to the question of whether there are liberals I love. I do love plenty of Democrats. (And not just one Chester James Carville.) Donna Brazile is one of my closest, dearest, soul-mate friends. When Donna and I talk politics—and, yes, we do—it's never about ideological purity. It's a real conversation, an open-ended back-and-forth. Neither of us claims to have all of the answers. And there are plenty of nonfamous liberals I love too, for similar reasons. If you could hear what these people say outside the hearing of the Liberal Mind Police, you'd like them too.

JAMES

IT MIGHT SURPRISE A LOT of people, but I've genuinely liked a lot of hardcore Republicans over the years, and not just my wife. I like Johnny Isakson, the senator from Georgia. Personally, I like Louisiana Governor Bobby

Jindal just fine. I like Sean Hannity. He's an affable guy. What you see is what you get.

A lot of the big Republican fund-raisers down in Louisiana I really like. I consider them good friends of mine. Hell, I convinced some of them to give money to Barbara Boxer in California.

I like Scooter Libby. He's a really personable guy. I think a lot of Ed Gillespie. He ran the Republican National Committee, worked in the Bush White House and advised Mitt Romney—that's like a trifecta of everything I'm against. But I think he's smart and motivated.

I actually don't even loathe Karl Rove. I've done a bunch of events with him, and we used to go at each other really hard over everything. I mean really hard—verbal body slamming. But he's also sort of grown on me over time.

I'll never understand how modern conservatives have managed to be massively and totally wrong about nearly everything since the turn of the century. Weapons of mass destruction, financial deregulation, abstinence-based education, the idea that tax cuts raise revenue, the exportation of American-style democracy, Terri Schiavo, creationism, self-deportation, global cooling, the notion that running a deficit is going to wreck the country, the IRS "scandal," Benghazi—they've just had a bad, bad century so far.

In the last century, they had their moments. Communism was evil, and they weren't afraid to say so. As I said, they were tougher on crime than many Democrats. Still, what is it about a modern political movement that contains likeable, educated people, but nevertheless is a) repeatedly wrong and b) completely incapable of any type of self-analysis or second-guessing?

That said, I don't think of Republicans as evil. The truth of the matter is, deep down inside—other than the ugly partisan experiences during the Clinton "scandals"—I'm really not too mad at anybody. It would be easier to list the people I *don't* like than the people I do. Most of the time, my experience has been that most Republicans are just wrong, as opposed to nefarious or ill intentioned.

That doesn't necessarily make it less of a problem, of course. We learned as a country during the Bush years that there's a real price for being wrong. That's why I keep fighting with them about all their boneheaded positions. But at the same time, it doesn't make them bad or malicious people. A lot of them are perfectly kind, honest human beings.

Those realities can exist simultaneously. It's an important truth to remember about politics, where it's so easy to always think of the other guy as nothing more than the enemy.

MARY

MY REFRAIN—AND BELIEF—IS that things don't change fundamentally. People are people. Human beings behave in the same ways—and have behaved in the same ways for centuries. But one change that happened in Washington while I was living there, at first gradually and then very rapidly, is that the sides were polarized not just on issues—but in personal ways too.

As the years in D.C. passed, James and I had fewer and fewer opportunities to socialize together. Our friends were bifurcated. The social events to which we were invited, or the parties we gave, were more divided, more partisan, and it was increasingly hard to find issues and causes that we could agree on—or even people we both liked. I'd throw a fund-raiser for a worthy conservative. James would have a fund-raiser for somebody he thought was a worthy liberal. And we didn't go to each other's parties.

10

Name Dropping, D.C.-Style

MARY

I'VE ALWAYS LIKED MANLY men and strong women. Of course, it all goes back to your parents and what they were like. My mom and dad were both tough, straightforward and hardworking. And maybe that's why I don't like mealymouthed, wussy wimps. I like strong people who take risks and don't wring their hands over it. I like decisive people who measure twice and cut once. When they make a decision, they've arrived at it through some logical, methodical process. And if there's a risk component to it, they have the testicular fortitude (and I mean that in a gender-free way) to take it and run with it.

Dick Cheney is everything I admire in a man and a leader. He embodies all the qualities you hope everyone engaged in public service would embody. Well, don't hold your breath. Because, while there are many unique and admirable people in politics and public service, only a handful are in Cheney's league.

He's steady, patient, prudent, consistently honest, good-humored and generous of spirit. He can work through an unanticipated, labyrinthine issue and all the related politics quicker than most people can figure out they have an issue.

And he's funny. He has a dry, wry, witty Oscar Wilde kind of humor. He can laugh at himself, and the Dr. Strangelove jokes and the whole Darth Vader skit on *Saturday Night Live*. One of our favorite end-of-day, on-the-way-home-from-wherever, really fun *Air Force Two* things to do was to grab a glass of wine and pop in a videotape of the SNL skit, "Darth Cheney." The skit with the coffeemaker in his chest always got a big belly laugh out of the viewers in the cabin. The VP and Lynne even dressed up their black and yellow Labs in Darth Vader costumes one Halloween.

I wouldn't say that he enjoys—or doesn't enjoy—his reputation with the media, but I can say he was never perturbed about it, not in the way his family and I were always made crazy by the political caricatures and parodies of the man we know and love. He always seemed more vexed with my concern about it than anything else, and he would always tell me to just chillax and stop worrying about him or his image.

One of my biggest regrets is that I listened to him about that. I could have spent all my time fighting the attacks against him. He didn't deserve the trash talk, and he was 99.9 percent right in all things. But an 11 percent approval rating could be a bit of an impediment to getting things done because his detractors ceased debating and started demonizing anything Dick "Darth" proffered.

You probably have a read on Cheney one way or the other. And if you love him, you don't know even half of what is so cool about him. And if you don't adore him, I guess that's your loss, because you ate up all the toxic garbage about him without bothering to think things through or think for yourself, and now that toxic stuff is still circulating in your system.

When it comes to Dick Cheney, "what you see is what you get." He isn't hiding or playing games. That's my all-time favorite thing about him. And at work or play, office or home, he is always chill.

The most riled up that he's ever gotten, as far as I know, happened one Thanksgiving. If you've read his or Lynne's books, you know that he makes Thanksgiving dinner every year. One year, when he was cooking at his daughter Liz's house, she and I were on the phone jabbering about kids or whatever. Midsentence, she asked me to hang on, because she had to go see why her dad was making so much noise in the kitchen.

He wasn't happy, it turned out, because someone had fed his beloved Labrador retrievers bananas against his strictest orders—and the dogs were upchucking them while he was trying to get the turkey in or out of the oven. Wow, he was really unhappy about that. I wasn't even there and felt the need to apologize.

JAMES

PEOPLE THINK DICK CHENEY is such a mystery. I don't think there's much mystery at all. I don't agree with his politics. I despised the Iraq War. I thought the "enhanced interrogation techniques" were bullshit.

But Mary adores him. He's not a big backslapper or anything like that, but he's nice enough. He certainly doesn't pretend to be somebody he's not, so give him credit for that.

There was this Showtime documentary that came out in 2013, *The World According to Dick Cheney* by the filmmaker R. J. Cutler, whom I'd known since he did *The War Room* about Clinton's campaign back in 1992.

It goes through the terrorist attacks and the wars in Afghanistan and Iraq and waterboarding and the really controversial national-security policies he helped put in place. And Cheney says right off the bat, "I don't spend a lot of time thinking about my faults." As in, I did what I thought was right and didn't worry about what was popular.

I sat there thinking, *That's it in a nutshell*. And I told Mary this after the movie came out. I said, "If somebody is a Dick Cheney fan, he's going to like this movie. If somebody already dislikes him, there's nothing in there to change that either."

The bottom line is, whether it's in a documentary or in real life, Dick Cheney gives you the distinct impression—which I suspect is accurate—that he doesn't really give a shit what you think. If you share the worldview that he's a guy who knew best what had to be done to protect the country and went about it come hell or high water, then the movie sort of reinforces that narrative. If you think that he was a guy who used 9/11 as an opportunity to do a bunch of crazy shit that wasn't well thought-out and harmed America's reputation, as well as undermined the Constitution, then you can find that in the story too. Both sides can take away what they want from it.

But whichever side you're on, the truth is he's not very upset about whatever you think. He's not losing any sleep over it. I've met the guy plenty of times. I've flown out to Wyoming with him on *Air Force Two* and spent time with his family. And I can promise you, that's exactly the way it is. If you were hoping that maybe he had started reconsidering what he'd done as he grew older, or questioned any of the decisions he'd made in office, you'd be disappointed.

This is not a man sitting on the rocking chair on his front porch, second-guessing himself and weeping over the mistakes of the past.

MARY

I'VE BEEN CALLING George H. W. Bush Poppy for years. I don't know when or why I started. But I certainly called him Mr. President when I worked for him and wouldn't think of calling him anything else when I see him in any formal setting. On this, James and I have bipartisan agreement; we respect politicians, or at least people who get in the arena.

If you are addressing somebody with a long and auspicious career that has produced many titles, you might assume they'd want you to use the biggest title, but that's not always the case.

For instance, a lot of governors like to be called Governor or Guv forever, no matter what other office they've been elected or appointed to, which is understandable, because being a state governor would be my all-time favorite job, were I ever to think of running, *which I am not.*

Another thing to know is that you should never mistakenly interchange the titles "director" (e.g., CIA) and "secretary" (e.g., State). There are other jargon matters that might interest you, such as when you are referencing the CIA, you say, "Agency" and the FBI is always "Bureau." Otherwise you're safe calling any of the other branches of the intelligence services simply "intel," although most people like to note if they are talking about "humint," as in "human intelligence." Ironically, the bigger our intel community grows, the less human intelligence we seem to get. Unless we are being lied to by the United States government, which in another age would be unthinkable.

As a general rule, the lesser the position, the greater the desire of that person for deference to all this title business. The least accomplished are always the most insistent that they be titled for life. But you probably already guessed that.

Ridiculing the "alphabet soup" of national departments and government bureaus is easy. And batting around these titles and jargon with aplomb does make you feel like an accomplished insider, even if you aren't. But, in most cases, acronyms are a product of efficiency, not ego or insider status. If you had to say "Environmental Protection Agency" every time you talked about the EPA, you'd get crazier than you already do get just *thinking* about that place.

Anyway, I digress. But it does bring me to this point: in a universe populated with self-serving impressed-with-themselves people, I have always been enchanted when anyone in politics introduces themselves by their God-given name, even if I must use their title when addressing them. And that's how the whole Bush family introduces themselves: with their names and a nice, confidence-instilling handshake. They look you right in the eye, not in an intimidating way but in a way that makes you want to hang out with them.

If you live in a real town, where real people step up and do what needs to be done for the good of their neighbors and community, you know what selfless service looks like. Of the many things I love about Poppy, he has always believed pubic service is an honor and acted like it. He brought honor to any post in which he served.

Much has been written and gummed over about the Bushes. I just want to say one thing, once again, without equivocation: *they are the real deal*. Do you have any idea how hard it is to hang on to your real self in the parallel universe of politics? And in a family of so many politicians?

They are the exception to the norm. And it is why they have so many trusted, loyal and steadfast friends in a profession that requires most people to get a dog.

All's Fair ends with an illustrative moment of Poppy's authenticity. After the campaign was over and there were no champagne corks to pop, my wingman, Dave Carney (aka "Stud Muffin"), and I were invited to join Poppy in the presidential private dining room next to the Oval Office in the West Wing. One thing was verboten with President Bush 41: pity parties. While he has great and consistent empathy for all, he does not allow wallowing or wound licking. And in the case of the 1992 defeat, he blamed only himself, despite his staff's well-chronicled snafus.

So Dave and I were gathered in the dining room, where *the president apologized to us* for the campaign outcome. To this day, I still wonder who else on the Earth and particularly in politics—a world of cover-your-ass types and blame-everybody-elsers—would have the generosity and big heart to do such a thing. We tried not to have a pity party after this apology, even if it was still happening inside our heads, when our lunch was interrupted by a consoling phone call to Poppy from a group of leaders from South America, which he took only because they were all friends, not because they were presidents. The guys just wanted to say how much they were going to miss him and his leadership.

And Poppy burst into tears. And then I burst into tears. This was something we managed to avoid throughout the whole campaign, but for one or two instances (confessed in *All's Fair*) where a person would have to had ice running through his veins not to cry. But sitting at the table in the dining room, every time we tried to collect ourselves, Poppy would look at me or I'd look at him, and we'd start boohooing. He was never going to finish the South American call at this rate, so I got up from the table and stood behind him as he resumed his phone conversation. I hugged him from behind. He hugged me. And we laugh-cried, because we were both more than aware that we were acting like ninny girls by this point.

We've been in pretty regular contact since that campaign and he never failed to call whenever he came to D.C. He would gather his little merry band at the Georgetown Club (previously an all-male institution, which still bars jeans and anyone not invited by a member). One day I forgot and showed up in my uniform—jeans—and was summarily dismissed even though no one else was there but our party and I was wearing ridiculously expensive designer jeans, unlike the Levi 501s I wore every day of the campaign.

Whenever I see Poppy, he says, "Mary, come sit by me." And we return to our time-honored, end-of-the-day campaign tradition of having an adult beverage together. And by that I do not mean a white wine spritzer, which many of the uptight D.C. crowd took up in the 1990s just when martinis were coming back everywhere else under the sun. But for Poppy and me, they'd never gone out.

How did we meet? In 1981, we met at the vice president's personal residence. I was a total newcomer to town who had just moved from the Midwest for a bottom-rung political job, which was literally in the basement of the RNC. It was a step up from my $11,000-a-year political job in Illinois. I was making the princessly sum of $13,000 a year.

The Illinois campaign manager, Maxene Fernstrom, had found me the job and was putting me up in her own home while I got settled. Political people—then and now—look after each other. And young people arriving for political jobs in Washington are met with open doors, party invitations and a lot of vertical mobility. Even so, when I met Poppy, I had no idea what a rare event it was for a bunch of RNC grunts to get invited to the vice president's house. But Poppy wasn't like most VPs. He had been the chairman of the RNC during the Nixon "unpleasantness" and threw one of his first parties in his new residence for everyone at the committee out of loyalty.

As we filtered into the expansive grounds of this mansion—I'd only ever seen anything like that house in the movies—it was clear Poppy knew everybody because he seemed to have a personal and very kind word for one and all. He knew the janitor, the printing press guy, the front desk clerk, the people who'd been in the institution for ten and twenty years. He knew them all, and he knew everything about their families.

That impressed me, not because he was the vice president, but because it was such a Midwestern thing to do.

His five kids were sprinkled around the party. They were all about my age—some a little older, some younger. They had lived all over the world, which, being a sheltered Midwesterner who'd rarely ventured out of Illinois, where my siblings and I grew up in one house, I thought this was kind of sad and screwed up. Where was their true home? But whatever concerns I had about their childhood vanished as soon as I experienced how cool and normal they were. And how together they were as a family. It was something you couldn't miss. They were connected and intact—unlike my own family after my mom passed.

Like many moms and grandmothers, my mother had been the family glue, the one who held us all together. I was still reeling from her unexpected death—and the loss of all the things in life that she had held together. And even though the Bushes weren't like my own working-class family, watching them together filled me with joy. Their bond was immediately recognizable—a love and commitment to each other, the way close and strong families are, no matter where they grow up—one house or a dozen—or how much money they've got.

One more testament to the Bush family: so many kids of my generation, and way too many "celebrity" kids, had been ravished by the drug culture of those days or messed up in some other Iron Butterfly "In-A-Gadda-Da-Vida" way. Not these kids. They were composed, approachable, superconfident and supercompetitive, not in that insecure way, but in a fun way that only close families are together. It was and remains a beautiful thing to behold. From that night on, I adored Poppy and his whole family. And for me, the magic has never worn off.

There was an unfortunate dynamic in that administration, the Reagan team versus the Bush team. And there was much jockeying around in the White House early on, with folks picking sides. Much of this has been detailed in other books. I don't need to expand on it, except to say that Poppy rose above the internecine maneuvers. He rose above the mattress mice and side pickers.

He rose above so many things and always has.

All of America has seen the integrity of this man since he left office, especially the amazing dignity and inspiration of his aging. He is never without jokes and humanity and grace, while he always retains his essence. (Let's not forget, he was jumping out of airplanes on his eightieth and eighty-fifth birthdays.) And after it was clearly dangerous for him to still be racing around like a teenager in that wacky speedboat of his, he started speeding around in a bright-red scooter. He really likes to speed down corridors, making people jump out of his way on all sides.

"Come on, Mary, let's go for a ride," he is always saying to me backstage at various events, daring me to speed along with him in that red racer. That wonderful human being gave me the ride of my life, but I only took one trip in his speedy cart. It reminded me of why my mother never let me get on a motorcycle with high school boys.

But declining a ride from Poppy could be just as treacherous. Once, at Texas A&M, home of the George Bush Presidential Library and the Bush School of Government and Public Service, he tried to run me off the "road"—which really amused him, since I guess watching me panic and run away in high heels on a slippery corridor floor in a crowd of self-possessed folks was pretty comical.

My longtime friend and fellow Bushie, Andy Card, asked me to give a short speech for the Aggie half-year commencement. It was supposed to be just me—and not James. But I got in touch with another longtime buddy and Bush "daughter," Jean Becker, who made arrangements for James to come too and surprise everybody.

For years, Barbara Bush couldn't stand James. She avoided him at all costs, and there were many events they both attended. She literally referred to him for years as "He Who Shall Not Be Named," which is an indication of what a classy lady she is when you stop and think of all the things James said about her husband in 1992. (And please don't stop and think about it, because I'm still trying not to. And I can't help but wonder, when I think about G. H. W. Bush serving only one term, how much I have to thank James Carville for that.)

We all know, and politics demands, that time heals all. But there are also some situations that just don't allow for forgiveness. And I had a hunch that this moment could break bad. But I also had a feeling that surprising Poppy would be a good thing. He was just beginning to lose a bit of the zip in his step—and he always loved surprises and he, weirdly enough, always loved James.

So at the end of my speech, I said, "I have a surprise guest for you Aggies," and I brought James out. Everybody in the audience went completely nutso—in a good way. It was fabulous, it was beautiful, and the best thing of all was the look on Mrs. Bush's face. She forgave James in that moment and stood up in front of everybody and said how much she loved him. James was beaming like a little boy.

At the dinner following the ceremony, I was seated next to Poppy, where we promptly took up our ritual: vodka on the rocks. Though others had cautioned me that he wasn't as spunky as he once had been, the surprise was now on me: he was completely Mr. Spunk. (Which I already knew since he had made me run down the corridor before dinner in high heels.) We had the best trip down memory lane, which I especially cherished since he finally let me take the blame for 1992.

Thank you, Mr. President. I accept.

JAMES

BARBARA BUSH ALWAYS INTIMIDATED ME. I can't explain exactly why. She's just always had that effect on me. Whenever I was around her, my mouth would get a little drier. I'd sweat a little more. Kay Graham at the *Washington Post* was the same way. Mrs. Graham intimidated everyone. Tough-as-nails, no-nonsense women, both of them.

In 2012, Mary and I participated in a fund-raising event down at the Bush 41 library in College Station, Texas. It was one of these dinners that they invite a bunch of people to and all the big donors show up. I've done similar events in the past at the Clinton library and the Reagan library.

For whatever reason, Barbara Bush decided that I was going to sit beside her at her table that day. I was nervous. I didn't want to say the wrong thing. I usually don't care much what people think, but I found myself really wanting her to like me. So I steered clear of politics. I avoided my usual bad language. And I turned to a tried-and-true Carville rule for charming someone: I asked about her grandchildren.

Trust me on this: you can say something too nice about somebody's mother. They'll brush it off. "Oh, no. You didn't have to live with her," they'll say. Or "Well, have you ever tried her home cooking?" You can say something too nice about somebody's spouse. "Are you shitting me?" they'll say. "He snores all the time." But you never can say something too nice about someone's children or grandchildren. You can go as overboard as you want, be as flattering as you want, and people are going to believe every word of it and like you for it.

It is one of the great secrets of life. I learned that in Austin, Texas, in 1984, during Lloyd Doggett's Senate campaign against Phil Gramm. We had ten days to go and we were twenty points behind. It was over. We were going to lose. So we were basically just drinking a lot and telling jokes and biding our time until Election Day.

One afternoon, the phone rings in the campaign headquarters. I pick it up. It's the mother of one of the staffers, asking to speak with her son. He was a decent enough guy, but kind of prickly and a little socially awkward. I don't know what came over me, but I launched into this long monologue, telling his mother what a saint he was.

I said, "Ma'am, I could not pull this phone away from my ear without telling you what a fine, upstanding man you've raised. And that boy has come here and been part of our team, and I can tell you right now that you and your husband have done right by your son. This man is just a delight to be around. He's got every kind of solid value that you could hope for. If I had children, he's exactly the kind of person I'd want them to become."

She was floored. "Oh, my God. Thank you so much," she said. She loved it.

After that, everybody in the office started getting their parents on the phone with me just to see how overboard I could go. And you know what? What I learned during my drunken stupor that October night in Austin is that, you can't go too far. It's not possible. Don't try it with spouses; don't try it with parents. They'll think you're full of shit. But with kids—it's a blind spot.

Anyway, after that dinner in College Station, Barbara Bush told Mary that she liked me. I felt like I'd just won the lottery.

MARY

I HATED GOING TO the White House when the Clintons were there. It felt like I didn't belong, and I tried to stay away. I went a few times with James, for an engagement party and something for George Stephanopoulos, and one state dinner. It was painful.

In 1996, I was a volunteer on Bob Dole's campaign because I was doing *Equal Time* and I had a radio show, so I couldn't really become an official paid member of the campaign. Then, while I was advising the Dole campaign pro bono, one of the party chairmen trashed me on the front page of the *Washington Times* for being married to James.

"On a scale of one to 10, with 10 being the most stupid choice, this is a 14," Florida GOP Chairman Tom Slade, Jr., told the newspaper. "There is little doubt that she is a talented political operative, but there are lots and lots of talented political operatives on our side of the aisle."

Later that day, the Dole campaign called to fire me.

"I'm a volunteer—you can't fire a volunteer," I said feebly. And even though I didn't understand, and it hurt, I decided to relent without more of a fight. In politics, the one thing you cannot do is become a distraction. And I guess they were afraid I would become one.

Bob Dole called me at home later that night. I said, "Sorry, sorry, sorry. I'll do whatever you want, sir." He said, "This is absurd. You're unfired. Or you never were fired. No one consulted me." Then he asked to speak to James. And James says, "We'll do whatever you want, sir." And within seconds the whole contretemps was over. We have always loved Bob Dole and now you can see why.

So, there I was, an unofficial adviser on the Dole presidential campaign against incumbent Bill Clinton, and James and I were invited to a state dinner. That's a big deal invitation—I don't care who you are, even working for the enemy as I was. But really, I just wanted to see Stevie Wonder perform. Even though I couldn't ease the awkwardness of being there, as I was in the nondrinking phase of a megapregnancy with my second—and looking like I did in my first: a beached whale.

As I walked into the White House, I heard the sound of genuine hostility escaping from every corner of the room, like a very distinguishable *hissssssssss*. I felt like Moses, and not in a good way, as the hissing red carpet parted and I walked through the daunting hall, praying to get through the night before my water broke.

As I waddled uncomfortably (for many reasons) down the fancy foyer, President Bill Clinton did what he always does in those awkward situations: he finds the most unworthy low-status human being in the room and comes to their aid.

So he made a beeline for me, and he started telling me everything he would do if he were Bob Dole—to beat the Clinton reelect campaign.

He was giving me a complete, perfectly thought-out Dole strategy, and he seemed more excited about telling me all the ways that Bob Dole could really challenge him, and win, than by anything else happening in that moment. I hadn't expected to like him. I hadn't expected to have a good time at all (except for Stevie Wonder). But just being with Clinton was so arousing and compelling (but not in *that* way). Talking politics on that level with a fellow lifelong junkie was and still is a singularly thrilling event. Who could imagine it? Not me, and certainly not before that night, despite years of being subjected to James's adoration of the man.

Even with my surging pregnancy hormones and bloated belly, the irony was not lost on me: Bill Clinton was telling me what to advise Senator Dole so he could beat Bill Clinton right after I had been basically fired as a volunteer from the Dole campaign because I was married to James, who had put me in proximity to Clinton.

What was his advice to Dole?

"Let Bob Dole be Bob Dole. Get off his neck. Let him be a full-throated Republican. Quit trying to make him something he's not. And make him stay on *his* message. He has a message, but you all have him jammed up with *your* message and anyone can tell he doesn't believe it."

This is a very truncated rendition of a very long gabfest. I am making it sound like standard stuff, but his articulation and passion for the topic was very sophisticated and compelling—and totally dead-on.

JAMES

I'VE LEARNED SOME GREAT lessons in life from Bill Clinton. And one was his rule for working a room: the moment you walk in, you pick out the most vulnerable, least powerful person and you go talk to that person first and foremost. You knock the MVP over to hug the guy who dropped the game-winning pass. Everybody notices it. And he's probably the more interesting guy to talk with, anyway.

Clinton has a sixth sense about that. If there's somebody in a room whose mother died the day before, he's going to know it instinctively. He just knows who needs the attention most. That's who he focuses on, and people instinctively understand it.

He's the best at it. But it's a good rule for anybody. That and complimenting people about their children and grandchildren. Those are two rules that are never, ever going to fail you.

MARY

WHEN YOU ARE IN A CAMPAIGN, your total window on the world is politics. But when you are a mother, your prism narrows to your kids and their immediate world. Politics aside, when you are the mother of daughters, you want them to see successful, strong, articulate, accomplished women in positions of power. You hope your daughters won't necessarily listen to some of the things being propagated by these women, but you do hope your girls will be encouraged by their example to be bold in their lives and follow their passions.

Such was the case with Hillary Rodham Clinton. The three of us gals—Matty, Emerson and I—of disparate and opposite politics, sat in the kitchen and cried when the news came over our little TV that her coronation was not to be.

JAMES

LET ME PUT IT THIS WAY. If Al Gore had been president, 9/11 never would have happened.

The reasons that people don't like Gore are the very reasons it wouldn't have happened. First of all, he is very, very anal. Very detail oriented. He used to read the Presidential Daily Brief, or PDB, and if he had a question, he would go out to Langley and ask the CIA analysts about it directly because he understood how things sometimes got filtered or watered down as they went up the food chain.

If Gore would've gotten that brief in August 2001, the one headlined BIN LADEN DETERMINED TO STRIKE IN U.S., he would have understood the gravity of the threat.

Plenty of people knew that summer that something was brewing. Richard Clarke and lots of other folks in the intelligence community were running around with their hair on fire, warning about a possible al-Qaeda attack, but they couldn't get the top Bush people to pay attention. Gore would have had the entire government on high alert.

Bill Clinton was acutely attuned to the dangers of al-Qaeda by the latter part of his tenure, and so was Gore. They'd been through the U.S. embassy bombings and the bombing of the USS *Cole*. They knew how determined al-Qaeda was.

Gore could be a cumbersome, difficult guy, but he was an extremely thorough man. He was nothing like George W. Bush, who was very casual, very cavalier about making decisions. Bush had a supreme confidence; he didn't spend a lot of time second-guessing himself. Gore would've been a president who would have second-guessed himself. He would have studied things. He would have had doubts. And he would have followed up.

Of course, you can't prove a hypothetical. There's no way you can go back and know for sure. But knowing the nature of Gore's past conduct and the type of person he is, I'll go to my grave believing that if he were president history would have turned out differently; 9/11 might have been just another sunny September day.

People ask me why I keep crisscrossing the world to work on foreign political campaigns. The answer is pretty simple.

There's this story about an up-and-coming, really ferocious boxer. They put him in the ring with this washed-up thirty-six-year-old fighter who's only getting paid $500 for the fight. And predictably, the young guy just bloodies the shit out of the old guy. Knocks him out in three rounds.

Afterward, everybody's clamoring to interview the rising star. But one reporter goes over to the old fighter and asks him, "Why do you keep doing this? There's not much money in it. There was no way you were gonna win."

And the guy says, "A fight is a fight."

That's what the foreign stuff represents to me. The money is fine, though not what people might imagine. I'll spend it. But the main reason is that it's just what I do. I like the challenge. I love politics, whether it's America or Africa or Afghanistan. A fight is a fight.

The most important campaign I've taken on since Bill Clinton's took place in Afghanistan in 2009, but it began with a meeting in Washington.

I met one afternoon with Steve Cohen, a Harvard-trained psychologist who runs the Institute for Middle East Peace and Development. He's a really decent, thoughtful guy who genuinely believes peace in that region is attainable.

A woman came with him named Clare Lockhart, an incredibly bright woman who'd spent years working in Afghanistan and had developed a deep understanding of the place. She'd advised the U.S. military and various governments on everything from how to put in place a new monetary system to how to create a national police force. Back in 2005, she'd cofounded the Institute for State Effectiveness with a guy named Ashraf Ghani, who had been Afghanistan's finance minister in the new government that took over after 9/11. The two of them had written a book about fixing failed states and the mistakes people so often make in nation-building.

Steve and Clare were gushing about Ghani, saying he was the sort of guy— smart, ethical, hardworking, charismatic—who could actually put Afghanistan back on a path toward economic and political stability. Ghani, an ethnic Pashtun, had gotten a PhD from Columbia and taught at the University of California-Berkeley and Johns Hopkins. He'd done all this research about transforming failed states. He was a Fulbright scholar. He'd worked at the World Bank and the U.N. After decades abroad, he'd come back to Afghanistan after the U.S. invasion in late 2001 to work as the country's finance minister, a job he did pro bono.

The guy sounded almost too good to be true. I was intrigued, but skeptical. Also, if I went to advise him on his campaign, I would be going to work for someone who the U.S. government hadn't backed. Technically, the United States had made clear that it wasn't endorsing any of the dozens of candidates in the upcoming election, but it had stood behind Hamid Karzai from the very beginning.

I called up Richard Holbrooke, who I'd known forever and whose opinion I really valued. He was working as the White House's special representative for Pakistan and Afghanistan.

I said, "Richard, I've just been contacted here about this Ashraf Ghani, who is running for president of Afghanistan. What do you know about him?"

He said, "Ashraf Ghani is simply one of the finest people I have ever met in my life."

And I said, "Well, I don't mind doing something like this if you say he's so good. But I'm pretty sure they can't pay me much. I don't even think they can pay my expenses to get over there."

Richard said, "James, you're a member of the Kennedy generation. You don't get a chance to work for somebody like Ashraf Ghani very often. You have to do this."

I said, "Well, shit. If you're going to pull out John F. Kennedy on me, I guess I'll go."

So I went. It ain't an easy place to get to, because you've got to go through somewhere like Dubai, and then spend the night, then catch a plane into Kabul. It's like an entire day of traveling. And by the time I showed up, I was tired. I was restless. I still wasn't sure this was a good idea.

It turned out to be worth every ounce of effort. I went to see Ghani. And the guy is literally—and I use this word with great caution and understanding— almost saintly. I don't know how else to describe it, but I had the sense that I was almost in the presence of a holy man. He kind of reminded you of Gandhi. Bald head. Soft-spoken.

He said, "Well, I can't pay you very much. But I'll give you this rug." Fine with me. I rolled it up and put it in my suitcase, and we got right to work. I helped him on his strategy and tried to figure out how to win over certain people quickly, because there is only a short window to campaign before the presidential election in Afghanistan.

The way it works, basically, is everybody pretty much has to cut deals with various warlords. One guy had control of this area; another guy had control of that area. And you have to convince these guys that they should tell their people to vote for you. A campaign, in the traditional sense, didn't really matter that much in Afghanistan. It wasn't like Ghani had a message he was trying to get out with stump speeches and TV commercials. It was about who you knew and who with power you could win over. I said in one interview that I felt right at home because it reminded me in some ways of Louisiana.

But it also felt like meaningful work. I told the AP one day that this was the most important election held in the world in a long time and that "this is probably the most interesting project I have ever worked on in my life." I meant it. Ghani was a fascinating, engaging, brilliant guy. He would have made a great president.

Of course, in the end, he got only about 3 percent of the vote. In a place like that, you don't always win on your merits. Sometimes, you lose badly. But I've never once regretted that experience.

As I said in *40 More Years*, if Barack Obama the human being was born on August 4, 1961, at 7:24 p.m., then Barack Obama the presidential candidate was born at 12:50 a.m. on October 11, 2002. That is the day, the hour and the minute that Senator Hillary Rodham Clinton voted to go to war in Iraq. It was what sank her in 2008. There was a lot written and said about the '08 campaign team and the personalities and delegate strategy, but that vote was the single most important factor in her defeat that year.

11

Katrina

MARY

JAMES IS HIGHLY ATTUNED TO WEATHER. When a storm is forecasted, he isn't one of those people who says, "Oh, they always exaggerate, they always get it wrong and overhype." James doesn't even bother with TV. He is one of those people who knows every special weather website that has Doppler radar and every imaginable type of technology. When a storm is coming, especially a hurricane—which James always references as a "weather system," like he's some TWC weather babe—he is the first one on high alert and the one to make predictions, which are 99.9 percent accurate.

In 2003, when Hurricane Isabel came to the D.C. metro area, he was racing around like a crazy man doing his storm-prevention activities, sandbagging every door, hoarding food, ice and Maker's Mark—and crabbing at me for not letting him buy a generator. *What a drama queen*, I thought. I was laughing at him until the first floor of our brand-new Alexandria house (the boxes were still unpacked from the move) was floating in Potomac River muck. I don't laugh anymore.

JAMES

IN THE DAYS AFTER Hurricane Katrina hit in August 2005, my phone never stopped ringing, and I never stopped calling Louisiana. The images rolling across the television—of the submerged city, of some people being rescued from rooftops and others enduring the abysmal conditions at the Superdome and the convention center—were hard enough to swallow. But the stories from friends and family made the devastation personal and painful. I felt like someone had punched me in the gut. I felt as far away from home as I'd ever felt.

I have a sister who lost her house in Slidell, a community northeast of New Orleans near Lake Pontchartrain, which got hit as hard as anywhere in Louisiana. Her family was staying with another of my sisters near Baton Rouge, not knowing when or if they'd ever get back home. The school she worked at was flooded, and her husband worked for the Exxon Mobil pipeline in St. Bernard Parish, which also flooded, and neither of them knew when they might get back to work.

My brother, a contractor, had a business associate whose father had terminal brain cancer and had to be evacuated from his home. The father ended up staying at my brother's house in Baton Rouge. When the electricity went out, my brother borrowed a generator from his business so the guy could have air-conditioning in the sweltering heat.

That was just the story of my family. One family. I kept thinking of the hundreds of thousands of other families impacted by the storm—many far worse than mine—and about the hell so many people were experiencing.

In public, I tried to put a positive spin on the situation.

"Sure, it's going to be rebuilt," I told Wolf Blitzer one day on CNN. "A lot of people love New Orleans, not just me because I lived there and got married there and my kids love it, but people from all over the country."

"Maybe it comes back stronger," I told a reporter from *USA Today*. "No one forgot how to play the saxophone or how to cook or write. Or have a good time. That's all still there. Calamities and disasters are part of New Orleans' history. This too shall pass."

But the truth was, I didn't know if it would come back stronger, or come back at all. I wasn't sure I believed my own spin.

What I was sure of was that I needed to do something, anything, to fight the helplessness I was feeling from one thousand miles away. I called up Chris Farley, who owns the Pacers running stores around Washington, where I was a regular customer, and we decided to hold a charity 5K called the Gulf Coast Relief Run. The city of Alexandria quickly agreed to permit the event, and a handful of corporate sponsors also signed on. Tony Kornheiser, who's a dear friend of mine, jumped in to help out. Mary pitched in too.

A race like that normally would take months to plan. You have to take out permits and line up sponsors. You have to get the local police to give their blessing. We put it all together in two weeks. Those hectic days of organizing made me feel like I was at least contributing to the recovery in some way, and it kept me from dwelling completely on the horrors still unfolding in Louisiana.

The run took place on Saturday, September 17, at nine a.m. We thought we might get five hundred people. More than three thousand signed up. I couldn't have been prouder. At the end of the day, we handed the Red Cross a check for $114,000. It was a drop in the bucket given all the need in Louisiana, but it was something.

A strange thing happened after that: the phone stopped ringing. The only way I can describe it is that it felt like when somebody dies and people are calling you or coming by to express their condolences. Then there's the funeral and the rush of planning that comes with it. People come and shake your hand and say how sorry they are, and please let them know if they can help. Then, at some point, everybody is gone. It's quiet. And the phone stops ringing.

That's exactly what happened after the race. One day, there was this sudden silence. That's when the stark reality of what had happened back home began to set in. I began to grasp the magnitude of the devastation and how New Orleans really might never be the place I had always known. I started to cry, and I literally couldn't stop.

MARY

WE WERE AT THE FARM BEFORE KATRINA, and James had been in Doppler mode 24/7 for days. He was obsessing about a "weather system" in the Gulf. I knew better than to question him after our Isabel debacle, but to me the system looked like one more swirling multicolored cotton-candy cartoon. And it was far, far away from our quiet Shenandoah Valley.

It's not easy to distinguish the normally crazy James from the abnormally insane one, but one telltale sign is that he focuses like a rabid dog that's gotten ahold of raw steak bone. That was James as he stared lasers into that "system" on his computer and the TV.

Much has been written about Katrina and most of the political accounts are flat-ass wrong. I remember being surprised when my White House buddy Steve Schmidt told me while the storm was still raging, "We will be defined by this." Usually my political instincts trump all other reactions. But in the case of Katrina, there was too much personal going on to think politically.

For one, James's family was possibly in harm's way. For two, my beloved Donna Brazile's family was literally underwater. Those she could find.

JAMES

I'LL NEVER FORGET THE first LSU football game after the storm. It was September 10, 2005.

A few days earlier, the *Washington Post*'s Michael Wilbon had written a column quoting me and talking about what that game meant to the Gulf Coast. I thought he got it exactly right.

"You see the devastation and despair in Louisiana and Mississippi and figure the last thing in the world you ought to be thinking about is . . . football,"

Wilbon wrote. "But if you listen closely to the people in despair, to the people who have lived in those flooded streets and know intimately what matters down around the Gulf Coast, and you realize football is a good thought, that anything that might bring joy for even four hours to people in for such a long haul is a very good thing. It is one of those times, political analyst James Carville reminded me yesterday, that sports helps people remain sane, even hopeful, especially when there's no light, no fresh water for drinking or a bath, when there's no food and for some the only clothing they own is what they're wearing."

You almost had to be from there to understand. Louisiana is this mix of all different races and cultures and classes—white and black, Protestant and Catholic, urban and rural, rich and poor. LSU football is the great unifying force. It's something everybody could rally around, especially during a time when people needed a reason to cheer.

A lot of the LSU players were from New Orleans or the little parishes around it. Their families were suffering. Their friends were suffering. Refugees were living on the LSU campus, so it's not like the players were shielded from the devastation. This was a very real and emotional time for them, as it was for everybody.

Arizona State was supposed to come to Baton Rouge for the game that Saturday. But the field house and the assembly center across from Tiger Stadium were treating Katrina evacuees, and there was a makeshift morgue there. Baton Rouge itself was flooded with refugees. So they decided to move the game to Tempe.

I watched every single play of that game at home in northern Virginia, feeling a million miles away but also feeling every soul in Louisiana pull for the Tigers alongside me. Arizona State was up 17–7 heading into the fourth quarter. We'd made a bunch of mistakes. It wasn't looking good.

All of a sudden, we blocked a field goal attempt and ran it back for a touchdown. We forced another fumble and returned that for a touchdown. We would score, then they would score. The lead just kept changing. Finally, LSU faced a 4th-and-10 on Arizona State's 39-yard line with a minute and twenty-three seconds left. Do-or-die time. JaMarcus Russell took the snap, rolled right, ran back left and launched a prayer. Early Doucet made this unbelievable freaking catch in the end zone. Tigers win, 35–31.

That moment was just pure, unfettered joy. I remember it like yesterday. It was exactly what we all needed at that moment.

Race is one of the inescapable issues in New Orleans. Like many cities, it has a long and complicated history with race. In a lot of ways, a really ugly history, from slavery to the Jim Crow segregation laws to the societal failings that Hurricane Katrina laid bare.

Back a century ago, the neighborhoods were really fairly mixed. Maybe the schools weren't and the churches weren't, but people of all races lived side by side in the neighborhoods, at least before the great black migration to the north. The neighborhoods were a real patchwork. You had African Americans, Sicilians, Irish—all these different cultures blending together. It was like the city was its own racial gumbo, and that's part of what gave New Orleans such a unique character. That's when some of the best art and the best music and the best culture emerged.

Today, the neighborhoods have become more segregated, no doubt about it. But people of different races live in closer proximity to each other than in a lot of American cities. If you go to Washington, for example, there's a huge disparity between where the white people generally live and where African Americans generally live. There's a giant demographic dividing line between northwest Washington and southeast Washington.

When you live here, it's abundantly clear that there's no separating race from everyday life. Everybody understands this in Louisiana. But the issue of race didn't get any less complicated after Katrina. If anything, it grew only more complicated. Part of the reason for that has to do with the geography of New Orleans. There are exceptions, but as a general rule, the closer you live to the river, the higher ground you're on. And, in general, the higher the ground you live on, the whiter you are.

Katrina happened in August 2005, and people started talking about how to rebuild the city. And they formed a commission to study ways to do smart urban planning, rather than just a half-assed reconstruction. It all sounded like a great idea. They rounded up the usual suspects—a local bank president, a black pastor, lawyers, businessmen, an academic from Tulane, the Catholic archbishop and so on. Ray Nagin, who was the mayor at that time, got behind it.

The commission studied the situation and issued some recommendations. One proposal they received suggested that the sensible thing to do was to start building from the high ground out. The panel eventually recommended a moratorium on building permits until each neighborhood could prove that enough of its residents were returning and that it could come up with a rebuilding plan.

It didn't take long before somebody said, "Aha! This is a plan to keep black people from coming back to the city." Because, remember, historically, the higher ground you're on, the whiter you are. And there was a lot of uncertainty around that time about who would come back and how the demographics of the city might change after Katrina.

So that's about the time Nagin, who originally supported the idea, came out and said in a speech in early 2006 that New Orleans would always be a "chocolate" city. He was telling his political base that he was not for all of these elites telling people who could move or who couldn't move back into the city. But it only deepened the racial tensions that already were there. It polarized a city that already was on edge about what the future would look like.

Like I said, race is never easy in New Orleans.

But after Katrina, and after I tell you a little more about my heritage, you'll see why Mary and I eventually had to move back.

The Carville, Louisiana, I knew is mostly gone now, but I can still see it clear as day, just the way it was. The old Illinois Central railroad track. The mighty Mississippi River, winding its way toward New Orleans. Bobby Wintz's meat market. The juke joints out toward St. Gabriel.

I can see my grandparents' place, with its circular drive and the big tree out front and the peach orchard in back. That house hasn't stood in decades, but I could still draw every inch of it from memory. I must have spent half my childhood at their place.

I can still see the house where my daddy was born, the green one off Monroe Street, named after Henry Monroe. I can picture the house I grew up in a little ways up the same street. It was about a mile and a half between my grandparents' house and our home, and I must have ridden my horse along that stretch thousands of times.

A little ways up the road sat the general store my father ran. It actually was attached to the post office where my grandfather was the postmaster, like his mother before him and his son after him. We were the only third-class post office in the United States that had a branch.

Just on a little farther was one of the only hospitals in the United States to treat Hansen's disease, which most people know as leprosy. It used to be called the Louisiana Leper Home (though what might have been acceptable a century ago isn't now; never use the "L" word to describe someone with Hansen's, as it's extremely pejorative). By the time I came along, the federal government had started running the place, and it was called U.S. Marine Hospital Number 66. Books have been written and films have been made about some of the legendary patients who spent time there. The correspondence to and from the hospital, all those tales of struggle and loss and hope and separation—all of it passed through my grandfather's post office.

The chemical plants have moved in now and cleared out a bunch of land and brought in a lot of truck traffic. But back then, other than my daddy's store and the hospital and a few other ramshackle places, Carville was truly rural. We'd travel a few miles over to the old white clapboard Catholic church off Highway 75. It's the oldest church in the Louisiana Purchase territory. I went to the elementary school nearby, where I still remember my fourth grade teacher, Miss Gert, telling us stories about visiting Paris and New York and other places I could only dream about. She made my friend, Cathy Jo, and I read *Little Women* to the class.

That was the world around me; that was the world I knew. We used to have to follow the river to get from Carville to Baton Rouge. What now takes twenty-five minutes took about forty-five back then, so you really did feel pretty isolated.

It was an idyllic way to grow up. To be honest, I'm not sure that what my kids have is as good as what we had back then. There's so much pressure on them these days. There's angst about college and exams. There's Facebook and Twitter and a million different ways to always be connected and plugged in, but very few ways to escape and be carefree and alone with your thoughts. There are a lot of forces that you don't have any control over that control your life.

When you grow up rural, and your daddy runs the local country store, and you got all your brothers and sisters to play with, and you come from a big family with tons of aunts and uncles and cousins—there's not a lot to reject you out there. There's no doubt about who you're going to spend your free time with because you're surrounded by family. There's no doubt about where you're going to college because LSU is right around the corner. And your daddy went, and your uncles went, and your brothers and sisters went. The idea that you'd go anywhere else never crosses your mind.

There was something to be said for having basically everything and everyone you knew exist in a twenty-mile radius. I loved my world as it existed, and I didn't know what I didn't know. Huck Finn was always running away, floating down the Mississippi trying to find freedom. I lived right there on the banks of the river and felt as free as any boy ever has.

People know I grew up in Carville, but they probably don't know just how strange and complicated the Carville family story really is, with immigrants and carpetbaggers and all sorts of characters who found their way to the South a long time ago. It's an unpredictable tale, and that's part of what I like about my family.

On one side, my ancestors were part of a Belgian colony in Guatemala before they came to Louisiana. My daddy's grandfather was born in Denmark, and his last name was Slangerup. There's still a town west of Copenhagen called Slangerup.

Most people assume Carville is a French name, both because of the way it sounds and because we settled in Louisiana. And I used to correct them and say that the Carvilles are all Irish until I learned differently on a trip to Ireland last summer. Actually, Carville is a French name, and our ancestors came over with William the Conqueror in 1066 and settled in Northumberland County in England, and then came into Ireland in the mid-1700s. My great-grandfather's people eventually ended up in County Monaghan and County Down in Northern Ireland.

What's really interesting is that there is a village in Normandy to this day called Carville. My mother's maiden name was Norman because her people emigrated direct from Normandy to Louisiana. So, if anything, the dominant ancestral gene I have is probably French-Norman.

My great-grandfather, John M. Carville, emigrated from Ireland to America in 1853 when he was eight years old. He served in the Union army, taught school in Janesville, Wisconsin, then migrated south to teach school in Iberville Parish. He eventually opened a mercantile store in what's now Carville, near St. Gabriel. He and my great-grandmother, whose parents were French, had eight kids.

Our family never really left after that.

My mother grew up in a place called Avoyelles Parish, which is the northernmost parish in Acadiana. It was the home to F. O. "Potch" Didier, maybe the only sheriff ever to be incarcerated in his own jail. He served a seven-day sentence after being convicted of malfeasance. I remember how her side of the family would have these big, raucous French family reunions. They called it a *boucherie*.

If you look at the Carvilles today, we still all look Irish, even though we have a French-sounding name. Some of us still drink like we're Irish, and we certainly have an Irish sense of humor. It's in our blood.

I remember when I was about eleven, I got to wondering about the Carville name. My grandmother pulled me aside and said, "You have a really good last name. It's easy to spell; it sounds just like it spells; and there's not a lot of other Carvilles around so you're not going to be getting confused with people all the time."

After that, I grew up really liking my name, really proud of it. I just never really knew the full history behind it, or what a diverse background I actually have and what a winding road my ancestors took to end up on the banks of the Mississippi. When we moved back down here, I finally began to research my family and connect all the dots. It helped me understand more about who I am and the people I come from. It reminded me that Louisiana is a mix of many backgrounds and cultures, ethnicities and experiences, and the Carville family was no different.

What was it that William Faulkner said about the past? It's never dead. It's not even past.

MARY

THE 2006 MIDTERM ELECTION cycle was a killer. James and I were on the road constantly. We came up with a new boredom-relieving game in that travel season after I couldn't take one more gin rummy loss to that supercompetitive, card-counting clown—we called it "where would we live if we ever retired?"

It was only a way to help us forget how often we were actually gone from the place we did live—and loved. And as much as we loved it, and as entrenched as we were in D.C. doings and as happy as our girls were in their Alexandria schools, every time we played the game, it got more serious.

Before we knew it, we had assembled a must-have list for any post-career, postkid potential move. The game maintained its fantasy status since no place on this planet or any other (I am a sci-fi nut to the point of sickness) could fulfill the dream list we concocted.

We had our standard demands, quite a lot of them. And if you got dizzy reading the laundry list of what we were looking for in a house earlier in the book, you might want to skip this part about what we were looking for in a post-D.C. environment, except that its complete disconnect from reality might make you laugh.

Me: I wanted a stimulating city that was manageable and family oriented, with good schools and restaurants, near water and art and amazing gardens and other botanical wonders. Quality but affordable living. I wanted a vintage house, no debate on that. In my mind, the total ideal would be a college town without liberals. See, I told you it was a fantasy.

The Ragin' Cajun's list was the same one he'd had for the last eighteen years. A place to run, warm, no snow, sports, fresh produce. Unlike me, he's a predictable human being with realistic desires. But as our game progressed, he added something new that in retrospect makes me think he was one step ahead of the sheriff.

He wanted to teach and he wanted to walk to work.

We pored over maps; we went through college towns; we looked for locally grown produce. We tried to imagine ourselves ensconced in a creaking old home in Fantasyville, USA. I tried to ignore his dream-killing distractions. "How much would that cost?" "Will our furniture work there?" "You can't buy anything else ever again."

Lord have mercy. I was about to reconsider gin rummy. Then something happened that we knew was coming, that we didn't want to think about, and that we had been dreading for a long time. My father died.

JAMES

I THINK MARY AND I had known for a while that we wanted to move. We knew it was time. But the answer never seemed simple. We had kids who had grown up around Washington. A lot of our work relied on our being there. We'd talked about coming back to Louisiana, but the details always got in the way. Would we uproot the kids in the middle of a school year? Would we sell our house in Alexandria? And where exactly would we move? Most of my family was in Baton Rouge, and while Mary loved them and they loved her, I don't think she would have been happy there. She needed a bigger city and at least an hour's drive between her and the full force of the Carville clan.

To some extent, the upcoming presidential election in 2008 made the decision to leave that much easier. There was going to be a new regime coming in, and for the first time in sixteen years, neither Mary nor I would have our guy in the White House. We'd endured the Clinton years and the Bush years. That's a long stretch. Just the thought of either of us being part of another administration was tiring. I felt kind of tuckered out with politics at that level, and I think she did too. Hell, our kids had already been to more than a decade of Easter egg rolls at the White House. It was time to move on.

Besides, the last thing you want to be is somebody just hanging on, like the guy who keeps trying to relive his high school glory days after everybody else has gotten on with life. One more dance. One more ball game. There are plenty of those people in Washington. I didn't want to become one of them.

The price of staying would be constantly having to prove your relevance, and it was something I thought I'd look foolish doing. I could have evolved into something else, I suppose, like a government-affairs consultant or another job where people wear suits to work every day. But I knew I'd never be happy doing something like that. I'd rather leave on my own terms.

MARY

MY FATHER HAD BEEN wrestling with cancer for seven years. The summer of 2007, on a visit that ended up being in the dialysis center to which he was now tethered three days a week, he gave me a folder with all his funeral instructions and some assignments for me, his eldest child. Since he had always been such an uberorganized man (unlike I am) and we always had a no-drama, man-to-man kind of relationship, I didn't cry while I stood over him, even when he did. But a while later, when I arrived at the airport to fly home, I called my sister and I couldn't stop weeping. I sat on the airport floor and sobbed and sobbed. I missed my plane, in fact.

My father kept working that fall, not that he had to, but his work ethic wouldn't give up even when his body did. Each day got tougher and tougher, but not working would have been way worse by his standard.

That winter, my precious baby brother, sainted sister and our kids confabbed at my Old Town home, in what we all suspected would be our last with Daddy. We had some laughs and good eats. He gave each of us a little private chat. He told my sister not to do what he did and work until she couldn't anymore. He died a couple of weeks later.

Christmas came and it wasn't the same—anybody who's lost a parent or family members knows what I mean. We tried our usual get-together in Virginia with my sister, Renie, and her family, but we were all shell-shocked and grieving. Renie doesn't drink, but she managed to put down a couple mimosas. I do drink, but no amount of red wine could ease my grief.

On Christmas Day, after Santa's generosity was revealed, we decided to head south to get James to the warmer climes he likes. So we packed up and took off for Carville country. To Louisiana. The first semihappy moment I'd experienced in seemingly forever was getting off the plane in sunny New Orleans. Who wears T-shirts at Christmastime? That blast of warm air was a godsend.

The Carville group lives near or in Baton Rouge, but we always liked to stay in our favorite city, New Orleans, only an hour away. We kicked off festivities with a giant, rollicking, comforting family dinner at James's sister Gail's new lovely home, and the warmth and laughs of the night totally distracted me from my grief. And another thing. It was Christmas, but there was no snow. Not a flake. For once, James wasn't spending Christmas crabbing about the cold, and all his sisters were fawning over him, which makes him so happy.

What tipped the scales? What made us know that we had found home again? It's hard to say exactly. When we got back to Windsor Court, a New Orleans hotel that we love, the girls and I went shopping (because Santa must not have gotten the secret list) and James went to the race-track. He loves horse races, hates shopping. (Do I ever ask him, "How much did you lose today?" No. I. Do. Not.) But, given my sad state of mind, he forwent his automatic "How much did you spend today?" question when we joined up for dinner.

The night was balmy and warm—unseasonably so for a Yankee girl like I am. And the twinkly lights and stars and Christmas carols and fake snow wasn't so bad looking either. And suddenly I felt better than I had in months, like I'd cracked open and the warmth and sunshine of New Orleans—the spirit of the people on the street, even though it was just a couple years after Katrina—were sinking in and healing me.

James and I looked at each other and knew.

The game was over. We were moving to New Orleans.

I like to think of the ease of that decision as my daddy's last, and lasting, gift to me and my family.

JAMES

BY THE TIME THE holidays rolled around in 2007, Mary and I had begun seriously discussing a move to Louisiana. We still hadn't quite figured out the details of how and when and where exactly, but one thing was certain: we both finally felt ready to let go of Washington.

We went down to spend Christmas with my family that year and to secretly scope the place out and make sure we really wanted to make the leap. One day between Christmas and New Year's, my brother Steve and some of our friends headed over to the Fair Grounds in New Orleans to bet on the horses. It was a cool, sunny winter day. After one race ended and before the next began, I sidled up to Steve. "Mary and I have been talking about moving back down here," I told him. "If I had to guess, I think this thing is probably going to happen."

Steve seemed excited, which made me that much more excited about the prospect of being reunited with my raucous band of Carville siblings. Of course, I had no idea at that moment just how fast the move actually would happen.

I called Walter Isaacson, the journalist and biographer, an old friend who also was on the board at Tulane. I told him that we were thinking of moving to New Orleans, that I knew I wanted to teach, and that it seemed to make more sense to do so in New Orleans rather than driving back and forth to Baton Rouge to teach at LSU.

"Well, well," he said. "Stay right where you are."

The next thing you know, my phone rings again. It's Scott Cowen, the president of Tulane. "So, I heard you're thinking of moving to New Orleans," he said. Shortly thereafter, Mary and I met Scott and his wife, Marjorie, for breakfast. Marjorie talked to Mary about what life was like in New Orleans and how quickly they had come to love it after moving to town in 1998. By the end of that breakfast, Mary was sold. She'd pretty much been ready to pull the trigger before that. But if she needed one last push, for whatever reason, that meal with the Cowens did it.

Almost immediately, I called a cousin of mine, Anne Milling. She and her husband, King, are a legendary New Orleans couple. They know everybody; everybody knows them. I told her we needed a real estate agent, and she got right on it. It seemed that Mary had a house picked out in a matter of days, if not a matter of hours.

Moving to New Orleans went from an idea to a reality in the span of a few months. At Christmas 2007, we were still wrestling with whether to end our two-decade stay in Washington. By May, we had bought a house and were beginning to pack our boxes. When the kids' school year ended in Alexandria, we headed south. After a quarter of a century, I was actually going home.

12.

Are We Really Home?

MARY

WE DIDN'T PRETEND WE were 100 percent sure of the decision. We just woke up every morning and looked at each other and asked:

Right decision?

Wrong decision?

While we waited to move, we waited for answers. We waited for signs, portents, any validating omen—anxious to be assured that we were doing the right thing. There were no rational reasons to move so we turned to looking hard for any reason, any indication, even irrational ones.

JAMES

LOOKING BACK ON IT, we didn't know exactly what we were getting into. It wasn't clear at all that it was going to work out. So much of the city was still a mess. The political leadership was tenuous. Our daughters were going into fifth grade and eighth grade, which is a tough time for such a big move. It was a risk any way you looked at it. But sometimes you have to take that leap of faith.

I've found that it's always better in life to be part of something that's trying to make it as opposed to something that already has it made. The real thrill is trying to build something new or save something worth saving as opposed to only protecting what you have. It's more fun to be the guy coming from behind than the guy trying to stay out front.

That was part of the appeal of New Orleans. In Washington, you can go to a fund-raiser for the Kennedy Center. You can give money to this cause or that museum. It's a nice thing to do. It's a tax deduction. But it doesn't exactly move the needle.

In New Orleans, Mary and I thought we might actually be able to move the needle. For better or worse, it's a smaller pond, and one in much more need. The idea for me, at almost sixty-five, that I would be able to throw a pebble and actually see the ripples we were making here was very appealing. Our hope was that whatever we did we might literally be able to see the impact.

MARY

IN THE FIRST MONTHS of residing in our new home, I was overwhelmed with the endless tasks of setting up a house, settling kids, finding my way to the grocery store without getting lost for hours—and the really critical mission of locating a hairdresser and manicurist and all those services you take for granted after thirty years in the same location.

Plus the presidential election was approaching, never fun at the Matalin-Carville homestead, though this one wasn't the marriage mauler all the previous ones had been since James's enthusiasm was tempered by Hillary's unexpected defeat and I wasn't all that attached to the McCain operation, though I admired him and adore Sarah Palin. And the wet blanket of grief lingering from my father's passing, and Tim's, kept my mood in check despite the ubiquitous enchantments of New Orleans.

While I fretted nonstop about the girls making new friends, it never occurred to me that I wouldn't have any pals myself to whip up spontaneous adventures with. You know, the kind of buddies you can drop in on unannounced, happily digging through their iceboxes, hunting through their wine collection, and taking over their TV. The kind of gal-pals who could take one look at me before I opened my mouth and say, "Girl, you're a hot mess. What's the matter?"

Maria had been that pal for more than thirty years. But Maria wasn't transportable to New Orleans. She was a Buffalo gal, not a Southern belle, and she couldn't stand the heat. That added to my list of things to be sad about, but we still had the phone, and she could detect any hot mess without any physical prompts. We both traveled a lot over the years, and when the going got tough, a call would come in out of the blue.

"What's the matter?"

"Nothing."

"Don't BS a BSer."

"You're a worrier."

"And you're a hot mess."

And so it went—and still goes.

My first response to extreme stress is to pretend it doesn't exist. Which is fine when Maria or my sister were around to take one look at me and go into fix-it mode. I didn't realize how entrenched my unhealthy neurotic dependency on them was until one day, after weeks of repressed hot messiness, Anne Milling showed up at my door with a bouquet of white lilies and I burst into tears. And couldn't stop.

Anne is James's lovely cousin, which blows every New Orleanian mind as there couldn't be two more different people. Anne is the epitome of what you think of when you hear "gracious Southern lady" and James epitomizes everything you'd imagine a crazy coonass would be, if you had such an imagination. And if you do, I am sorry for you.

As it turned out, by sanity-saving coincidence (if you believe in them, which I don't), Anne was our neighbor in Uptown and, as good fortune would have it, the queen of New Orleans. At the time, I didn't know that since I was still getting lost getting groceries and didn't have the mental bearings to study the social structure of my new place yet.

All I knew was that Anne was uniquely gracious, tremendously loving and inordinately helpful in getting us settled. She knew everyone, she was in the middle of spearheading countless Katrina recovery efforts, and she invited us to everything and generously threw parties and lunches and dinners to introduce me to her astounding array of friends. In addition, praise be to Jesus, she possessed an uncanny hot mess detector.

Anne was my first NOLA friend, a sister, mentor and protector.

JAMES

SO THE WANDERING SON came home. It only took a quarter century, but I'd finally made the journey back south, as I'd always suspected I would one day.

I was the only one of eight kids who had ever moved outside the borders of Louisiana. Hell, only two of us ever left the Baton Rouge television market. I had one sister who moved a little more than an hour away from Baton Rouge, and you'd have thought she moved to the moon. Washington might as well have been Mars or Jupiter.

Everybody else stuck close to home and, needless to say, stuck together. That made perfect sense. Ever since we were kids, we'd been intensely loyal to one another. We'd fuss and fight at home—being the oldest, I probably harassed my siblings more than anyone—but out in the larger world, the Carville kids watched out for one another.

Partly, that sense of loyalty came from my parents. My father was a deeply loyal man—loyal to his business, loyal to his friends, loyal to his family. My mama, Miss Nippy, always believed fiercely in her children. She demonstrated time and again how she had our backs, whether one of us got into a neighborhood scrape or whether I was on the verge of failing out of LSU (again). I suppose that from watching them we learned the lesson that looking out for your family was a duty, as well as one of life's greatest virtues.

Even in all my years away from Louisiana, the closeness of the Carville clan never waned. I missed more birthdays and christenings and LSU games than I would have liked, but never have I lost that tightness with my brothers and sisters. Whenever any of them would come to see us or when we'd visit home, we'd slip back into the same old conversations, tell the same old stories, laugh at the same old jokes.

Some of them are Republicans. They don't believe what I believe about abortion, or religion, or whatever. As with Mary, it doesn't really matter at the end of the day. We love one another dearly, and we don't spend much time sitting around talking politics. We talk about our kids. We talk about food. We talk about football.

Without a doubt, one of the highlights of the move back to New Orleans was reentering the orbit of my siblings and my nieces and nephews. I felt all the years apart begin to melt away as if I'd only left for a brief time.

They still consider me the black sheep, of course, given that I actually live eighty miles away in New Orleans. But that's about the perfect distance. Mary adores my family and loves my siblings to pieces. But she's more of a loner than most of us, and living with me is enough of a trial; I'm not sure how she'd do surrounded by the whole sprawling mess of Carvilles all the time. We can be a little overwhelming.

When you're in Baton Rouge, the Carvilles still operate as one unit, like a loud and unruly flock of geese. My sisters are still all best friends with one another. The joke is that no one has ever seen a single Carville girl. They always run in packs. Along with my brother, their families hang out together almost every weekend.

If LSU has a baseball game on a Saturday night, I guarantee you they're all going over to my sister's to watch, which is exactly what they did for the game the night before, and probably what they'll do for the game the day after. There's something very endearing about that to me.

Families in America keep getting smaller. People get married later in life. They wait longer to have kids. That's all fine; I went that route myself. But I'm sure glad that I come from a big family. Those same siblings you complained about when you were a kid because there were eight of you in three bedrooms and they got on your nerves—you learn as an adult that you can't live without them, nor would you want to. They sometimes felt like your enemies growing up, but over time they become your closest friends and your most ardent defenders. Coming from a big family, I never have felt alone in this world.

My siblings also give me a deep sense of comfort that trumps any life insurance policy or 401(k). I know that if I got hit by a bus tomorrow, there's a big group of loving people eighty miles up the road who would swoop in and look after my wife and kids. There's just no question about it; they'd be there in a second. Big families breed loyalty.

MARY

THE SPECIAL HOSPITALITY AND expansively embracing nature of New Orleanians is well-known and well documented. But to actually move there and see it firsthand—and feel it up close—is a thoroughly beautiful experience. Another facet of life in New Orleans, and equally cool, is the genuine eccentricity of Crescent City characters.

In my meandering life journey, I've been blessed with the friendship of many characters, but nothing prepared me for the large personalities of NOLA. And I mean LARGE. No one feels obliged to smooth their nonconforming edges or subdue their originality.

One day I walked unannounced into James's work space and there, sitting in a chair, was an uncommonly handsome man radiating energy, charisma and a king-of-cool vibe. I recognized him from somewhere, though I couldn't place him. I glanced over to a table and there on the cover of a local magazine, I saw this same specimen of male perfection staring back at me.

Turned out, he was the ridiculously talented King of Swing, the heart-stopping trumpeter and jazz maestro Irvin Mayfield, who also has a nonstop devotion to service. (Don't miss his Jazz Playhouse at the Royal Sonesta on Bourbon Street or any of his other New Orleans establishments.) With his longtime friend Ronald Markham, a classically trained pianist and MBA (by night, rocking in Irvin's band; by day, running the New Orleans Jazz Orchestra or NOJO), Irvin and his gang have launched countless projects to preserve indigenous New Orleans music and heritage, saving many a young kid in the process. From Carnegie Hall to the great concert halls across Europe, his music has mesmerized the masses. And along the way, he has provided schools and instruments and inspiration for the next generation of New Orleans musicians.

Everyone had a profoundly heartbreaking, gut-wrenching Katrina story—Irvin found his daddy drowned on Elysian Fields when the ghastly mud and murky waters subsided—but you never hear anyone complaining. Ever. For those who remained in New Orleans, they were only trying to put it all back together.

And it was a purely 100 percent citizen effort too. The people of New Orleans were the ones who prevented their city from becoming a "sliver on the river," a constant tortured thought of my husband's. In the long, hard slog after Katrina, they have buried their dead, collected tons of storm debris from the ruined jungle of dead foliage, cleaned out mangled appliances and waterlogged furniture from warehouses, scraped the black mold from what remained of their demolished homes, comforted their shell-shocked kids, fed their displaced neighbors—and housed them.

When Hurricane Gustav threatened a Katrina redux soon after we arrived, stark terror gripped the city. More than one new friend told me, "That's it. Can't take another one. I am out of here. For good."

That's when any personal reservations I might have had about our move began to pale in comparison to my sudden realization that this wondrous city was heading for trouble if we didn't get our political act together. Pronto. The city needed leadership. Even the most industrious citizens can only do so much if their government is undoing it right behind them.

I could tell James was working on a plan, but for the first time in our lives, I feared even my Superman was about to crash into a mountain of kryptonite. It was one hot mess for sure.

JAMES

ANOTHER REAL UPSIDE OF COMING HOME: the chance to teach at Tulane.

Even after the move, I still went on television plenty, and I continued to jet off to foreign campaigns. But back home, I loved being a professor at Tulane. I've got a great office. I've got great kids who teach me every bit as much as I teach them. I started teaching back in 2005 at Northern Virginia Community College, and it just grew on me. Now, when I fly overseas and they ask you on the entry form to fill out your occupation, as often as not I'll write "professor," because that's how I tend to think of myself these days.

And as a professor who takes the job seriously, I get pissed off at the notion that universities are some sort of giant brainwashing factory. That's certainly not why I came to Tulane to teach. I'm not there trying to churn out a new generation of Democrats. Ask any of my students, and they'll tell you my mantra: "It doesn't matter what I think; it only matters that *you* think."

I tell them, I'm sixty-nine years old (as of October 2013). You are in an elite class at an elite university. Why do you need some old man telling you what to think? You don't.

But what they can benefit from is somebody who knows people, has experience and can give them the framework to think about important things. That's really my job—to get them to think. That's the whole reason a university exists.

Take the Tea Party, for example, which has played an interesting role in U.S. politics in the past few years. I think it's a cockamamie thing, but that doesn't really matter. If you're my student, I want you to understand it. If you think it's a cockamamie thing, and you don't understand it or take the time to learn about it, what good is your opinion? These are people with a grievance.

If you don't understand the nature of their grievance, then what good am I as a teacher?

In fact, one of the first things I did after the Tea Party began to gain steam was to call the office of Congressman Steve Scalise, a hard-core conservative who represents Louisiana's 1st District, and ask them to put me in touch with the local Tea Party leaders. They referred me to these guys in Baton Rouge, who I then invited to come speak to my class. One guy was an engineer at a chemical plant. Another guy knew one of my sisters. They talked a lot about the Constitution, a lot about the deficit—the normal stuff you'd expect.

But at least the students got to hear it straight from them. Suppose I had sat there and told my class, "Here's the deal. The Tea Party is full of shit. They don't understand the real Constitution. They don't understand the Articles of Confederation. They don't understand true Hamiltonian values." You could regurgitate all of those arguments, all of which are arguments that I would make, but you would not understand who those people are. You would understand my point of view, but you wouldn't understand their point of view. I'd see that as a failure.

Each semester, I've lined up a string of guest speakers, and I've always had people from across the political spectrum, as well as journalists I admire. Sure, I've had Democrats such as Stan Greenberg and Eliot Spitzer. But I've also had plenty of conservatives, from Erick Erickson and Newt Gingrich to Governor Bobby Jindal. I've had Art Laffer. I've had Neil Newhouse, who was Mitt Romney's pollster. I don't discriminate. I want the students exposed to every imaginable viewpoint.

In fact, when I make an assignment, I don't ask students which side of an issue they want to argue. I tell them which side they're going to take, and you can't swap with anybody. I say, "This half of the class is for the Keystone pipeline. This half is against." I'll make half of them argue for economic stimulus and the other half argue for austerity. I want them walking out of there with an understanding of the topic. You can't really know an issue until you know both sides of it.

What they choose to believe after that is their own business. But there's no credit for agreeing with me.

MARY

THERE IS NOTHING MORE beautiful than a person and his passion converging. James loves, loves, loves teaching; he loves, loves, loves bright young minds. And he loves, loves, loves to talk.

He knows something about everything. And on those rare occasions he doesn't know anything, he can get smart on any topic with his truly amazing lightning quick-study capacity. The girls call him Answer Man. I could make a joke about his having an answer for everything even when he just makes it up, but the truth is he has both a strategic mind and an abnormal reservoir of disparate knowledge. That, combined with the reality that he could have done stand-up in the Catskills, makes him the teacher you wish you had in college—especially in law school.

Teaching the brightest kids in the country at an elite university is a lot of work. He puts more effort into his Tulane class than anything I've ever seen him do. I don't get it because, to be honest, I don't like to teach as much as I like to learn. And a lot of college kids opine with an authority not supported by fact or argument, which I find grating. But I do love his kids, whom he regularly has over to the house after class for jambalaya or crawfish boil. They are unfailingly earnest, polite, poised and thoughtful.

I've attended a few of his jam-packed classes, and he does demand the kids think, not regurgitate. And he's especially effective with those kids you always hated because they were the smartest ones in the class and made sure you knew it. Those precocious ones are his faves. He makes them earn it big-time.

And contrary to his public persona, James is also relentlessly open to and respectful of opposing views. My all-time dream class was with

Peter Berkowitz on his book, *Constitutional Conservatism: Liberty, Self-Government, and Political Moderation*. Like all visitors to Tulane classes, I am supposed to be only an observer, but I was such a guest-speaker hog, James quit calling on me.

That was fine too. Because I was just as happy to watch in silence. As beautiful as seeing a person and his passion collide is, it is even better to witness it overtaking the person you are most passionate about. I am happiest when he is.

JAMES

IN UPTOWN NEW ORLEANS, the natives don't necessarily take too well to new-comers or strangers. It's not exactly like the rest of the South. It's sort of its own society, with its own traditions and its own rules. It's hard to break through if you're new in town; it doesn't matter if you're rich or famous or whatever. They take some pride in that.

One of my favorite stories, which illustrates that wrinkle of New Orleans society, happened not too long after we got to town. My youngest daughter loves tennis, and there is this private tennis club not far from our house. So I told Mary, "We ought to join the tennis club." She went and talked to this federal judge she knew in town who was a member there, a nice fellow who'd been appointed during the Reagan administration. "Oh, that's great!" he said, promising to put our name forward for membership.

We get this call a couple weeks later, and he says, "I don't know what to tell you. It's embarrassing, really, but y'all were blackballed."

And I said, "Really? How cool is that?"

We had moved down South from Washington. I was teaching at Tulane. We were raising money for all kinds of causes and trying to help with the recovery. But apparently we weren't good enough for the tennis club.

I was ecstatic. For starters, it saved me thousands of dollars. Even better, I felt like I was finally a real New Orleanian. I'd now been shunned and felt the sting of discrimination. The same people who were toasting us in public were blackballing us at the tennis club. They didn't need these uppity political types polluting their tennis club.

I never got to set foot in the place. The judge who'd put our name up was furious. He wanted to quit. I wasn't beat up about it at all. I thought it was great.

It's like the old Groucho Marx line: "I don't care to belong to any club that will have me as a member." Or, in this case, won't.

MARY

EMERSON WANTED TO JOIN a private tennis club in New Orleans, which I normally would have balked at, but I was thinking maybe it would make her less homesick for the swim and tennis club where she and her Virginia posse had hung out all summer. I asked one of my new girl-friends in local politics what she knew about it. Stacy Head, who is now a big-deal city councilwoman-at-large, said all the right kid-friendly things about the club and took me over to see it, showing me around and volunteering to sponsor us.

I didn't think much about it, even though it was way pricey, but I could never put a price on my kid's happiness. I figured I would just re-duce the cost by 80 percent when I told James the price and he would be cool. I think we needed more than one sponsor, and I don't remem-ber who else weighed in, but they all were wonderful new pals. So I was pretty embarrassed when they had to tell us that we'd been re-jected. It was a neighborhood tennis club, after all, and we only wanted to join so our fifth-grader could hit some balls and possibly make some friends.

Not that I was upset; I have had lots of practice with rejection. But I just couldn't wrap my head around this latest one. It didn't jibe with the enthusiastic new neighborly embrace that we had otherwise been enjoy-ing. And even more, I felt awful for my new friends, who were mortified. They put on a big campaign to change the rules after that so new members couldn't be anonymously blackballed—or, at least, to require more than one person to kibosh a new applicant.

JAMES

TO UNDERSTAND WHAT IT meant for the Saints to win the Super Bowl in 2010, you have to understand more than just Hurricane Katrina. You have to understand the whole sorry, miserable, soul-crushing history of the Saints. You have to understand how many loyal fans had waited so long to have even a decent team, much less a Super Bowl champion. The horrors of Katrina, the slow and painful rebuilding of New Orleans—all that made the Super Bowl win that much more emotional and special. But trust me, a lot of the unbridled joy that engulfed New Orleans that day in February 2010 came down to the fact that we'd gotten so used to having one of the worst teams in football, it felt awfully damn good to finally have the best.

I'd been waiting as long as anyone. I was an original Saints season-ticket holder from the very beginning in 1967, when their home field was Tulane Stadium. They played their first game ever that fall against the Los Angeles Rams, and I was in the Marine Corps, stationed at Camp Pendleton, watching on a little television in a bar near the Pacific Ocean in La Jolla, California. I'll never forget John Gilliam running back the opening kickoff ninety-four yards for a touchdown. I scared the bejesus out of everyone in that bar, howling like some sort of possessed swamp creature. How could you not be hooked after a start like that?

After that first play, it was all downhill for about twenty years. Year after year, the Saints were abysmal. The absolute definition of futility. In a way, it didn't matter. The true fans stuck with them. What else could you do? New Orleans didn't have a pro basketball team until the Hornets arrived in 2002. You had to drive three hundred miles to Houston to find the closest major-league baseball team. LSU was right up the road in Baton Rouge, and I'm as big an LSU fan as anybody, but that's an entirely different experience. When it came to pro sports, the Saints were the only game in town. Football is one of the five F's of Louisiana, the other four being family, food, faith and fixing flats.

By the time 2009 rolled around, a lot of fans, including me, had been suffering with the Saints for more than four decades. Mary and I had moved back the previous summer, and being there to witness that season made being back home that much sweeter. I'd been to plenty of Redskins games during my Washington days. It's an enormous pain in the ass to get out to the stadium in Landover, Maryland. You sit in traffic forever. You walk a country mile to get to the stadium, and another one once you're inside the gate. You sit outside in the blazing heat, at least early in the season, and if they make the playoffs, you freeze your ass off. Now, it was maybe twenty minutes from my living room chair to my seat inside the cool comfort of the Superdome.

After all those horrid years, the Saints were finally, mercifully, amazingly good. They finished the regular season 13–3, then kept on winning right through the playoffs. They destroyed the Arizona Cardinals. They squeaked out a really tight game against the Minnesota Vikings in overtime to make it to the Super Bowl. Un-freaking-believable.

Off the Saints went to Miami. No way I wasn't going too.

I was on pins and needles that whole night, like pretty much everybody else in New Orleans. Even when the Saints took the lead in the fourth quarter against the Indianapolis Colts, I never actually allowed myself to believe they could win the Super Bowl. So many of us had been conditioned by the years of mediocrity that we couldn't fathom a moment like that. But when Tracy Porter intercepted Peyton Manning in the fourth quarter and ran it back seventy-four yards for a touchdown, it dawned on me. Holy shit. We're going to win. It was a great night for the city, and a great night for that marine corporal who started pulling for the Saints forty-two years earlier in a bar in La Jolla.

Another great memory from that night: Rita Benson LeBlanc, the granddaughter of the Saints' owner, Tom Benson, invited me up to the owner's suite during the game. After the win, we all went down on the field, and Drew Brees was holding his little boy in one arm and the Super Bowl trophy in the other. Confetti was raining down. There was glitter everywhere. Pretty magical moment. And somebody said, "Let's get on the team bus, and we'll ride back to the hotel with the team and go to the after-party."

So we got on this bus, and there sat Archbishop Philip Hannan. He'd served as a chaplain to the 82nd Airborne Division in World War II and been the archbishop of New Orleans for more than twenty years until he retired in the late 1980s. He was a legendary figure in town, and here he was at ninety-five years old, sitting on the team bus after the Super Bowl win, surrounded by a couple of other priests. About that time, here comes Kim Kardashian, who was dating Saints running back Reggie Bush back then. She's wearing tight black jeans and a low-cut black shirt.

I should have taken a picture with my cell phone to memorialize the moment, because that bus could not have held a motlier crew—a revered Roman Catholic priest and a reality-TV star with her own sex tape. I think Kim got as far away from the archbishop as she could get. I doubt the archbishop knew who she was, anyway.

But I couldn't help thinking that this was New Orleans in a nutshell. The holy and the unholy, together in one spot.

MARY

JAMES HAS MANY LOVE songs to New Orleans, the theme of which is usually *our unique way of life*. But he hits a high note when he croons his long, inspired riff on the funerals here.

Until we moved to New Orleans, funerals were no occasion for anything inspiring for me. As a society, we often claim to have planned our funerals according to what we know our departed loved ones would want. But this is rarely true, as far as I can tell. For me, the experience of attending one runs the continuum from somber dread to unendurable pain. As I think I've mentioned, in my youth my parents kept my sister and brother and me from all wakes and funerals, leaving me ill equipped in adulthood to fathom their main purpose, which is to be comforting or comforted.

Wailing, I literally ran from my mother's graveside. And silently, I sat zombied-out at my father's, trying to comprehend being orphaned at age fifty-four. In our decades together, James and I have lost parents, many family members and a shocking number of friends. Some losses were harder than others. Some were bittersweet blessed leave-takings, like Lee Atwater's who suffered too hard for too long. Some were breathtakingly painful, like Ann Devroy's, also struck down in her prime, leaving a precious eleven-year-old girl and beautiful young husband. There will always be a hole in our hearts for Tim Russert, but as discordant as it was for all the many who adored him, his funeral was an unexpected gift for us. It completely eradicated whatever residual concerns we had about moving our family to New Orleans.

We may not agree on all the life issues but James and I are in aggressive agreement on the life-affirming way New Orleans deals with death.

Unlike the whispering, weepy Midwestern funeral or the Washington command performance—a New Orleans funeral is a celebration of life in every way. It echoes the way life is savored and lived fully here. With a death comes dancing and music and second lines and food and fun for days. I know that can sound disrespectful, so I should point out the prayer vigils and faith rituals preceding the festivities are plenty mournful; as deeply sad as the aftermath is riotously happy. The bereaved in New Orleans are always very comforted by the yin-yang juxtaposition. The party goes on and on. If you have lost a truly loved one, you know the pain goes on much longer. New Orleans funerals don't stop the pain, but in that moment when your heart is shriveled up, they do foretell a future when memories of your dear lost one will put a smile on your face. And I swear, you can feel your angel hovering above the music and dancing. It's definitely the way I want to be sent off.

JAMES

MARY GREW UP IN A METHODIST CHURCH. But in fundamental ways, she was born to be a Catholic. It's tailor-made for her. She loves the traditions, the rituals, the beauty and the ornateness of the churches.

Since we moved to New Orleans, she has taken to Catholicism with the fervor of a convert. She doesn't just go on Sundays. She goes during the week. And down here, people take their religion seriously. Everybody either knows the name of the archbishop or knows him personally. Mary's definitely in the latter crowd

I'm a cradle Catholic, born and raised. But these days I think of myself as more of a cafeteria Catholic. I pick and choose what to believe, and what not to believe.

I obviously don't buy the "no birth control" argument. Doesn't make a lick of sense to me. In terms of abortion, I'm not sure if you'd really want to be part of a church that was actually pro-abortion. I'm sympathetic to difficult choices people have to make in life. I obviously believe abortion should remain legal. But I don't find the Church's opposition to it particularly surprising or troubling. It's understandable. What other position are they supposed to take?

On the topic of gays and gay marriage, I can kind of understand the prohibition on getting married in the Catholic Church. Okay, fine. But the Church's whole vehement opposition to gays in general, it's just ludicrous. It makes the Church look out of touch and unrealistic. It's a battle they're going to lose, if they haven't lost already.

In Louisiana, like in so many other places, it's staggering the number of people who have little or no health care, who are suffering from mental illnesses, who are underfed or underemployed. The world has enough crises. And Church leaders are spending all this time and energy fighting gay people? It's more than a waste of time. It's a colossal misrepresentation of what they should be doing.

The truth of it is, I'm not going to change the Church. The Church isn't going to change me. We just sort of live with each other.

MARY

THE MOST FREQUENTLY ASKED question I get about faith comes from non-Catholics, who always want to know what epiphany triggered my conversion to Catholicism. Whether convert, revert or a cradle Catholic, most of the community of faith will tell you the gift of faith is an ongoing journey, not a slap-across-the-face revelation. There are certainly blessed moments of clarity and joy and humility, occurring through deep prayer or sometimes just out of nowhere.

My religious journey started way before faith and is based on reasoning. The beauty and order of the world is too great to be the result of a random collision of particles. And the truth of love and evil is too undeniable to occur by happenstance. I am a faith and reason gal, of the JP2 variety: *Fides et Ratio.*

I wish—I pray—I could convey what the gift of grace is and means to me, but its one of those things: if you don't get it, you just don't get it. And if you do get it, you know it is inexpressible, though some great minds through history have given expression to it, which sparkle and delight and stop you in your tracks. Thomas Aquinas, C. S. Lewis, Archbishop Sheen, Dietrich von Hildebrand, G. K. Chesterton. Blessed John Paul II and Pope Benedict XVI and our new Pope Francis have the voice of angels. And George Weigel can explain everything and open your mind to the inexplicable issues.

If there was one catalyst it was the timely presence of a very learned and dedicated man of faith, Monsignor Christopher Nalty, who returned from the Vatican to New Orleans about the same time we did. It's a daunting path to get on and a harder one to stay on, but he is a born shepherd.

Something beautiful and true occurs almost daily to validate my "nothing is random" belief. But Monsignor Nalty is a walking-talking-spot-on consistent validation of God's will on earth. Try to imagine this scene last winter at the conclave in crowded St. Peter's Square. There he was crushed in the hordes, being bustled about in the rain, responding to the barrage of believers' questions, explaining in depth the meaning and possibilities of every airborne whiff of smoke emanating from the Vatican fluently in four different languages (which didn't include English or Latin, which he is also a whiz at). How could that be random?

So if you are wondering about the Catholic faith, do some reading and find another miracle like Monsignor Nalty.

In the meantime, I offer these thoughts.

This summer, on the day I decided to write some thoughts about my Catholic faith for this book, I went first to a little chapel in Cortona, Italy, a beautiful city on a Tuscan hilltop, where I was staying for part of the summer. In the dark quiet space, I searched for words to describe how such an unworthy one as I have been blessed with such a gift. Faith: what greater gift is there to be given in middle age—or any age? I got down on my knees on the cool marble and prayed and prayed and prayed.

All that came to my mind were the words of the great Christian, Saint Augustine, also a late-in-life convert, whose gratitude for grace comes down to us through the centuries as immediate and pure, and full of feeling, as the day he first wrote his confessions:

Late have I loved you, beauty so old and so new: late have I loved you. And see, you were within and I was in the external world and sought you there, and in my unlovely state I plunged into those lovely created things which you made. You were with me, and I was not with you. The lovely things kept me far from you, though if they did not have their existence in you, they had no existence at all. You called and cried out loud and shattered my deafness. You were radiant and resplendent, you put to flight my blindness.

You were fragrant, and I drew in my breath and now pant after you. I tasted you, and I feel but hunger and thirst for you. You touched me, and I am set on fire to attain the peace which is yours.

But as is the case, great writing like Saint Augustine's can inhibit rather than inspire. How could I ever come within a million miles of saying it better? Or even just something vaguely original? I have learned that God has multiple ways of communicating and works on his own schedule, which, of course, is totally cool with me.

So I opened my daily prayer book that I use at home, which contains the *Magnificat* (*The Song of Mary*), and was so-not-surprised to find the meditation of the day that followed the Gospel of Matthew 13:18–23. Again, the words are not my own, but they say exactly what I feel—and certainly much better than I ever could. And believe me, I've tried. Thank you, Walker Percy, the Catholic convert, novelist, essayist and medical doctor who wrote this exchange below.

THE CERTAINTY OF THE HUNDREDFOLD

Q: What kind of Catholic are you . . . a dogmatic Catholic or an open-minded Catholic?

A: I don't know what that means. Do you mean do I believe the dogma that the Catholic Church proposes for belief?

Q: Yes.

A: Yes.

Q: How is such a belief possible in this day and age?

A: What else is there?

Q: What do you mean, what else is there? There is humanism, atheism, agnosticism, Marxism, behaviorism, materialism, Buddhism, Muhammadism, Sufism, astrology, occultism, theosophy.

A: That's what I mean . . .

Q: I don't understand. Would you exclude, for example, scientific humanism as a rational and honorable alternative?

A: Yes.

Q: Why?

A: It's not good enough.

Q: Why not?

A: This life is too much trouble, far too strange, to arrive at the end of it and then to be asked what you make of it and have to answer "scientific humanism." That won't do. A poor show. Life is a mystery, love is a delight. Therefore I take it as axiomatic that one should settle for nothing less than the infinite mystery and the infinite delight, i.e., God. In fact I demand it. I refuse to settle for anything less. I don't see why anyone should settle for less than Jacob, who actually grabbed aholt of God and would not let go until God identified himself and blessed him.

Q: Grabbed aholt?

A: A Louisiana expression . . .

Q: How do you account for your belief?

A: I can only account for it as a gift from God.

Q: Why would God make you such a gift when there are others who seem more deserving, that is, serve their fellowman?

A: I don't know. God does strange things . . .

Q: But shouldn't one's faith bear some relation to the truth, facts?

A: Yes. That's what attracted me, Christianity's rather insolent claim to be true, with the implication that other religions are more or less false.

Q: You believe that?

A: Of course.

The other question I am asked: did my conversion change my views on abortion?

Abortion. What an issue. In a league of its own. Thinking of abortion as an "issue" is like thinking of life and death as just another day at the office.

When you are a young woman, even in this age of prolific birth control options and sonograms and so many couples having problems making a family, abortion is about you, not babies. The moral compass is your rights, your life, not a baby's and certainly not anything to do with the morality of the culture.

Young women today—not all, certainly fewer it seems than when I was young—think of abortion as I did before I *thought* about it. When you don't think about what abortion really is, it's easy to put it in the basket of "I am woman, I am strong" stuff; to think of it as your personal province: your body, your decision.

And I really do get the desire and need for women to be able to control their professional and personal destinies. And yes, at some level it seems unfair that our window of time to create life often conflicts with our peak career and earning years. And, of course, there can be no greater or more horrific dilemma than the one an unwanted pregnancy presents to a woman.

But the sound of a heartbeat beating separately from your own, long before there is anything in your body that looks remotely like a baby, completely and thoroughly washes away those concerns. Or at least it did for me. And if that heartbeat stops, the world stops, or at least it did for me.

I remember how I felt when I discovered Maxene Fernstrom, my first campaign boss, a woman I looked up to more than anyone, was pro-life. She was a close friend and supporter of Henry Hyde, the pro-life champion of his day. In those days, I did not know one woman that was pro-life. Not that any of us "I can bring home the bacon" babes thought about abortion as having anything to do with a life other than our own. We were "doing our own thing" and on a fast track to glass ceiling crashing.

I know my girls at their young ages have a deeper understanding of the "issue" than I did, due to their Catholic instruction and modern technology and their mother's haranguing, but still theirs is the age when the "issue" is just not all that *real*, in the sense that wanting a family is in the far distance. I get that. I do not get grown women not having a deeper conversation about abortion.

Even when I was pro-choice, I did not like the state butting their big all-knowing selves on either side of this most personal business, but even then, I understood a culture that doesn't revere life and the dignity of individuals was on unsteady ground.

I am pro-life for many reasons and support many pro-life causes; it is literally inconceivable to me that *anyone* of *any* party or philosophy or gender or age could support partial-birth abortion. And I hate the politics of abortion, that it is treated like any other political football, as though it were ANWR or taxes.

Americans do revere life, and America was built on both the sanctity and dignity of every individual. And we are uniquely moral. Yet we talk past each other of the most life-affirming and moral issues of all time.

Monsignor Nalty prayed every Saturday for years outside an abortion clinic in New Orleans. And the clinic closed. No telling how many lives he saved, mothers and babies. Many have thanked him for making them stop and think about what they were doing, and for their decision to not do it, but I suspect there are many more families out there he saved and will never know about.

In life, and especially in this country, there is a do-over opportunity for almost everything. Except abortion. That is one bell that can't be unrung.

JAMES

WASHINGTON IS A DIFFERENT WORLD from New Orleans. Even the stories in Louisiana have a richness and a depth that you just don't find in Washington.

Everything is related to everything else, probably because everyone is sort of related to everyone else. There are voodoo priests and jazz legends, Cajun swashbucklers and Mardi Gras marauders, and any number of wild-ass heroes and scoundrels.

I can't count how many Washington stories I've heard over the years about Congressman So-and-So who was a committee chairman, and how he passed this or that legislation. Or how they had to get an amendment to this certain bill, and so they got a certain congressman drunk, and it all worked out in the end.

That's all fine, as far as it goes. But the stories down here tend to be a little spicier, a little more irreverent, a little rougher around the edges. Some are mystical. Others are just downright dirty.

I first began to discover this when I was about fifteen years old and my grandfather was on the board of a bank in Baton Rouge. They gave me a job delivering checks and files around town. I used to walk from downtown to the State Capitol during my rounds. They had this huge statue of Huey Long on the Capitol grounds.

This was the late 1950s, only a couple decades removed from when Long was still alive and a very powerful figure. So I'm standing there one day looking up at this statue and wishing I'd been around to see Huey Long in his prime, and along came this groundskeeper I used to stop and shoot the bull with.

I remember saying something like "Huey Long—that guy must have been the biggest thing to ever hit Baton Rouge."

And the groundskeeper looked back all serious and said, "No, son, he ain't the biggest."

I said, "Well, who's bigger?"

He said, "A woman named Big Red. She come from Port Arthur, Texas, to the inauguration in 1946. Brought the blow job to Baton Rouge. She's a bigger legend here than Huey Long will ever be."

I mean, he had her name, the date, even her hometown. I suppose we'll never know the whole truth about Big Red. She'll never get her own statue at the Capitol. But I began to understand that day that people down here know a good story when they see one.

MARY

WHEN YOU MAKE A dramatic move to a new planet, it is almost impossible not to compare all your experiences to the ones you had on the previous planet. This is just how human beings are. So along with the questions we asked ourselves—Right decision? Wrong decision?—we also couldn't help but think of our old home a lot and try to put it in perspective.

Everything in New Orleans—and I mean *everything*—was different from Washington.

JAMES

HERE'S ANOTHER DIFFERENCE: beignets are an indication of an advanced culture. Doughnuts, they're an indication of a culture in decline. You can't even compare the two.

For starters, beignets have a shelf life of like three minutes. You can't take them home. You don't eat them as leftovers. They're delicate, just like New Orleans itself.

The truth of the matter is they are a pain in the ass if you're the shop owner. Because they only last a few minutes when they're fresh, you've got to keep them coming. If you make too many, you have to throw them away.

Think about any other pastry. The chef comes in at five o'clock in the morning, and he bakes a bunch of croissants and you line them up and sell them all day.

In many ways, beignets are an art form. To make them well takes persistence and dedication. You have to have the oil temperature just right. You have to pace the entire operation throughout the day so you don't make too few or too many. Many places don't have the patience or the passion to turn a pastry into art.

That's the whole story in a nutshell. Washington is doughnuts. In New Orleans, you eat beignets.

MARY

THE RE AREN'T CHURCH BELLS after dark in Washington. It is considered a disturbance of the peace.

JAMES

IN WASHINGTON, IF YOU WANT, you can basically avoid the other side. You can work with people from your party, socialize with people from your party, expose yourself only to media that espouse the beliefs of your party. It's possible never to leave the confines of your own tribe.

That's not the way it works in Louisiana. I may not particularly like the Republicans in Baton Rouge. I may disagree with Bobby Jindal on a lot of his policies. In fact, I can't stand that his idea of an education plan is to cut funding to state colleges and teach creationism in the schools. I find it offensive to every bone in my body that I've got to pay one nickel in taxes for that kind of crap, and I've said as much to people who work for him. So I don't have to agree with Jindal, but I also don't have the luxury of not getting along with him. I don't think that makes me a hypocrite. It's just the reality. If we're working on the Super Bowl or trying to put together an improvement project in New Orleans, the road almost always passes through the governor's office. I live in a Republican state, and that's not going to change anytime soon. I have to deal with that and play nice whenever possible.

Mary faces the same predicament. She lives in a Democratic city. There's not going to be a Republican mayor of New Orleans—not now, not ever. So unless she wants to completely withdraw from the community, she has to deal with it and put aside partisan politics and work with people on the other side. And she's done exactly that. I think what we both discovered very quickly is that there are too many things that need to get done here, important things that matter profoundly, to worry too much about anyone's party affiliation.

We have to get along with the politicians here, no matter whether they have an (R) or a (D) after their name. We don't have any choice, because if people down here didn't work together, nothing would ever get done. That's true to some extent for local politics around the country. Politics takes a backseat to progress, not the other way around. Washington could learn a thing or two from that.

Without question, the most consequential political person in my life these days is the mayor.

I can live with a half-ass governor. I could even live with kind of a crappy president like George W. Bush. As long as a president doesn't do much, and doesn't do really stupid things, he can cause only so much harm. But a mayor matters, man. At every level.

When I first got down here, my first thought was, you can rebuild all the damn houses you want in the Ninth Ward, and it's not going to save the city. If we don't have some political leadership in this city, we're done.

I decided I needed to get some data and find out what really was happening with the city. People were saying New Orleans was hopelessly racially divided. There was a lot of bad blood, a lot of anger to go around over Ray Nagin's whole "chocolate city" remark. So we did some research. I tapped my class at Tulane, but we did most of the work through Democracy Corps, the nonprofit I founded back in 1999 with Stan Greenberg.

Ultimately, we discovered some really interesting things about New Orleans. First of all, it has the most female-heavy electorate of anyplace I'd seen anywhere in the world. Females make up 58 percent of voters. Among African Americans, it's 62 percent. Part of that, unfortunately, is because of the high male incarceration rate. The other thing is, there's staggering church attendance among black females. It's almost like 70 percent once a week or more. For white males, it's more like 20 percent.

We also found that Mitch Landrieu, a Democrat and the son of a former New Orleans mayor, was in a commanding position to be mayor. He'd run twice before, in 1994 and 2006, and lost both times.

He had said he wasn't planning on running again. But I really kept at him that year. Every time I'd see him, I'd say, "Look, you have to do this. The city needs you. You're going to win."

He'd say, "Oh, I don't want to drag my family through this again."

I'd say, "Man, you can't not do it."

Privately, I was thinking, *If this guy doesn't run, this place is screwed.* I had to convince him to run. It was literally almost a selfish impulse. I'd just moved my kids down South. I'd bought a house. I didn't want to live in a New Orleans that doesn't have a strong and competent mayor. There was an element of panic.

I'd been around the world. I'd seen the political landscapes in Colombia and Venezuela, in Israel and Nigeria. I knew what a difference real leadership made. And I wanted that for New Orleans. I knew that it mattered profoundly. And maybe the smaller the place, the more it matters.

I told Mitch, "Look, Mary is going to be for you. She's going to round up the Republicans for you." And Mary was behind him, a thousand percent. She knew he had the talent to do it, that he was the right guy for the job.

When he finally threw his hat in the ring, we did a lot of the data work for his campaign. Hell, we ran part of the operation from our dining room table. When he won with more than 65 percent of the vote, it came as no surprise to me at all. But it was still a big relief.

First of all, the attitude here has totally changed in recent years. They're still having a terrible time with the murder rate. There's plenty other problems. But they've really done some remarkable things.

There are really able people running the various city departments, but just like any other place in the middle of a recession, we've seen some tough fiscal times.

They've cleaned up the cabs. The airport has improved drastically. The city's image has completely changed for the better. We're hitting bigger tourism numbers than pre-Katrina.

Mitch came in and did what's easier said than done, but what he needed to do, which was raise taxes and cut spending—and not by a little bit. He's putting the city on more solid ground. He pays attention to the details, right down to the potholes. It's still far from perfect, but then no city ever is.

I'm certain about this much. Mitch was elected on Saturday, February 6, 2010. The Saints won the Super Bowl the next day. Of the two, which was the most important? Not even close. The mayor.

Don't get me wrong. New Orleans was a lot happier place because the Saints won. No doubt about it. Having a great football team is a blessing, and that win came at an important time for the city. It was a hell of a celebration, and I think people felt good about themselves, good for the players, good about the city. But it ain't real life.

Give me a choice between a great football team and a bad mayor versus a bad football team and a great mayor, and I'll take the great mayor any day.

Because in the end, what I've really come to learn—and this applies all over the world—is that it really matters who's running the show. If you're a company, a city, a country, a newspaper, a university—I don't care. It just matters.

MARY

DINNER PARTIES IN WASHINGTON, as everybody knows, end at ten-thirty p.m. on the dot. As a general proposition, it is very rare to go to bed after midnight and come downstairs in the early morning to find your dinner guests still in your living room, deciding to cheer you up with a competition to see who can squirm under your coffee table the quickest—and somebody has a stopwatch.

If that sort of thing happens, you know you are in New Orleans.

JAMES

MARY AND I BOTH have managed to make friends in New Orleans who are outside of politics—actual, normal, interesting human beings who don't wake up thinking about the latest Gallup polls or debating who might win the Iowa primaries in 2016.

That's been an incredibly healthy development and something I'm not sure was ever quite possible in Washington, considering the nature of that city and our chosen profession. There, politics is the industry. It's the first topic, the middle topic and the last topic of conversation. That's not so unusual or surprising. If you're in Hollywood, people talk about entertainment. If you're in Detroit, people talk about the auto industry. It's not that people in New Orleans aren't political or don't have a point of view, it's just that it's much easier to go to a dinner or to a party and actually not talk politics.

That kind of change, in my opinion, has been especially good for Mary. Conservatives, for whatever reason, tend to politicize everything. They politicize what kind of car they drive. They politicize French fries. One time, at the 1996 Republican convention, I heard Newt Gingrich politicize beach volleyball. He was introducing Olympic beach volleyball gold medalist Kent Steffes, and he said, "A mere forty years ago, beach volleyball was just beginning. No bureaucrat would have invented it, and that's what freedom is all about." How the hell do you even think something like that up? I would never look at a beach volleyball game and see something political. But that's how it goes. Almost every conversation in Washington carries the risk of having a political meaning that it wouldn't have anywhere else.

In a way, it reminds me of when I was a teenager in Carville, and I grew so tired of people talking about race. It's no surprise it was such a hot topic, considering the seismic shift that was taking place in the country and considering I lived in a town that was 80 percent African American. But you heard about it everywhere you went. I remember thinking, *Shit, can we have another conversation?* And I didn't mean like grand conversations about equality and justice and the dignity of man. I meant, can we talk about literally anything else? The latest LSU Tigers game? School? Anything. I found it so tiresome after a while. I didn't understand why we couldn't just move on. That's similar to how I came to feel about the political talk in almost any social setting in Washington. Can we please just have another conversation? In New Orleans, you can always have another conversation.

Another truth I discovered is that despite the reputation to the contrary people do not booze very much in Washington, as a rule. You go to a party, and people are having wine spritzers or whatever. It's always the same scene. People are looking around to see who is there. People are trying to work the room—"Good to see you, Bob. How are you, Bill?" If there are journalists there, they're always kind of working, sniffing out potential stories. People are careful not to get too tipsy. They are worried about embarrassing themselves or saying the wrong thing. Compare that to New Orleans. Here, if you host a party, you'd better have two bottles of brown whiskey with you, because they're coming after it.

The restaurants—same story. They're generally way quieter in Washington. People eat gently. They talk in hushed tones. They dress well. I remember going out to eat in New Orleans the first few times after we moved back and thinking, *This is the way people are supposed to sound.* There's not much of a social penalty here for laughing a little too loudly or talking a little too loudly or cursing a little too much. If somebody slips up and says the wrong thing, people don't hold it up as some sort of faux pas. They tend to shrug it off and say, "Oh, he was just drunk. What the hell?"

The conversation doesn't start and end with politics. You can let your guard down. That's been a good change for both of us.

MARY

OKAY, I know you are sick of hearing about my critters (but not as sick as James is of living with them). And while I don't feel a need to justify my adoration for all critters—large or small, mammal, amphibian, invertebrate or winged, domesticated, wild or feral—I would like a chance to explain how profound this connection and affection can be.

I have yet to encounter any creature in any category in any environment that didn't fit into the timeless order of things. You don't have to believe Noah to know the truth of a natural order. Ask Darwin, or even those crazy Malthusians. And it just so happens that the animal kingdom is a very reliable guide to the human kingdom.

You can do all the focus group studies and social networking spying you like. But how people interact with critters is a far more precise gauge of behavior, whether it's entire populations or individuals, than any poll or census data.

In my own field, you can bellyache forever about insolvable *partisan bickering*, but I know one powerful unifier that transcends political devotion: critter love. In his groundbreaking book, *The Righteous Mind*, Jonathan Haidt notes liberals presume all liberals are animal lovers and are always surprised to meet conservatives who are equally passionate about animals and so-called animal *issues*. (For the moment, I will forgo any diatribes on the closed and intolerant minds of liberals for the purposes of making my larger point.)

And my larger point is: people make instinctive (and correct) presumptions about other people based on their attitudes regarding animals. Yes, I know about Hitler and his dogs. And for every dog-loving Nazi, there is a cat-impaling Saddam Hussein—just like those neighborhood punks who tormented kittens and puppies and grew up to be junkies and perverts.

Those individuals aside, animals are an indispensible guide to people you might otherwise miss an opportunity to know or love.

One of the things that I most loved about our home in Virginia was its proximity to a fantastic dog park, which I renamed immediately "Dog Shit Park." (It was my walkway to the grocery store and Starbucks, so it wasn't an entirely 100 percent positive experience that so many dog owners don't bother to pick up after their canines.) The mitigating factor was all those happy, yapping dogs living large and loving life so nearby. They ran. They barked. Their exuberance was infectious. And they filled the whole park before and after the workday.

Even better than watching the dogs was witnessing the park's transformational power on people. All the dog people were delighted and animated and engaged with each other at Dog Shit Park. They laughed. They connected. Their eyes sparkled with warmth and humanity. Yet, so many of these same folks were less than friendly if you encountered them at the grocery or Starbucks.

The point is not that animal lovers are saints or that non–animal lovers are terrible people. The point is that animals connect us to something timeless and healing, life-embracing and deep.

If you have been involved with a wounded warrior at Walter Reed Hospital or anywhere else, or a battered woman in a shelter, or a terminal patient in hospice, or a troubled kid in a crisis school program, you have seen how animals can often reach and help humans, sometimes much more fundamentally and profoundly than another human.

I could never live anywhere that is animal restricted. NOLA is famously animal loving. Who could forget all the stranded Katrina roof sitters who refused rescue without their beloved pets? Even so, my first and lasting favorite NOLA friendships were forged and fortified by animal fondness.

The first week we arrived in New Orleans, Julia Trawick, a self-professed bleeding heart liberal, put a flyer on James car and signed it "from another good Democrat," presuming that he would want to engage her services as a dog-loving walker for the hounds she always saw him fussing with.

I usually roll my eyes at "good Democrats," but Julia's story was so New Orleans, I paused to pay attention. She had had a big job pre-Katrina, but the hurricane and its devastation transformed her from the inside out. She asked herself, What do I love most in life? Two things came to mind: dogs and New Orleans. From that epiphany, Julia never returned to her big job and, in a few short years, has established a mighty busy business doing what she loves: dog sitting. I love this woman. She is the kind of person who texts you videos of your beloved pups huddled together and sleeping peacefully while you are frantically on the road and missing home. And Julia does not discriminate among furry and feathered beasts: she loves rats, cats, dogs, birds and, of course, life. And what she gets from their love, she gives back. Who doesn't want to have a Julia in their life?

Another story that illustrates the animal-loving people and culture of New Orleans has to do with Matty and her struggle with math when we first arrived at our new home. Catholic schools may have curricula similar to public ones, but they are more serious about the basics, such as math and grammar. There are no remedial classes; it's sink or swim. But if you need extra help, there are some truly sainted teachers and tutors who are devoted. They will do whatever it takes to make sure you've learned what you need to learn. Without her amazing math tutor, Nina Kirk, I'm pretty sure Matty would still be retaking trigonometry.

I like math fine, but I was a little intimidated by Nina and initially didn't want to chum around with anyone that smart in a subject I can't really talk about—or, most days, grasp. But as it turned out, Nina is a big dog lover. Bingo. And then I learned that Matty's incredible eighth-grade teacher, Miss Graf, also a math maven, is a cat savior and saver. She kept a house and yard full of cats that had been displaced by Katrina, which evolved eventually into a place where people dropped off felines with such regularity that Miss Graf started sending around APBs recounting the wonders of another stray or adoptee or foster kitty who needed a good home. Robbie and Witchy (aka Fat/Killer Cat and Bagpipes) were abandoned kittens found under a house, and a good neighbor, rather than just leave them there, unloaded them at Miss Graf's.

Fully aware of James's feline antipathy, but feeling bad about Miss Graf's overcrowded kitty castle, I decided to take these two little ones and hide them upstairs until they were old enough to roam around the neighborhood. By then, James wouldn't know they were actually our cats. He'd think they were two more local beasts that I left food for outside. And my plan almost worked.

It's true. I had sworn to him—pledged an oath—*Yes, sir, no more animals*. But then Miss Graf sent around another APB about a recently discovered semiferal cat who had been living with a homeless person. When that individual found proper housing, the cat had moved to a car, which resulted in a tail-cutting incident we don't need to go into.

This cat had a few issues, and who wouldn't. She was not a people person, let's just say that. She hated the other cats and all dogs as well, probably due to her life as a drifter. After deciding I had to take her in despite her personality defects, I realized that she couldn't be hidden in the attic. She wasn't a kitten. But she was too crazy to leave outside. So I snuck her into my office.

But adult cats need to roam, and this one wasn't going to sit in an office after years as a restless roadie. To make matters more complicated, this cat—like all other cats—was very attracted to cat haters. So every time I opened my office door, she made a beeline for James's office and took over his big leather La-Z-Boy recliner, which no one—human or animal—was allowed to touch.

I named her Stubs, thinking it might help her recover from her recent indignity. So I was pretty confused when James called, screaming for me to get "Paula" off his throne and out of his life. *Paula?*

Gennifer Flowers, currently a lounge singer and previously a political pain in James's butt, had just moved to New Orleans. I wondered if this had caused him to have a Paula Jones flashback or something.

I ran into his office where he was swatting at poor Stubs—James will never actually touch a cat, so he swings his arms and hisses at them to get them to move. Meanwhile, he was saying, "Hey, hey!" and "Hey, hey, Paula!"—and then in one of those Carville mind processes you never see coming, he had started calling her Paula, as in the song "Hey Paula." The name stuck, so I took this as a sign that Paula could too.

Not long afterward, Stubs/Paula disappeared during one of my absences. I wasn't sure what happened and didn't want to grill James about what may have precipitated this. I trolled the neighborhood looking for her. I put up signs. I cried myself to sleep. But she was nowhere to be found.

A few weeks later, I ran into our neighbors Liz and Poco Sloss, who told me how much they loved my cat, who had taken up residence in their home. But not in their yard, on their bed! Totally unaware that she had gone missing—they hadn't noticed my signs—they did what New Orleanians do so habitually: they offered hospitality to any creature, large or small, that needed a bite to eat. They were happy to return her, they said. But in a testament to my love for James, I let them keep her.

To this day, Paula is enthroned on the Sloss bed, and James has one kitty victory under his belt. Lately, I've noticed that he likes to leave the doors of our house wide open in hopes that one or two other critters might wander away, which is why we end up at the emergency vet so often.

Lastly, I want to tell you about a man in New Orleans who has stolen my heart—and become one of my closest friends. We talk all day, every day. We call and text from overseas. We have regular dates and every one is special, from Sunday-night movies to the Dalai Lama. He plays piano and sings to me in celebration or sorrow. He knows when I need a good stress-relieving back cracking and knows how to do it expertly, as well as assess the inner turmoil of my daughters with far greater accuracy than their mother. And he has taught me everything about the beautiful things in life and even more about beautiful people.

I met Kevin Stone through a pair of stunningly beautiful and amazingly calm French bulldogs, Pascal and Henri. I was on a hunt for an oversized wooden chandelier and (being the occasionally obedient wife of James) I didn't want to pay much for one. And as always, I was in a hurry. I screeched into Kevin Stone Antiques, the shop that he and his partner, Mark Diamond, run on Magazine Street, and was stopped deed in my tracks by the handsome, friendly canines.

Forgetting all about my mission—and the big bottle of water in my hand—I fell to my knees to better admire these noble creatures in all their glory.

The water bottle dropped to the floor too, hurling its contents all over the shop, a virtual palace of rare and amazing treasures that was now sprayed in springwater. Across the room, a beautiful man shouted out, "Pascal! Henri!" and raced over to rescue me. I loved Kevin instantly; his warmth, empathy, kind humor, and those bulldogs, won me over. And ever since, he has come to my rescue too many times to mention. I had hoped to include one such rescue tale, but out of deference to the squeamish (which Kevin is not), I decided against a full description of how he and Mark saved me from an unfortunate belly-button-piercing incident.

My larger point here is to herald critters. They are good for the soul. And they bring kindred spirits together.

JAMES

MARY UNDERSTOOD THE SIGNIFICANCE of the Saints winning the Super Bowl. She gets the attraction of pro football. She understands the passion people have for the Saints because she grew up in Chicago, where everybody's crazy about the Bears.

But she doesn't get the college sports stuff, especially my obsession with LSU football. You can hardly blame her. She went to Western Illinois University. How could you understand big-time SEC football?

Of course, it ain't just football. People show up in their RVs and camp for days when LSU baseball's making a playoff run, and even I have to find a TV wherever I am to watch the games. My brother-in-law in Baton Rouge never misses a baseball game. He literally has one single season ticket. He goes by himself and is perfectly content to do so. He goes to basketball games, to softball games. I'm pretty sure he goes to a few golf matches every season. We're talking tried-and-true fans down here, not fair-weather fans.

Needless to say, Mary doesn't come to Baton Rouge with me too often during football season. Maybe if we have friends who are throwing a tailgate party, or maybe if it's a huge game (they're all huge games to me). But there's like ten preconditions before she'll agree to come.

It's a totally different story for me. I live, breathe and eat Tiger sports. Always have. I didn't miss an LSU home football game from the time I was in second grade until the time I went in the Marine Corps in 1966. I still go back every season, despite the crowds and the traffic jams and all the other small hassles that come with getting to the stadium.

It's an emotional connection that goes back very deep. I remember watching Billy Cannon make his unbelievable Halloween run in 1958. LSU was ranked first in the nation at the time; Ole Miss came in ranked number two. It was a bruising defensive game. Ole Miss kicked a field goal in the first quarter, then it seemed like nobody would score again.

All of a sudden, in the fourth quarter, Billy Cannon drops back to take a punt. He watches it bounce once and grabs it out of the air on LSU's 11-yard line. He goes eighty-nine yards for the touchdown and breaks like seven tackles along the way. It was total pandemonium, total jubilation that night in Tiger Stadium. I can still hear J. C. Politz, who was one of the great college announcers of all time, making the call: *"Billy Cannon races some eighty-nine yards for the touchdown! Listen to the cheers for Billy Cannon as he comes off the field! A great All-American!"*

The seat I saw Billy Cannon's run from in 1958 is the same spot where my sister and brother-in-law still sit today, over in the southeast end of the stadium. Umpteen times over the years, they've had the opportunity to move up or choose another spot. Not a chance. Those seats have been in the family since 1955, and that's where they're staying.

That's just the way it is when you've had such a connection to something your entire life. The old wins still give you joy; the old losses forever gnaw at you.

I remember the season after that 1958 national championship, when LSU looked like it might go undefeated all over again. On November 7, the Tigers played a nail-biter against Tennessee on a freezing day in Knoxville. Tennessee had been up most of the game, but LSU scored a touchdown in the fourth quarter to make it 14–13. They decided to go for the two-point conversion that would have won the game. Of course, they gave the ball to Billy Cannon, and the refs called him down a hair short of the goal line. Billy later said, "I will go to my grave believing I was over." I too will go to my grave believing that he scored.

Why do I bring this up now? Because I've never really gotten over the treatment Bill Clinton endured during the Lewinsky scandal. Ken Starr, the Republicans, the press—they were all obsessed with this witch hunt over something that wasn't criminal and never had anything to do with his abilities as president. Same with Whitewater and all the innuendo and accusations around that, which never amounted to a pile of beans. All these years later, I don't want to let go of my anger over it all. I still want to taste it; that's how furious it made me.

MARY

LOUISIANA MEN CAN REALLY cook and they all do a lot of it. The first time we had Mitch and Cheryl Landrieu over for dinner, when we didn't really know him all that well, he bypassed the polite public areas of our house and walked right to the stove. He uttered an indigenous saying I'd never heard before—but have heard many times since: "I need to get all up in your pots."

This "pot-getting-up-into" is reserved for the best of peeps—not just anybody. After all, you can't just let any-old-body get all up in your pots, now can you? So I loved Mitch from his first takeover of my kitchen.

Since he's the mayor and all, Mitch's pot marauding is somewhat limited—he's got bigger and more important things to do—but he still does try, even at catered events for him. But my most frequent kitchen raiders are Monsignor Christopher Nalty and his merry band of better-than-professional chefs.

Sporting events are only one thing that brings us together to eat, to drink, to spectate and holler. In New Orleans, any and all occasions, or no occasion at all, demand celebration and things frequently get out of hand, or at least out of hand by a Midwesterner's standard. We are intrin-

sically more reserved, though we do enjoy a good steak and rowdy free-
for-all sports event, but my new home has made a convert of me on every
level. I understand how sports and food and drink go together—and not
because it's a business or networking opportunity, which is how it always
felt in Washington, D.C. Dining was about deals and schmoozing.
Sports was about more deals and schmoozing. In New Orleans, sports
or any event with food offer a moment of beauty, truth and possible
redemption.

The monsignor likes to eat God's creatures that he has felled on the earth
or from the sky, or pulled from the warm Gulf waters, and then cleaned
and butchered himself. His hunting skills are legendary, and his gathering isn't bad either, as he grows his own herbs and veggies—all of which
help to make him a delightful dinner guest. He brings his kill and harvest
to our house, prepares a feast and always cleans up after. Did I mention
that he can make any kind of martini you can think of and is an oeno-
phile with an extensive cellar of unobtainable rare bottles? He also has
an endless repertoire of stories and, in the event of necessity (ghost
sightings, weird noises, bad history, etc.), can bless your house.

We have a fairly regular weekly gathering, mostly on Friday nights,
and it is always memorable, always an extravaganza. Just to give you a
flavor, here are some printable deets from our last dinner before we all
hauled out of the hot city for the summer.

Monsignor brought freshly caught tuna and red snapper, along with
venison sausage made from another personally felled beast. With herbs
from his garden, he made special sauces for each, and a kale salad, which
he dressed to perfection.

His Jesuit classmate, Eddie Connick, whipped up some kind of flaming extravaganza for dessert—something he calls peaches Julie Ann
after the wife he adores and never stops talking about . . . in a good way,
the way all wives wish their husbands would talk about them—while

our other dinner regular, the only noncook of the bunch, Terry White, provided entertainment by riffling through all my kitchen-gadget drawers and imagining alternative uses for each exotic (to him) utensil. And he didn't just tell the predictable and pedestrian "take my wife" jokes while holding a turkey baster or meat thermometer, but he regaled us with bust-a-gut, previously unimagined applications for everything from an avocado peeler to a garlic press to a hand-cranked tomato masher. Though Terry always marches to the beat of his own creative drummer (for instance, arriving at his own parties in footies, togas, animal skins or some antique velvet he took off a chair that Kevin was re-covering—though he wears Nehru jackets on a normal night), we were all very impressed with this sustained riff and it more than made up for his being clad in a polo shirt.

Though we can all cook, the "little women" (a term no one would use for any of us), the beloved wives of Eddie and Terry, Julie Ann and Frog, and I were reduced to menial food prep, table setting and hanging out on the back porch. The monsignor doesn't trust me with the guts of his dinners. After the third time I drained the pasta and didn't leave any preseasoned water to finish his sauces, I temporarily self-deported from even prep work to spare him further frustration and spare myself further humiliation.

Which was fine with all of us, because after a couple of James Bond martinis and copious gallons of rare wines, who wants to get up in any pots?

So I went to bed on that one typical night, and the monsignor went home to prepare for early Mass (and I do mean *early*, since he has many adoration hours a day, including a daily one at four-thirty a.m.), and the wives bid a fond adieu to their clowning partners, who proceeded to party on.

Sometime later, I got up with heartburn and came down to a kitchen that looked like a bomb had gone off. I promptly texted the "boys," berating their kitchen etiquette lapse, and as luck would have it—which happens all too frequently in New Orleans—they had retired right next door and were partying at the home of another routinely misbehaving couple, Parker and Julie LeCorgne.

To cure my heartburn, they rushed right over with icy mojitos made with muddled mint that had been raided from Julie's garden. Yum. And instant heartburn eradication.

But before we could get around to cleaning up, we had to have a cook-off, because New Orleans men are nothing if not competitive and they have limitless appetites. Because soft butter is always available in my kitchen, I chose the vehicle for our completion: grilled cheese. In the Midwest, gourmet grilled cheese consists of white bread slathered with butter and two slices of processed American cheese. Because I am a true epicurean, I substituted fresh sharp cheddar cheese.

Terry and Parker were the judges and seemed to be anxiously awaiting Eddie's entrée. Eddie was the focus of everything. I should have known, whatever I chose to make, the game would be rigged.

Eddie found some fresh-frozen deveined local shrimp in the freezer, discovered much better cheese hiding somewhere in an icebox drawer. He used "artisanal" bread and garden tomatoes and about three seconds later, with none of the smoke that always accompanies burning butter, served up the most delectable grilled cheese ensemble known to mankind. As I said, I was robbed of victory.

Since I was unable to remain good-natured and uncomplaining about my loss, they placated me by doing cartwheels over my family-room chairs.

It was just another night in paradise, but it provided the sort of memories and magic that in twenty-eight years I'd never experienced in our nation's capital. Could it be that people take themselves a little too seriously there?

JAMES

OF ALL THE THINGS getting rebuilt and restored after Katrina, the Saenger Theatre in the French Quarter has to be one of the most recognizable landmarks. It's this beautiful old space built back during the 1920s, with a pipe organ and ornate carvings around the walls and lights in the ceiling arranged like constellations. It's got this great marquee hanging over Canal Street. The Saenger has seen it all over the years—silent films, Broadway shows, classic movies, comedians, concerts. It fell into disrepair a couple times but always came back.

Katrina really did a number on it. The flooding rose above the stage line. The place was a mess. Nobody was sure what would happen. A few years back, the city entered into a public-private partnership and raised something like $40 million for restoration. It's as gorgeous as it's ever been. Jerry Seinfeld performed at the reopening last fall (September 2013). Garrison Keillor brought his radio show (October 2013). Wynton Marsalis came and blew his horn. Diana Ross did a concert. It's back.

When I saw that restoration start to happen, I got to thinking that if we can rebuild the Saenger why don't we rebuild the Dew Drop Inn down on LaSalle Street, across from the old Magnolia housing project?

A lot of people don't know the history of the Dew Drop the way they know the history of the Saenger. But they should. It's a hell of a history. In the forties and fifties and sixties, when segregation was still the law down here, it was one of the hottest nightclubs in the African American community. So hot that even white people sought it out because the music was so good. Deacon John Moore, a local blues legend and a great guy, who played a ton of shows at the Dew Drop, told me they used to have a COLORED ONLY sign in there. I hope to God it still exists.

Every big musician played there back in the day. Ray Charles played there. Billie Holiday, Louis Armstrong, Little Richard. Allen Toussaint. Earl King. So many legends. In its heyday, there was also a barbershop, a restaurant and a hotel on-site. Some of these jazz and blues legends would live there for days or weeks at a time. They'd have these nightly stage shows with magicians and comedians and all kinds of performers in addition to the music.

The sign is still hanging out front, but it's been shuttered as a music joint since the early 1970s. I'm certainly not the only one who's wanted to restore it. A lot of people would love to see the Dew Drop make a comeback. But after I started looking deeper into the history of the place and understanding its significance, I couldn't shake the thought that it needed to be returned to its former glory. I've talked to a lot of people about the project. We're hoping to get Tulane behind it, maybe get the architecture and law schools involved. My hope is to see a concert there again someday. Or educational programs for kids. Or historical tours.

As I've become more cognizant of the culture and the history around every corner in New Orleans, one of my goals is to play a role in giving people markers about their past, so that it never gets completely lost. If places like the Dew Drop get torn down, they'll vanish into memory. You can't really recapture it.

13

BP

JAMES

THE SAINTS WON THE SUPER BOWL. Mitch Landrieu got elected mayor. The early part of 2010 was shaping up pretty nicely in the Crescent City.

Then BP's *Deepwater Horizon* rig exploded on April 20, 2010. For more than a month, a lot of us down in Louisiana watched with disbelief and growing anger at the lack of an effective federal response or any real cleanup efforts by BP.

By the middle of May, I was fuming. Eleven crew members had died. Millions of gallons of oil were gushing into the Gulf. The federal government had neglected New Orleans during Hurricane Katrina, and everybody worried it could happen again. The government should have been much, much more aggressive on the oil spill from the beginning. Washington was dragging its feet while so many people were suffering along the Gulf. Just look how long it took us to get an actual shot of the oil gushing out.

I knew what was coming out of that hole. Finally, I couldn't stand it anymore. I started making the rounds on TV, trying to stick up for New Orleans and not pulling any punches. I was genuinely angry, and I thought that if I could cause a stir some good might come from it.

"The political stupidity of this is just unbelievable," I told George Stephanopoulos on *Good Morning America*. "It just looks like [Obama] is not involved in this. Man, you got to get down here and take control of this, put somebody in charge of this thing and get this moving. We're about to die down here."

I kept the drumbeat going on any show that would have me.

"I think the administration has done some good things. [But] they are risking everything by this go-along-with-BP strategy they have," I said on CNN. "They seem like they're inconvenienced by this, [like] this is some kind of giant thing getting in their way, and, somehow or another, if you let BP handle it, it will all go away. It's not going away. It's growing out there. It's a disaster of the first magnitude . . . I think that the government thinks they're partnering with BP. I think they actually believe that BP had some kind of a good motivation here . . . They're naive."

I was pretty emotionally raw at the time. But I meant what I said. For numerous reasons—the potential environmental damage, the economic interest along the Gulf of Mexico, the public perception—it was dumb for the administration not to be more forceful and proactive from the start.

My rants got a lot of media attention, which was the point. I wanted to help keep as much pressure as possible on the White House and BP. Even after President Obama visited the region and promised to remain committed to the cleanup—which I saw as a very positive step—I kept making a ruckus, letting Washington know that it couldn't forget about Louisiana.

"We're not going away," I told Anderson Cooper one evening on CNN. "Every time somebody comes, if it's Katrina, if it's offshore drilling, if it's the canals, we lose our coastline; people are just sick of it. If this would have happened in Nantucket, happened in San Francisco Bay, if this would have happened in the Chesapeake Bay, if this would have happened in Lake Michigan, the response would have been entirely different."

It's not that I thought Obama or other people in Washington didn't care. I'm not that cynical. But I have a theory on why certain things too often fall through the cracks in Washington, and I think it applied in the BP situation. In my experience, people who go to work in the White House—whether it's the Clinton White House or the Bush White House or the Obama White House—generally come in wanting and expecting to do important things. They want to change the world in big ways, and that's a very valid motivation. No one says, "I want to go into government and clean up fucking crude oil on the Louisiana coast in the middle of the summer."

So a disaster like the BP oil spill happens, and the people back in Washington are busy working on health care implementation or saving the financial and auto industries from themselves or fighting terrorism. All these great, noble causes. Then this giant turd gets dumped right in their laps. It's complicated, and you've got to deal with the Coast Guard, you've got to deal with the Energy Department, you've got to deal with a global oil company. Louisiana's not a swing state. All these factors come into play.

The tendency is to hope that it takes care of itself, that it works itself out. It's not "Fuck those people in Louisiana, we don't care about them. We're going to screw them because they voted for McCain." It's nothing like that. It's just that a catastrophic oil spill in the Gulf of Mexico is not what they came to Washington to spend their time doing. There's no upside; there's no glamour in it. Even if you do an amazing job, it's just a less shitty ending than it could have been otherwise, and the world will forget about it either way.

MARY

I WAS SITTING IN THE KITCHEN, pretty settled in my new home, thinking it was all going to work out, when *blam*. Oil well explosion in the Gulf. At first, I wasn't too concerned, as it is a big gulf with hundreds of rigs. It's literally a floating city down here. Also, I had some expertise in hydrocarbons and knew they were no match for Mother Nature's curative powers.

But the oil flowed and flowed, actually gushed. Without end. It is not an exaggeration to say I saw my life flashing before my eyes. What fragile progress we had made in New Orleans getting out of the water was about to be swept away in a flood of goo.

I got even more scared when James went into his dog-with-a-bone focus mode. Without end.

JAMES

VERY MUCH ON PURPOSE, I'd been a scourge to BP officials week after week during the oil spill. I went on television calling for criminal investigations because of their negligence. I pointed out how they had lied about the resources and manpower they were pouring into the cleanup effort, about how they cared more about their shareholders than about the small towns and the fishermen affected by the spill. I kept saying they would abandon Louisiana in a heartbeat if they could get away with it, and I believed it.

"Justice has to be done here. BP and its senior officers have to be subject to a grand jury investigation. If they're guilty of something, they've got to be brought to the bar of justice," I said on CNN one day in late May 2010. "And then if you give them the choice between going to jail or paying the claims in a fair way, they're going to pay claims in a fair way. Because I'm going to tell you what, [BP chief executive] Tony Hayward—he would not fare well in a Louisiana prison. I promise you that. It would not be a good place for him to be."

As luck would have it, several nights later I wandered into Eleven 79, one of my favorite hangouts in New Orleans. Sitting there at a table off to the side was Admiral Thad Allen, who'd done a great job running search-and-rescue operations after Hurricane Katrina and now was overseeing the federal government's response to the BP oil spill. He was having dinner with Tony Hayward.

Allen motioned me over to his table and introduced me to Tony. We all shared a little small talk. I'd just been down to Colombia, and Allen had done work for the Coast Guard down there. As I recall, one of Tony's kids was born down there when he worked in Colombia for BP. So we talked about that.

But it was awkward, even a little icy. I'd been railing on these guys and the job they were doing for days. I'd basically been calling Hayward a criminal. So, yeah, the conversation was a little uncomfortable. I was trying to be cordial, but I wasn't about to apologize.

Finally, Hayward said something like "Look, Jim, I have to tell you that some of the things that you have said lately have not been helpful."

"Well, they really weren't meant to be helpful," I shot back. "I wasn't really trying to help you."

He assured me that the company wasn't going anywhere, that BP had every intention of sticking around to clean up its mess. He asked me to give the company a chance to prove it would do the right thing. I told him I was skeptical of such promises. It was a polite enough conversation, and he's a charming enough guy, but we clearly weren't going to agree on much. So I said good night and went on my way.

I'm glad I at least got the chance to talk with him face-to-face. At the time, he was a true villain in my life. I'm sure I wasn't exactly his favorite guy either.

14.

We Are Home

JAMES

EVENTUALLY, THINGS GOT BETTER FOR THE GIRLS. They brought more and more friends around. They'd scamper off to hang out in the French Quarter. They'd settled in and become New Orleanians. I think they understand that they live in a unique place, a place unlike any other in America. They realize that they're part of something other people view as exotic and cool.

MARY

TIME HEALS ALL. New Orleans became home for all of us. Moving to a new place turns out to be a little like marriage. You take a vow of sorts, a promise to make it work, for better or worse. (Except, sometimes, when you really miss your old home and old life, you can fly back and visit—kind of like the residential equivalent of drunk-dialing an old flame.)

How we adjusted, how we dealt with the changes, and adapted and thrived was different for each of us. James reached a state of residential happiness and pride. I was having more fun than I'd had since I was really young and irresponsible. The girls had roots, a neighborhood, a community where politics didn't dominate their lives or overshadow them. Living with James and me is bad enough.

In time, the girls will be able to tell their own stories, and funny ones too—since, besides their love for each other and us, they seem to have two things in common, a wacky sense of humor and writing ability.

That is not just puffed-up mother-speak because, as they say, *It ain't bragging if it's true*. In her senior year at the Academy of the Sacred Heart, Matty won the alumni essay contest, which I was told afterward was awarded by a unanimous decision on the part of the judges, the first time ever.

If you are a Sacred Heart girl, and they are global, you probably saw it, as it was posted around the world—people actually stopped me in Italy, France and Ireland last summer to comment on it. (Are these women quietly taking over the Earth? I hope so.) Suffice to say, it was so good that when she read it aloud at the chapel ceremony the whole assembly laughed and cried. It was better that *Cats*, as they say.

Matty also wrote political pieces for *PolicyMic*, a respected millennial site when she was a high school sophomore, which caused some awkward moments, not because her views are annoyingly divergent from my own but because she articulates them so much better than I do my own.

As for Emerson, here is a typical random text, sent while she was on an East Coast trip with her girlfriends. It was to her sister in New Orleans:

MATTY- I am going to need all hands on deck for mission "Save Private Emma." I can't find my wallet and Dad only gave me 90 dollars to last me for 5 days. I have officially gone from Princess Diana to a Real Housewife. Most probably Theresa. As I am now poor, I plan on learning how to save my soap bars in little shavings in a sock like they do in prison. Please look for my wallet while I'm away. It's scared and alone. Until I am reunited with my baby I will take on the identity "Barbra Q" like BBQ. Get it? Anyway, wish me luck and bring my wallet back to safety. Over and out—Barbra Q

JAMES

LOOKING BACK, it was a damn near irresponsible gamble for us to uproot our family and move to New Orleans. The New Orleans of early 2008 was not anything like the New Orleans of today. The city still hadn't really come back. You could see remnants of Katrina almost everywhere you looked. It was in rough shape.

We've turned a corner now. The city's moving in the right direction. My family is happy. It turned out to be a good move in so many ways, but it could have gone another direction entirely.

I don't think we realized at the time what a gamble it was. Maybe we don't really even grasp it now. It's like if you were to walk up to a roulette wheel and put $1,000 on black. Well, the New Orleans experience came up black for us. But it just as easily could have hit red.

MARY

WE RAISED OUR DAUGHTERS to think for themselves and make their own decisions. We wanted to teach them how to make a case—plead their case—and convince us. We trusted them to make wise decisions, until proven otherwise, and they never failed us.

In 2011, after four years of bouncing around various New Orleans schools, making good grades and friends, Emerson felt like she fit into what was a loving but somewhat insular culture, but she never stopped missing her familiar posse and former life in D.C. She never complained, but mothers don't need words to get the drift.

One day, in a totally confident and clearly thought-out announcement, she told me that she wanted to go to boarding school.

Boarding school?

Leave us?

Aren't you still a preteen?

Do you know how hard boarding school is?

Do you know how hard it is to get into boarding school?

Do you know how expensive boarding school is?

You do know your father will spontaneously combust?

She had a quick and irrefutable answer to all my questions, including the lucid declarations that she would be leaving someday, no matter what, that she preferred hard work, she would take an SSAS course to fulfill the rigid entrance requirements, and, finally, that she would swap out the cost of boarding school for her college fund and attend a cheaper state university. As far as Daddy went, he was never far from a meltdown no matter what and that was my problem, not hers.

Her closing argument, as I remember it, was "Mother, you just don't provide the structure I require."

She had me. What could I say? My stalling tactic was "If you do well on the test, I will talk to your father."

Damn, if that girl didn't research all the boarding schools, providing the pros and cons for herself and me; she researched and found the best exam tutor; she studied the practice tests like each and every one was a career-determining LSAT; she got up early Saturday mornings and took all the simulated SSAS exams.

She was one smart cookie, but a tepid test taker, so I held out hope, as the SSAS exams were every bit as rigorous as college entrance exams.

Damn, if that girl didn't get a near perfect score.

I was so impressed and proud of her, I became her number one advocate and was certain James would see it the same way.

What *was* I thinking?

Suffice to say, talking him into letting his precious baby "abandon" him was harder than any house purchase or animal acquisition. Long experience—and *Godfather* reruns—taught me how to deal with the "implacable" James. And it wasn't with rational argument. You just had to make him an offer he couldn't refuse and convince him it was his idea.

Emerson's ace in the hole was reminding me that her daddy and I had survived her monolingual, quasihomebody sister Matty's decision to take an Oxbridge program and study expat literature and European history in Paris, alone, when she was Emerson's age. At least, Emerson argued, she knew the language of the country where she planned to study. Matty left home with some spotty Spanish and came back a fluent Left Banker, a top award–winning, exponentially confident and cool kid. Emerson calmly reminded me how adamantly opposed we were to that decision and how well it turned out.

But Emerson was wrong about how her daddy and I would survive. When Matty went off to France, it was hit or miss for us on the Champs-Élysées.

Anticipating I might not make it out in one piece, I begged our great New Orleans friends, the Hebees and the Fayards, and their kids to come with us when we took Matty a week early to her Oxbridge program.

Jennifer Hebee is a lay preacher and one of those special beings with the gift to heal all. Over our years here, despite having her own mothering handful—twin girls Sarah and Anna—she has walked me back from the edge too many times to count. I love that woman and knew if she was tootling around the city with me, getting the lay of the land and being there with her unusually strong hand to hold, I might be able to leave Matty thousands of miles away. Alone. Without me. For a month.

Jennifer kept a close eye on me while we ran around getting Matty more than she would ever need. Jenny never said what I am sure she was thinking: *Girl, this is more stuff than Matty could use for a decade in Paris.* And I have to admit that even I was not sure how useful all those stuffed animals would be.

We dragged a truck full of mostly useless stuff to the campus, which was supersafe and beautiful. The instructors were top-notch, and Matty's fellow students were wonderful. I started breathing, or at least stopped hyperventilating. Then it was time to leave.

Matty walked into her dorm without a look back down the long tree-lined walk where I stood on the curb. Good thing, because *standing* quickly became not an option.

Matty called me that night and said, "You are never going to believe what happened. Right after you left, some girls got on the elevator with me and said some crazy woman had a seizure on the sidewalk in front of the dorm! She was on her hands and knees, wailing and thrashing! Were you still there? I hope you were able to help her."

I think you know who the crazy woman was.

JAMES

I ALWAYS LIKED EVERYBODY at CNN just fine. I think Mary did too. I've got nothing but mostly good memories of my tenure there.

But what always seemed a little odd to me—maybe because I'm just used to the tight-knit nature of campaigns—was that there didn't seem to be much camaraderie, at least that I could see. I never really felt like I was part of a team. If one person had a show, he or she had his own little empire. Another person with another show had her little empire, and so on. There didn't seem to be much overlap or collaboration between all the fiefdoms. It was sort of every man for himself.

At the same time, I never really understood the charge that CNN was a liberal network. They always struck me as being more corporate and structured. They seemed to have a formula for how they wanted to do the news and do their talk shows, and they stuck to it. There was no underlying ideology that I ever saw.

When Mary and I ended our contracts with CNN in early 2013, we walked away on good terms. It was a pretty simple equation: they wanted their contributors closer to Washington. They wanted us available at a moment's notice. I totally get that. I understood. We're not always available. And we no longer live in Washington. So we called it a day. I think it made sense for us, and it made sense for them. I wasn't mad at anyone. I wasn't upset by anything. If they ever needed me to help out or sit in for someone, I'd still gladly help out.

The truth of it is, I've been on television plenty, and I still show up on TV several times a week. Being on another show is not something to which I aspire. In a way, leaving CNN felt like one more link we severed to our old Washington lives, one more affirmation that New Orleans is now truly home.

I'm staring at seventy, and a number like that makes you think about how many years you have left. You find yourself thinking about your kids growing up and moving away, how you'll miss them. You find yourself studying all the stairs in your house and thinking we'll probably have to sell it at some point, maybe move into a flat in the French Quarter.

I'm certainly not exempt from nature. This body has some miles on it. Right now I'm a healthy sixty-nine. I still run every day. I eat healthy. I travel hundreds of thousands of miles a year. But no matter what your lifestyle is, your bones grow old and brittle; you fall down. Until that time, my strategy is to go full speed ahead. I'm not young anymore, but I still can't stand sitting around.

When my health starts to deteriorate, I know I'll have to adjust. Like anybody else, I'd prefer to live as long as I can and be healthy, but you don't have any choice in the matter. You don't get to pick. But living to ninety-two is not something I lie awake dreaming about. I know I'm going to die one day.

But here's what's important to me: I don't want to grow old among strangers.

Washington, it always struck me, is a city all about power. That's why it exists. And if you live there, the fact that at one time you had power or influence doesn't really help you much. You don't even have to get old. Just lose an election, and people trample right over you to get on to the next thing. That's the way it is. Time marches on. New players arrive on the scene. Your moment passes. I get that.

I think it would be miserable to be holed up in some luxury apartment building in northwest Washington, sitting around all day while a caretaker wipes your drool and hoping that your kids come by to tell you hello or somebody remembers who you once were.

Down here, people have such a different attitude toward the elderly. They are more respectful. Maybe that's the French culture. Maybe it's a Southern thing. But older people are revered here in a way that they never would be in Washington. When you grow old here, you don't have to exit the culture. You can still be a part of the fabric.

You see all these old guys around here, still going to all the events. The Mardi Gras parades. The jazz clubs. The Saints games. I can just see somebody wheeling me into a bar in my wheelchair. "Oh, there's old man Carville! What's going on, man? How you doin'? How about that LSU game? Remember the Super Bowl?"

And there's this: when I'm somewhere else, people know *who* I am. They've seen me on TV plenty of times. They know the Clinton story. But when I'm in Louisiana, people know *what* I am. We have a shared history.

I'll never be among strangers here.

MARY

THE DAY ARRIVED FOR Matty to leave for college. Since her birth, I had dreaded this moment, but by the time she was actually going, we both were ready. This was partly due to her departure being preceded by a six-month descent into a hell that made Dante's look like Sunday school, and mostly because she had worked with such diligence on her journey to maturity—academically, emotionally and every other way—I was more proud than sad about my little bird leaving.

Speaking of which, I have never liked the term *empty nest* for the transition to independence and a new parent-child relationship. But Tim Burns, the headmaster of Sacred Heart, did give me a great companion phrase for that overused and abused term, which completely captures the vicious twenty-faces-of-Eve phase girls go through during their final months at home: *soiling the nest*. They have to make one big hot mess of their home base and everyone in it, which thereby forces them to jump out or be kicked out.

Anticipating it and understanding it didn't make it any easier to go through. There is way more pain to teenage leaving than baby birthing. But you will have to read Matty's Great American Novel in a couple of years to get her version of it. I'll just say, for me, there was no epidural to ease the pain of having your heart ripped out, sliced and diced, stomped on, lit on fire, doused with acid and returned with the faintest of beats to your pulverized chest.

Thinking back to the summer before she left, it was the kind of experience for which the phrase "Someday we will laugh about this" was coined. I hope.

And she couldn't help this behavior. She did what she was supposed to do. And although it does seem like an unbearably nasty bit of merciless and undeserved punishment for all parties involved, it is actually indicative of a healthy kid and healthy relationship.

On our way to upstate New York, where she was going to college, she and I made a final trip to the farm in the Shenandoah Valley where she grew up. We shared all our favorite music—a lot of Josh Ritter and about a thousand different versions of "Galway Girl."

We barely spoke as we traversed yet another amazingly scenic view through the mountains and across the rivers of the east, while Matty cued up one perfect tune after another, and when I started to flag on the final leg, she said simply and with authority, "This always works," and cranked up Ke$ha.

Sometimes—and this was one of them—words are neither an option nor memorable. The other time was when she came into this world.

I can remember, but only vaguely, how my own folks dropped me off in front of my dorm and then took off. A quick getaway wasn't a remote possibility for James and me. We were relieved to see we weren't the only hovering parents. Everywhere, on every dorm floor, dads mingled in the halls, trying to act all macho, and moms unpacked, trying to act all grown-up.

Everyone should have won an Oscar; we were all so good with our performances.

We weren't half unpacked when Matty kicked me out. She wanted to check out an orientation event with her new and already beloved roomie, Lindsey. Okay. Of course.

A small good-bye, a don't-embarrass-me hug, and she was off without a look back.

I returned to my rental car, closed the windows, revved up and replayed "Tik Tok" over and over at the loudest volume, and I got all the way out of town before I realized Ke$ha doesn't *always* work. I was crying so hard, I had to pull over. I am still not sure how I made the seven-hour drive back, but I am pretty sure I won't be able to hear Ke$ha again without returning to that feeling.

Matty's new life begins.

JAMES

BEFORE WE KNOW IT, Mary and I will be alone together. Matty's already gone up to college one thousand miles away in upstate New York. It won't be long until Emerson packs up and heads off for good too.

We've hardly ever known life together without them. Mary and I got married at the end of 1993, and Matty came along in 1995. So we've rarely lived alone, just the two of us. We've got this big house off St. Charles Avenue, and we're not getting any younger. I believe we'll probably end up in the French Quarter at some point—single-floor living, walking distance to everything, but a hell of a lot less boring than an old folks' home.

Every parent thinks about what life will be like after the kids move out. I don't expect it to be miserable or anything. But I know it will change.

I talked to my daughter before she headed off to college, planning out when she was coming home for Thanksgiving and the holidays, talking about when we might go there to visit. It dawned on me that she wouldn't really live here anymore. But it's not entirely bad. They get long breaks. She'll come back home. And considering she's at school in the tundra of upstate New York, I'm guessing New Orleans will be a popular destination. She's going to have plenty of friends eager to come with her down South.

Besides, Mary and I will still be on the road a lot. I'll have my foreign campaign work. We both will do our share of public speaking and TV appearances. Life goes on. We'll evolve.

It's also happening at the right time, I think. Mary and I have gotten along better than ever these past few years. Maybe that's New Orleans. Maybe it's just the passage of time. Maybe both. Whatever the case, if we'd have had an empty nest seven years into our marriage, it might not have been a pretty sight. We were both more focused on building careers back then; we were both more intense than perhaps we are now. We've mellowed a little, if only a little.

Thank God we always had the kids in the picture back then. They were a great mitigating force. Even when Mary and I could barely stand to look at each other, they united us in a way nothing else could. They got us through. I have far less trepidation about living alone with Mary now. We enjoy each other's company. We know each other inside and out. We have fun.

Mary and I will be fine. It's the absence of our girls, the silence they'll leave behind, that will take the most getting used to.

MARY

MY MOTHER HAD LOTS OF TRITE SAYINGS. They dropped from her lips all day, beginning with her first cup of coffee in the morning to our last kiss of the night. When I was growing up, I didn't remotely appreciate them—or give them much thought. Later on, I found myself living by her little quips. They floated into my mind regularly, like clouds. *Life is what happens when you are making other plans.*

That particular saying was a talismanic watchword for me, which for brevity's sake was converted to *Life is a bitch and then you die.* Now, as I enter my sixth decade of life and my senior years, the rushed exuberance of youth has given way to the wisdom of experience. I don't think about plans as much, or complaining that life is a bitch. I go by something different: *Life is a magic carpet ride. Buckle up!*

As far as I can tell, predictability has less to do with life than being totally surprised. If I were a betting woman, I wouldn't have to put a nickel on the prospect of a hand that held loving a husband or making babies, leaving Washington or finding faith, or making great new friends in the last part of life. And . . . oh yeah, pulling for any team other than the Bears, let alone the Tigers. Magical surprises all.

You can aim your magic carpet for a destination. And if you have responsibilities, like kids, it would be irresponsible not to. But aiming—and arriving punctually at your precise destination—kind of takes the magic out of the ride, doesn't it? And assuming that you are in control of the carpet in the first place, and where it's going, seems foolhardy to me. You can't know about the crosscurrents in the wind that will blow you off course. And what if the carpet has a hole?

Play a meditative game with yourself and think back to five years ago, or ten years ago, and try to remember what you thought would happen. Take my girls, for example. Even as their mother, I didn't expect at ages ten and thirteen they would be the remarkable human beings they are now at fifteen and eighteen. On this trajectory, in five or ten more years, who knows where they will be, what they will be doing, how many lives they will have impacted. I only hope—pray every day—I am here to see it.

Now play this game while thinking of New Orleans.

Seven years ago we were fifteen feet underwater. Today we are the fastest-growing city in America, a tech mecca, foodie mecca and music mecca that's also luring academics, bankers, doctors, entertainers, young professionals at the start of their careers and old politicos like James and me. The Crescent City has weathered Katrina, the BP oil spill and the recession—and is now leading the country in economic recovery.

As Mitch Landrieu said, "There's no other place, there is no other city in America that has been called upon to re-create the intricate fabric of their lives like we're doing here in New Orleans.

"And, while we've still got a long way to go, we're not only back—in many ways we're even stronger than we were before.

"We're not rebuilding the city we were, we're creating the city we want to become. We are proving that out of tragedy can come triumph."

On this trajectory, I am confident, if Mitch and reform leaders like him can continue to commit their talents and time and passion to the amazing city, seven years from now we will be a city previously unimaginable in all the world.

JAMES

I DO THINK WE'VE MADE A DIFFERENCE. Maybe not as much as some people think, maybe more than others think, but a difference just the same. We promoted the hell out of New Orleans as cochairs for the Super Bowl. We've flung open our home to dozens of fund-raisers for dozens of causes, from Teach for America to local small-business initiatives to the Women of the Storm, a nonpartisan group of Louisianans who have really helped draw attention toward rebuilding the city. In fact, Mary and I decided when we moved that we'd do very little personal entertaining at home. Instead, we try to do "purpose-driven" entertaining. After all, we moved here for a purpose.

Neither of us ever has cared much about honors or accolades. But we were both touched when we were named New Orleanians of the Year in 2012 by the local alt-weekly, the *Gambit*, which since Katrina hit has been giving that title each year to people who have helped lead the city's rebound. It's gone to first responders and local activists. It went to the Saints the year they won the Super Bowl. In the article that accompanied that announcement, Mitch Landrieu called us "wonderful ambassadors and great friends for the city." A columnist for the paper wrote, "In ways large and small, public and not so public, they generously and passionately embody the simple criterion that *Gambit* has used to select New Orleanians of the Year since 1983: They make a positive difference for New Orleans."

I certainly hope that's true. No doubt there's an element of correlation and causation. It's like the rooster that crows at four o'clock in the morning and then the sun comes up. That rooster didn't have a hell of a lot to do with the sunrise. New Orleans has really gotten back on its feet since we arrived in 2008, but it's hard to know how big a role we've played in making that happen. Rebuilding this city has been the very definition of a team effort, with hundreds and thousands of dedicated people pouring their hearts into it. I just hope we've played some small, meaningful part.

It's fun, at my age, to be in a fight that matters.

MARY

AND SO IT GOES. My magic carpet ride winds down, but is far from over. My daughters are just buckling up. The most awe-inspiring, astounding, breathtaking leg of my own journey began with their entrance and is pivotally punctuated by their departure. Equally humbling, exhilarating and enchanting is marking twenty years of a never boring, always loving—if not always blissful—monogamous relationship.

As for my lifelong and ongoing passion—politics—we are about to wend our way through the 2014 midterm and 2016 presidential election that I've been involved in, and I do plan to be involved in the upcoming ones, aged though I may be. I have lived through big and little, dynamic and imperceptible, political shifts in the last three decades, and the America my ancestors came to, loved and fought for without reservation has largely stood the test of time. But only because each generation has kept vigilant.

My parents, as did their own, shared a passion for generational vigilance. We were raised in a moment of hypersensitivity about the future; just like the times we all find ourselves now raising this generation. There's a reason they call it *wisdom of the ages*: change is certain, progress is not. All it takes for evil to triumph is for good men to do nothing.

From the Ten Commandments to the Constitution, despite detours, debacles and disasters, humankind keeps on trucking. And on the whole, no one can say the good didn't—and won't—outweigh the bad. We keep heading in the right direction.

God bless you, your ancestors and your progeny. See you in another twenty years. If anyone out there has any better thoughts for today or tomorrow, tweet me.

FAQ OF THE FUTURE

WE HOPE MOST OF YOUR WILDEST QUESTIONS ABOUT US HAVE BEEN AN-
SWERED IN THIS BOOK, ALONG WITH THE ANSWERS TO QUESTIONS YOU
DIDN'T EVEN KNOW YOU HAD. WE TRIED HARD TO MAKE YOU HAPPY. We always try hard. We are different in two million ways and don't agree on furniture and real estate and animals in the house, but we got all the way
through the book-writing process, which is no small marital feat (secret to
getting through it: nobody says you have to carefully read and consider
every sentence your spouse writes; a quick cursory skimming of their rav-
ings might be enough), and told lots of stories, or the ones our publisher
would let us put in print.

As for the next twenty years, or even the next four, here are a few questions we don't know the answer to yet:

- What is the chance you'd ever run for office?
- What is the chance you'll get matching tattoos on your thirtieth wedding anniversary?
- How many new pets are on the horizon?
- Would you consider marrying each other another time?
- Would you consider divorcing and then remarrying each other?
- Would you wonder if divorcing and then dying single and alone might be better than another day with him/her?
- What do your daughters really think?
- Can you imagine ever agreeing with each other on a presidential candidate?
- What if Hillary runs?
- How about Mitch Landrieu?
- Does make-up sex get better with age?
- Will you ever move again?

We'll check back in another two decades.

Afterword

MARY

SO HERE WE ARE at the updated paperback. To my profound pleasure, and I suppose shock, *Love & War* was treated fairly by the critics. More importantly to me, since I plan never to pen another, readers received this book in the exact way I had intended and hoped.

That is to say, the interest in and appreciation for New Orleans dominated the response to it. Of course, we got the mandatory queries on contemporary politics, but they were largely perfunctory. Certainly the well-documented, near universal fatigue with all things political played into that response, but the nature of the questions about New Orleans suggested a gravitational pull to positivism and optimism.

JAMES

AND HERE I GO AGREEING with my wife again out of the gate. I have to say that traveling around the country this time for the book tour, I was particularly impressed with this sense that most people would like the country to "get back together." There's this feeling that in politics, people used to get along much better. There's a nostalgia for Ronald Reagan–Tip O'Neill collegial relationships among people from both parties. They pine for a day reminiscent of the time when people from both parties were willing to compromise.

That certainly is what drives some of the curiosity about Mary and me. And I think it too is what is so appealing about what is happening in New Orleans. We've sort of put down some of the ideological arguments for a more pragmatic and practical sort of politics. Some of that is certainly driven by necessity given what the city has been through, but on the whole, that's been good for the innovation that's happening here—on education, health care, government reform and more.

MARY

AS WE TRAVELED, audiences of all political persuasions genuinely wanted to understand how the Big Easy moved on from such monumental difficulties. Not just moved on, but improved, excelled and became a national prototype for urban resurrection. How did we clean up city hall corruption; improve and expand health care, education, entrepreneurship; restore and exceed our traditional beauty; preserve our unique heritage and culture? And *how on earth* did we fix all those potholes?

To repeat the central message of *Love & War*, when individuals come together with elbow grease, faith and determination in their communities, magic happens.

We reelected our great mayor, Mitch Landrieu; we expunged hundreds of crooked pols; we rebuilt our infrastructure; we established a lively business and family friendly environment. We kept on task. We rewarded success and eschewed failures, no matter what or how much political force was brought to bear.

And we had (and are having) a lot of fun in the process. If you have been among the thousands of visitors who helped us garner the designation from *National Geographic* or *Travel & Leisure* as one of the top places *in the world* to visit, you know what I mean.

If you haven't visited us, well . . . your big-time loss.

You're not just missing only-in-NOLA fun; you are missing an opportunity to see history and regeneration from a front row seat.

We are in the early stages of preparation for the three hundredth anniversary in 2018, when all our glorious history and progress will be on sui generis display. *Be there or be square*—to which my daughters would say, "Mom, the 1950s are calling; they want their lame sayings back." Nonetheless, you must check it out.

JAMES

I THINK WE CERTAINLY NOTED it in *Love & War*, but there are few people Mary and I share a positive opinion about, and one is our mayor, Mitch Landrieu. For the city's sake, he was reelected in February with another mandate.

I've always believed that Democrats are better for the economy, and on the smaller scale, Mitch proves that in New Orleans. The city is open for business. I cannot drive around the damn city without hitting a construction site. There are ribbon cuttings and grand openings on a daily basis. In the six years that we've been back in New Orleans, there seems like no better time to be here. As we head toward the tenth anniversary of Katrina in 2015, there's a real opportunity to turn the page. New Orleans will be three hundred years old in 2018, and that seems like the perfect new rallying point for the city.

The only thing missing from New Orleans has been my girls. I can barely talk about it, but having them both out of the house has been something of a struggle. That's all I can say about it. But I am very proud of them.

Since the book was released, Matty got another dog (I don't think I'm even supposed to know about it). But it's more or less been more of the same.

I also joined Fox News, which, if you know anything about my past comments about the network, might seem strange. But hey, where else can you go punch holes through their vapid, inane arguments on a daily basis. On the downside, it complicates our marriage even further because now all Mary has is Rush. She can't even turn on the TV.

MARY

SPEAKING OF THE LOVELY FAMILY . . .

To all you (beautiful) critter-loving kindred spirits: as you are well aware, our four-legged and winged friends do age exponentially faster than we of the two-legged species. You would think such speedy disintegration might provide some small consolation (or at least distraction) if you are in that demographic cohort who is shocked—*shocked!*—by daily discoveries of new gray hairs, fresh crow's-feet and yes, stubborn belly fat.

It isn't.

But in the way that we learn so much from our animal kingdom kin, maybe we can stop and consider how gracefully and happily they embrace their "maturing" status.

Overnight, my beloved *Killer* cat morphed into Jabba the Hut with fur. He has few remaining teeth and sizeable swaths of fur fly off his body in a strong wind. His snorting and snoring make the ludicrous sounds your husband emits sound like gentle purring. And, unlike your hubby, you cannot dispatch him to another room to sleep because he follows you wherever you go and wraps his mammoth, toothless, furflying, wheezing carcass around your neck. Which is double annoying, since he sleeps all day. He sleeps through his sister-kitty's screeching tirades, which have increased in frequency as the days add up for her, owing to her deafness, I suppose.

Yet, they are both content.

They eat what they want, when they want, and loll around in the sun for hours at a time.

They do not mourn their departed furry and feathered friends (the rats and birds all passed since we last met) or miss their canine buddies, whom I reluctantly sent to our Virginia farm as a gesture of sincerity in my quest for marital tranquility.

They demonstrate their utter apathy at our daughters' departures by refusing to relinquish the sofa spots they've staked out when the girls come home on school breaks.

In short, we should all wish to be so chillaxed in the face of time marching on.

Okay, don't take this the wrong way, but I miss my critters more than I miss my daughters moving on. Maybe because they moved up and out rather than *on*. Actually, I am pretty much more on call than I was when we were all under the same roof.

Remember all the times your mother told you she'd get smarter as you got older? It is true! I am no longer the dorky loser-mom of yore with all the rules; I have been upgraded to dorky answer-mom . . . with an open checkbook.

Or maybe it is because I am so proud of them. Both have excelled in their academics; have made lovely and fun friends; are thoughtful, kind and compassionate in ways that make me think they might have been adopted.

They even learned how to cook and do their own laundry! Not that they're not amazed that their mother can do three months of laundry without breaking a sweat or whip up a tomato pie in the time it takes them to pick out a pair of shoes and put on their make-up.

Or maybe it's because they read books I've never heard of, know things I've never dreamed of, have aspirational dreams I never knew existed.

They've turned me on to things that make me belly laugh out loud; they inspire me, entertain me, enlighten me with almost everything that they say or do.

They have become flat-out the most interesting people I've ever known and the only ones I want to be with for all eternity.

So I am okay with their being home only episodically. Their home-comings are so rich.

James, on the other hand, appears to still be reeling. I say "appears" because we can no longer talk about it. Talking about their being gone would deconstruct our painstakingly crafted self-deception. They really aren't growing up and we really aren't growing old.

Good thing we are expert spinners.

Speaking of spinning, the national political universe is a veritable whirling dervish these days.

If you believed the punditry, you'd think the Tea Party was dead, or what lives on is a bunch of dumb hick shit kickers. You would be remarkably stupid to believe such a thing. The Tea Party was never a "party" or even a movement at all. It is a way of living, a call to the wisdom of the ages.

Whatever the electoral success, if you have any doubt a dedicated, resolute constitutional fervor hasn't impacted both traditional national parties, you must be kin to Rip Van Winkle or regular viewers of MSNBC.

JAMES

NOTE THAT MARY sort of dismisses the electoral success as if that is not what this whole thing is about.

Needless to say, in 2014, there is a lot of wind in the face of the Democrats. A high wrong-track number for the direction of the country, six years of an incumbent president and exposure in "red state" Senate seats held by Democrats. It all points to a pretty problematic year.

What almost always happens in these off-year elections is one party does better than the other. So the question is, "How many competitive Senate seats are there?" Charlie Cook makes a living on this sort of thing, but let's for simple math's sake say there are ten competitive US Senate seats. One party will typically win seven or eight of those in play. It doesn't split five to five.

I am only hopeful because recent history indicates that Democrats will outperform expectations. Since 2006, the Democrats have lost very few, and I mean very few, competitive Senate seats.

As for 2016, I think we know enough to draw a pretty large conclusion. And that is simply this—other than Hillary Clinton, there is not a particularly impressive candidate or potential candidate in either party right now. I am sure someone could have said that about Bill Clinton in 1990. And certainly, someone said that about Barack Obama in 2006. But if for some reason she doesn't run, there will be a mad scramble. And for Democrats that will be disconcerting.

The one thing that I know—and I'm sure Secretary Clinton knows—is that come 2016, the voters will not really be looking for an election to rehash old debates. It is not going to be about former president Bill Clinton's record, just as it is not going to be about Bush 43's record. Frankly, as highly regarded as Bill Clinton's presidency was, it was better than you think. Similarly, the way we loathed George W. Bush's time in office, it was worse than you think.

Any long discussions of these issues will turn voters away in droves. Believe it or not, given the trauma of the finance-induced horrific recession, voters are going to be looking for an election about their lives and about their futures. The truth of the matter is that there is an actual shovel-ready message for Secretary Clinton on how we can make Washington work to rebuild America's devastated middle class.

Rarely has there been a coming presidential campaign with such an obvious and effective message available to a candidate. We can continue to list what this will be about—Bill Clinton; George W. Bush; the attack in Benghazi, Libya; Monica Lewinsky; Whitewater; the IRS political targeting scandal—but none of that is going to matter one half of an inch outside of the right-wing echo chamber. Reince Priebus, the chairman of the Republican National Committee, said in February that Republicans will have a "truckload" of material to use against Secretary Clinton. Well, I will help Reince drive those trucks and show him where to park. It isn't what matters, and it is not what voters care about.

To a large extent it is going to be less about President Obama and what happened during his administration than people think. The Democrats and our nominee presumably—and hopefully, Secretary Clinton—will say the following: "Obama had a huge task; he had to wind down wars in the Middle East; he had to rescue the American auto industry; and, by the way, he had to fix a very broken health care system. And you know what, he did those things, but the task ahead of us is difficult and necessary."

The task ahead is about growing and expanding the middle class. It is about creating the conditions in which people who play by the rules and work hard can get ahead. The message is about expanding economic opportunity for the American people.

Regardless of the message, they will still need a candidate who can win. On the Republican side, that field is nowhere near impressive. Rand Paul and Ted Cruz have no shot at being nominated. The GOP has no history of nominating someone with that sort of experience.

Jeb Bush may run, but while he may seem impressive to the punditry, he is not viewed as that impressive by the American people. If you don't believe me, check out his polling numbers (see pollster.com for details). There's also any number of well-discussed prior business relationships that will draw much scrutiny (see "Lehman Brothers").

Wisconsin governor Scott Walker, as of this writing, is engaged in a brutal reelection campaign, part of it focused on less-than-promised job numbers.

So bear with me—I think they have two possibilities. And please hold your laughter until I'm through.

Number one is Rick Perry. The case that he can do better than you think is pretty simple—he's been around the track once. Granted, it is the same track he essentially finished last on, but Perry can raise a bucket load of money without even trying and he, unlike Walker, has a compelling economic story to tell. Certainly, more of that has to do with the energy explosion than any of his policies, but he gets credit nonetheless. *Washington Monthly* did a good job debunking some of his "Texas miracle" arguments, but I suspect his story will be pretty hard to combat in sound bites.

Number two is even less plausible today but could happen—Mitt Romney.

He too has been around the track once or twice and handled himself well. The Netflix documentary about him on the 2012 campaign trail couldn't do anything but help. This only has a chance if the process gets bogged down and the above-mentioned candidates sort of muck it up. If the convention were to somehow be deadlocked, Mitt could be their guy again. It's highly remote but— come on—people like me fantasize about this sort of thing. And hey, a guy can dream, right?

There's a lot of time between now and then, though.

At the end of the day, we all know that our democracy is not perfect. But I have come to the conclusion that our democracy is as imperfect today as any time in recent history. One of the reasons why *Love & War* resonates is because the polarization in Washington is here to stay, for several reasons: the proliferation of news organizations that are echo chambers for a point of view; the way we live—with Democrats in cities and Republicans in suburbs and rural areas; campaign finance; gerrymandering; and on and on.

If you look at it strictly from a political landscape lens, it's simple: It will be exceedingly difficult for the Democrats to win the House of Representatives. In order for that to happen, we would have to win the popular vote by 4.5 to 5 points—it would have to be a Democratic wave election due to the way in which the seats are drawn and all of the above reasons. Conversely—and as I laid out in *40 More Years*—it has become equally difficult for Republicans to win back the presidency. Their base, white voters, make up 2 percent less of the electorate every four years. In 2008, they made up 74 percent of voters; in 2012, 72 percent of voters. I suspect the trend will hold if not accelerate, and white voters will be only 70 percent of the electorate in 2016. In the last six cycles, the Democrats have carried states whose electoral votes total 242. That doesn't include any of the traditional "swing" states we think about. If you just add Florida and nothing else, Democrats win. The electoral college map favors Democrats for a long time to come.

So you have something close to a permanently entrenched Republican majority in "the people's house" in Congress that is dominated by a fringe segment of a political party and is constantly being challenged from the right in primaries. And absent some big compelling shift, you have a permanent Democratic presidency, where Democratic primary voters are charged with picking the next president.

Until this dual lock is picked, and both of these dynamics change, I think we are looking at more of the same.

MARY

IF YOU CONTINUE TO BELIEVE "progressives" are the second coming or that their policies are the salvation of our future, again, wake up and turn the channel.

Progressive policies have even greater unpopularity than they did when they spawned the constitutional concern that now grips the nation. National politicians from the Progressive Party up for reelection sound like Ronald Reagan while progressives in non-competitive seats sound like Nero off his meds. Still, the *conventional wisdom* insists the GOP has formed an insular circular Uzi firing squad.

No amount of irrefutable positive data from red state governors or commonsense mayors of either party can dissuade progressives from their utopian cognitive dissonance.

Initially, the progressives predicted a 2014 midterm takeover of the House and an expansion of the Senate ranks. Now they monolithically and delusionally just chant, "Hillary . . . Hillary . . . Hillary . . . 2016."

Initially, they huffed and puffed about Barack Obama going down in the history books . . . and they may be right about that, but certainly not as "the one we've been waiting for," more like "the one we can't get rid of fast enough."

Meanwhile, Republican governors keep racking up successes, conservative candidates keep coming up with commonsense policies and normal Americans have run the emotional gamut from surprise to fear to anger to disgust with Democratic policies and politicians.

The twenty-first-century Democratic demagogic and dictatorial primary thinkers have mutated into some obscene offspring of Woodrow Wilson and Saul Alinsky, who have in turn spawned policies producing the worst economic calamity and the greatest cultural degradation in our nation's history.

As Americans watch mouths agape at their communities and fellow citizens in unnecessary decline at the hands of progressives, liberals just keep freaking out over Rush Limbaugh and Glenn Beck and Fox and people of faith. Tyrannical political correctness masquerades as civility. The earth is melting; God is dead; kids belong to the state; free birth control for everyone!

Reality is soooooo yesterday, as is the history of progressivism. His Holiness Benedict XVI, Roman pontiff emeritus, fervently warned of liberalism's contemporary signature accomplishments: "We are building a 'dictatorship of relativism' that does not recognize anything as definitive and whose ultimate goal consists solely of one's own ego and desires. . . . Today the idea of truth and that of intolerance are almost completely fused, and so we no longer dare to believe in the truth or to speak of the truth."

Yet decades of liberal policies have produced the first generation to leave the country less well off than their forbearers. *But*, as has always been the wont of tyrants, liberals insist therein lies the road to restoration.

If you'd rather light candles than curse the dark, let us turn to the best news for and opportunity for our restoration. This generation of the so-called Millennials, so often maligned, is a truly exceptional cohort. For all their parents' selfishness and idiocy, they have grown up in an unprecedented era of quantum leap technology, which they are grafting onto a practical know-how, youthful energy and uncommon courage to produce real promise for a future better than the one handed to them.

Everywhere you look, if you care to see them, young people are applying themselves with all the best ideals to all the best ideas with astounding results. James's Tulane students, my own kids' friends, the happy hordes of young people jammed into St. Peter's Square for the canonizations of St. John Paul II and John XXIII, the swelling ranks of Teach for America kids.

They have the right stuff; we keep giving them the wrong policies.

So the other central message of *Love & War* is not a new one: to all things there is a season. You, your family, your pets, your community, your time and place.

The New Orleans rebirth and the kids we birthed should make everyone smile . . . and chillax. But, as always and for all time . . . stay vigilant.

ACKNOWLEDGMENTS

James is right about acknowledgments; someone dear and indispensable gets inadvertently left off, so apologies in advance if either space or my own brain limitations leave you on the cutting room floor. Pulling together a book really does *take a village*. This falls far short of an exhaustive list of helping hands on this project. You know who you are.

Twenty years ago, together we published *All's Fair*, a more cathartic-than-fun book. From then until now, between us we have published more than a dozen books—most by James and his cohorts, and my one singular effort, *Letters to My Daughters*, a tribute to my mother. After that, I swore I would never work on another book, describing the experience as akin to "giving birth without an epidural." Turning sixty this year, and hence, done with birthing, this book began with great trepidation but turned out to be as joyous as giving birth, thanks to **Martha Sherrill**. I've known for decades Martha was an unusually gifted and creative writer, editor, novelist and a beautiful person in every way. But who knew her work mode was so organized that she makes *The Seven Habits of Highly Organized People* look like a one-car funeral screw-up? Without Martha, it would have taken seven *times* the number of highly organized people to deal with the myriad substantive, logistical, administrative, technological and legal issues, not to mention divergent "personalities" associated with this project. And she did it all without screaming at the many who deserved it; indeed she's encouraging to the point of saintliness. Did I mention the book was a "crash" and she layered it on top of her other global projects? Space restrictions allow only a partial listing of Martha's multiple winsome features: she is unusually well read and well versed on any topic you can think of, an exotic cook (she made Nutella from scratch!), a versatile yoga, fashion, notions and medical expert and *the party gets started when she walks into the room.* Much of this book was put together in New Orleans and *to a man,* everyone who crossed her path (when we played hooky, which was often and necessary) adored her. I don't know when I've been as inspired by a person or had so much fun with one on a work project. The greatest gift, though, was rekindling a treasured friendship interrupted by time and space. Thanks also to her beloved family, the talented and handsome (King) **Bill Powers**, who kept us sane as best he could and deployed his critical eye without complaint, tendering indispensable contributions with the patience of Job and gentleness of Mother Teresa; and to (Prince) **William Powers**, whom I adore like a son, even though we've never met, because his mother loves him so much, she fills the room with his essence. Good luck at Milton, William. You come from good stock.

Brady Dennis. May I pay you the highest compliment I have: your mama raised you right. This handsome, intelligent and stunningly goodnatured Southern gentleman—and intrepid reporter at the *Washington Post*—worked nights and weekends over an entire summer with a new baby on the way and a big baby (my husband) on his lap. He made the process of writing another book with James a rare treat, almost blessing, and certainly not as much the hair-pulling raging nightmare that I worried it might be. James sang his praises. Martha adored him. When do I get my turn? Brady, please come back often and bring your new family.

There is no book (or much of anything else) without **Bob Barnett**.

"Thank you, Counselor." We wouldn't have anything to write about without the guiding hand and friendship of **Harry Rhoads**. And no one we would want to write it with beside the inimitable **David Rosenthal**. Boys, we have traveled some miles and we're just getting started. xoxox

We're also grateful to all the good folks at Penguin/Blue Rider Press for guiding us through the complications of two stories which constantly needed to be made one (on a short deadline, to boot). We're especially thankful to copy chief Linda Rosenberg, managing editor Meredith Dros, production editor Janice Kurzius, associate publisher and publicity director Aileen Boyle, publicity manager Brian Ulicky, senior publicist Carrie Neill, and assistant editor Phoebe Pickering. Nothing in this book scared them away.

Nothing in this book, or for that matter in any part of my life, would be remotely possible without the following friends. And by "I," I mean "us" because *if Mama ain't happy, ain't nobody happy*, as Tim and James never tired of pointing out.

No way to thank **Elizabeth Brown Long** for all she does, every day, 24/7/365, in good times and bad, always calm in our chaos, for *all* of us, and has for years. So much love to you and **Ramon Long**, our very special daughter and son.

With thanks and love to our Home Girl Queen, **Debbie Mantz** for our Valley paradise, keeping us in good order everywhere and always rolling with it all; and for sharing her multitalented, manly-man, **Ford**.

James likes to console himself with the quote usually attributed to French general Charles de Gaulle (but it turns out a dozen people had already said it before him), "The graveyards are filled with indispensable men." But it is just not possible to imagine a more robust and indispensable joy bunny in any world than **Ryan Berni**. And the whole Carville Clan agrees, no project would ever get off the ground, let alone be completed, without the Berni-touch. Who Dat, dear love. To Claire Drake, for your energy, good cheer, and sistering the girls so lovingly.

With gratitude and awe for their constant vigilance and continued sanity in the Matalin/Carville nuthouse: **Allie Olivier, Kees Nordin,**

Sarah O'Brien, Caroline Ponseti and Lily Lopez. Eternal thanks to Renie and lil bro. Hugs to Todd, just because.

To my hearts, **James, Matty and Emerson**: even if the words existed for me to write of my love for you, there wouldn't be enough trees on the planet to carry it. And that goes for all the critters too.